THE
Picture
Bible

Script by Iva Hoth

Illustrations by Andre Le Blanc

Equipping Kids for Life

COOK COMMUNICATIONS MINISTRIES
Colorado Springs, Colorado   •   Paris, Ontario
KINGSWAY COMMUNICATIONS LTD
Eastbourne, England

Faith Kidz® is an imprint of
Cook Communications Ministries, Colorado Springs, Colorado 80918
Cook Communications, Paris, Ontario
Kingsway Communications, Eastbourne, England

The Picture Bible
© 1978, 1998 by David C. Cook Publishing
© 2004 by Cook Communications Ministries

First hardcover printing, 1979
First paperback printing, 1981
Printed in Korea

Bible Editors: C. Elvan Olmstead, Ph.D., and Jim Townsend, Ph.D.
Revision Editor: Jeannie Harmon
Art Director: Andrea Boven
Designer: Paz Design Group
Interior Text Revisions: Cheryl Ogletree

The maps shown on pp.12, 544, and 644 were developed for Bible-in-Life
Sunday School Curriculum.

LC 79–67013

ISBN:0-78143-057-7 Deluxe Hardcover
ISBN:0-78143-055-0 Storybook Hardcover
ISBN:0-78143-058-5 Paperback

Table of Contents

OLD TESTAMENT STORIES

CREATION
In the Beginning 13
Temptation in the Garden ..19
Jealous Brothers 22
The Verdict 25

NOAH
When the Rains Came 28
The Great Flood 31

ABRAHAM
The Tower that Crumbled ..37
The Journey Begins 41
Into the Unknown 43
A Big Lie 46
Raiders of Sodom 48
A Strange Prophecy 51

WHEN MOSES SEES THE ISRAELITES WORSHIPING AN IDOL, HIS ANGER CAUSES HIM TO THROW DOWN THE STONE TABLETS.

▲ EXODUS 32 (page 157)

ISAAC
Lost in the Desert 55
Test of Faith 59
Secret Mission to Haran 65
A Bride for Isaac 68

JACOB
The Scheming Brother 72
Cry of Revenge 75
A New Start 80
Bargain in the Desert 85
Journey to Hebron 89

JOSEPH
Into the Pit 92
Slave Train to Egypt 97

ABRAHAM IS WILLING TO OFFER EVEN HIS BELOVED SON, BECAUSE OF HIS LOVE FOR GOD.

▲ GENESIS 22 (page 65)

1ST CHINESE DICTIONARY		1ST OLYMPICS	ALEXANDER	ROME FALLS		COLUMBUS	TODAY
2000 B.C.	1500 B.C.	1000 B.C.	500 B.C.	B	500 A.D.	1000 A.D.	1500 A.D. 2000 A.D.

◀ BEFORE RECORDED TIME

THE FUTURE ▶

ABRAHAM   MOSES   DAVID ELIJAH ESTHER JESUS BORN

B I B L E   H I G H L I G H T S   I N   T I M E

The King's Dream 101
Trouble in Egypt 105
The Stolen Cup 109
Joseph's Secret 113
South into Egypt 117
Death Sentence 121

MOSES
Cry of a Slave 125
The Fiery Bush 129
Pharaoh's Revenge 133
Plague of Death 137
Trapped 142
Crossing the Sea 146
Attacked! 150
The Mountain Trembles . . .154
Commandments of God . .157

Death to an Idol 161
The Tabernacle 164
Fire in Camp 167
A Family Divided 169
Spies Sent Out 173
Division in the Camp 177
Serpents in the Wilderness .181

JOSHUA
A New Leader 189
Crossing the Jordan 193
Siege of Jericho 197
Attack that Failed 201
Sin Brings Defeat 205
Forced March 209
Traitors to God 211

JUDGES
Battle in the Storm 214
Chosen by God 218
Philistine Raiders 224
Attacked by a Lion 227
Fire! 232
The Gaza Trap 235
The Big Bribe 238
Blind Captive 241
Samson's Victory 244

RUTH
Naomi's Strategy 247
A Joyful Wedding 250

▲ JUDGES 6—7 (page 218)

1ST CHINESE DICTIONARY   1ST OLYMPICS   ALEXANDER   ROME FALLS   COLUMBUS   TODAY
2000 B.C.   1500 B.C.   1000 B.C.   500 B.C.   0   500 A.D.   1000 A.D.   1500 A.D.   2000 A.D.

BEFORE RECORDED TIME   THE FUTURE

ABRAHAM   MOSES   DAVID ELIJAH ESTHER   JESUS BORN

B I B L E   H I G H L I G H T S   I N   T I M E

▲ **RUTH 2 (page 247)**

SAMUEL

Call in the Night 253
In a Heathen Temple 255
The Turning Point 258
Samuel Prays for a King . . .261

SAUL

Test for a King 264
By Order of a King 269
The King Disobeys 272
A Mysterious Visit 275

DAVID

The Chosen One 278
A Giant's Challenge 281
The Challenge Is Met 284
The Jealous King 287
Jonathan Defends David . .290
Trapped in a Cave 293
Saul Is Spared 295
David's Dilemma 297
At the Witch's House 300
A Voice from the Dead 303

On the Robbers' Trail 306
Front-line News 307
Rival Kings 310
Warring Kingdoms of Israel .315
Plot against the King! 318
Hail to the King! 321
Underground Attack 324
God's Promise to David . . .327
A King Is Tempted 330
King David's Sin 333
The King's Punishment . . .336
Flight of the Brothers 339
A Prince's Command 342
Treason? 345
Revolt! 348
Council of War 351
Hide-out in a Well 354
Father against Son 357

BECAUSE THE LORD IS MY SHEPHERD, I HAVE EVERYTHING I NEED.

▲ **1 SAMUEL 17 (page 281)**

1ST CHINESE DICTIONARY   1ST OLYMPICS ALEXANDER   ROME FALLS   COLUMBUS   TODAY
2000 B.C.   1500 B.C.   1000 B.C.   500 B.C.   0   500 A.D.   1000 A.D.   1500 A.D.   2000 A.D.

BEFORE RECORDED TIME   THE FUTURE

ABRAHAM   MOSES   DAVID ELIJAH ESTHER   JESUS BORN

B I B L E   H I G H L I G H T S   I N   T I M E

The King Returns 360
The Plot that Failed 363
Death of a King 366

SOLOMON

The Temple of God 371
A Queen's Visit 374
The King Is Dead 377

ELIJAH/ELISHA

The Kingdom Is Divided . .380
Idol Worship in Israel 385
A Prophet Speaks 389
Challenge on Mt. Carmel . .391
Answer by Fire! 395
A Voice in the Mountain . .399
Forged Letters 402
The Price of a Vineyard . . .405

▲ 1 SAMUEL 15 (page 272)

The Last Journey 409
Chariot of Fire! 412
A Miracle of Oil 415
A Prophet's Prescription . . .418
Surrounded 421
One against an Army 424
A Starving City 427
The Missing Enemy 430

THE KINGS

The Sound of Marching Men .433
Revenge of Israel 436
A Queen's Plot 439
The Temple Secret 442
Boy King of Judah 445
Dagger in the Night 448
Test of a City 451
A Foolish King 454
The Lost Book 457
A Prophetess Speaks 460

▲ ESTHER 7 (page 475)

The Fall of Jerusalem 463

EZRA/NEHEMIAH
Return of the Captives 466
Jerusalem Rises Again 469
Two Lines of Defense 472

ESTHER
The Search for a Queen . . .475
A Plot against the King . . .476
A New Law 479
A Queen Risk Her Life 482
The Unchangeable Law . . .485

THE PROPHETS
A Man with a Message 491
A Call from God 493
The Broken Vase 496
Surrender 497
Babylon Strikes! 500
Accused 503

A Prophecy Comes True . . .506
Ten Thousand Captives . . .509
A Message of Hope 512
Captives in Babylon 515
The Statue 518
Trial by Fire 521
A King's Boast 524
Handwriting on the Wall . .527
The Lions' Den 531
Twelve Men of God 534
The Final Message 537
The Years of Waiting 540

NEW TESTAMENT STORIES

JESUS' BIRTH AND MINISTRY
The Life of Jesus 545
A Secret from God 549
A Father's Prophecy 552
The Night the Angels Sang .555
A King Is Born 558
Flight in the Night 561
Boy in the Temple 564
Tempted! 567
Victory in the Wilderness . .570
Six Jars of Water 573
The Judge's Problem 576
In Enemy Territory 579
Through the Roof 583
One Man's Answer 586
Sermon on the Mount 589
Mad Man by the Sea 593

▲ **DANIEL (page 521)**

1ST CHINESE DICTIONARY		1ST OLYMPICS	ALEXANDER	ROME FALLS			COLUMBUS	TODAY
2000 B.C.	1500 B.C.	1000 B.C.	500 B.C.	0	500 A.D.	1000 A.D.	1500 A.D.	2000 A.D.

◄ BEFORE RECORDED TIME

THE FUTURE ►

ABRAHAM   MOSES   DAVID ELIJAH ESTHER   JESUS BORN

B I B L E   H I G H L I G H T S   I N   T I M E

AND SO I AM GIVING A NEW COMMANDMENT TO YOU NOW--LOVE EACH OTHER JUST AS MUCH AS I LOVE YOU.

▲ **John 13 (page 637)**

The Mocking Crowd 596
No Earthly Throne 601
Miracle on the Sea 604
A Boy and His Father's Faith .608
Seventy Times Seven 611
A Beggar Meets Jesus 614
Four Travelers to Jericho . .617
The Lord's Prayer 620
The Prodigal's Return 623
Called from the Tomb 626
Man in a Tree 630

Jesus' Final Days

Triumphal Entry 633
The Great Commandment 637
Secretly in an Upper Room 641
The Lord's Supper 644

Tried and Denied! 648
Condemned to Die 652
A King is Crucified 656
The Sealed Tomb 660
The Lord Is Risen 665
Behind Locked Doors 668
The Last Command 671

The Church is Born

Waiting for a Promise 674
Like Tongues of Fire! 677
Three Thousand in a Day . .680
Miracle at the Gate 683
The Pretenders 687
Missing Prisoners 691
Martyr for Christ 695
Simon, the Magician 698

AND WHEN THE CROWD THAT CAME TO SEE THE CRUCIFIXION SAW THAT JESUS WAS DEAD, THEY WENT HOME IN DEEP SORROW.

I HAD HOPED THAT HE WAS THE ONE WHO WOULD DELIVER US FROM THE ROMANS.

▲ **Luke (page 656)**

1ST CHINESE DICTIONARY · 2000 B.C. · 1500 B.C. · 1ST OLYMPICS · 1000 B.C. · ALEXANDER · 500 B.C. · 0 · ROME FALLS · 500 A.D. · 1000 A.D. · COLUMBUS · 1500 A.D. · TODAY · 2000 A.D.

◀ BEFORE RECORDED TIME   THE FUTURE ▶

ABRAHAM · MOSES · DAVID ELIJAH ESTHER · JESUS BORN

B I B L E   H I G H L I G H T S   I N   T I M E

On the Gaza Road 701
Mission to Joppa 705
God, a Roman, and a Jew . .708
Angel—Open Gate 711
Fall of a Tyrant 714

PAUL

The Story of Paul 717
A Light and a Voice 721
Man with a Mission 724
Foreign Assignment 727
The Enemy Strikes 731
Miracle in Lystra 737
Storm Warning 740
Council in Jerusalem 744
Second Journey 746
Call from across the Sea . . .749
Earthquake 752
Out of Trouble...Into Trouble . .755

Paul Explains the
  "Unknown God" 757
Talk of the Town 761
The Angry Mob 763
Riot in Ephesus 767
Bound Hand and Foot 769
A Boy and a Secret 773
Paul Pleads His Case 775
Apostle on the March 779
The Burning of Rome 781
Soldier Victorious 784
The End of the Era 786

Life in Bible Times 790
The City of Gates 792
Occupations in Bible Times .794

Scripture Index 796

▲ ACTS 9 (page 721)

Did You Know?

The Bible is filled with many exciting stories. Sometimes it is hard to keep everything in perspective. We have provided additional "Did You Know?" fact pages to help you better understand the people and events found in God's Word.

Old Testament World (MAP) 12
God's Wonderful Creation 17
Adam and Eve 18
Noah—Man of Righteousness 35
The Ark and the Flood .36
Abraham—Man of Faith 63
A Bride Is Chosen 64
Wrestling with a Stranger 93
God Turns Bad into Good 94
Moses, God's Leader 135
Countdown to Freedom 136
Traveling with the Israelites 165
The Journey Continues 166
The Roller-Coaster Ride of the Israelites . . .225-226
Prophet, Priest, and Judge 267
Israel's First King—Saul 268
The Road to Becoming a King 313
David, A Man after God's Heart 314
Two Kingdoms 383
Two Prophets—The Same but Different 384
Women Who Change Their World 489-490
New Testament Palestine (MAP) 544
Jesus—A Miracle Worker 599
The Great Storyteller 600
Arresting a King 663
Jerusalem in the First Century A.D. (MAP) 664
Paul, A Champion Who Switches Sides! 735
Spreading the Good News 736

STORIES FROM THE

Old Testament

Old Testament World

FROM GENESIS 1

IN THE BEGINNING

1st DAY

there was darkness—darkness and silence. God created heaven and earth. His Spirit moved through the darkness and across the waters. God said, "Let there be light": and there was light. How beautiful the light was! Then God divided the light from the darkness and called the light Day and the darkness Night.

2nd DAY

God made the sky.
In the sky He placed clouds
to hold the moisture.
And the sky was called Heaven.

3rd DAY

Then God gathered together the waters under the sky. He called these "seas" and He named the dry land "earth." On the land He made grass and flowers, and trees, and in each was the seed to replenish itself. The fruitful earth was to become a place of beauty.

4th DAY

To light the earth, God made the sun to shine by day, and the moon to shine by night ... The days, the years, and the seasons were also set by God. Then He made the stars and placed them in the heavens.

5th DAY

God looked upon the land and seas and said: "Let the waters abound with living creatures" —and the seas and rivers became alive with whales and fish....
"Let there be birds"—and the open sky above the earth was filled with winged creatures.
"Be fruitful and multiply," God said as He blessed the living creatures of the sea and sky.

6th DAY

Then God said, "Let the earth bring forth living creatures"... and animals of all kinds filled the earth. So the waters, the sky, and the earth were filled with life. To have dominion over all these things, God created the first man, Adam, and the first woman, Eve. They were the greatest of all God's creations, for He gave them a mind to choose between good and evil, and a soul that would live forever.

And on the seventh day God rested ...

God took Adam and Eve to the garden of Eden and showed them the beauty and fruitfulness of it. And God commanded: Of every tree you may eat freely ... but of the tree of knowledge of good and evil you may not eat, for in the day that you eat it, you will surely die....

God's Wonderful Creation

Before time, space, or the world existed, there was God. Nothing existed before God. And He created all that exists. His plan is perfect.

Here are some interesting facts about God's creation:

▶ God created day different from night. A day is the time it takes for a planet to spin around once.

▶ The largest tree can grow higher than 367 feet and wider than 20 feet across.

▶ About 71% of the Earth is covered by water.

▶ There are 4600 species of mammals—the largest is the blue whale. Adam gave animals names.

▶ A human child has about 200 bones which stop growing when he or she is 25 years old.

▶ God placed the Sun 93 million miles from Earth to perfectly heat and light our world. It is the closest star to us.

▶ The Earth is 24,859 miles around at the Equator.

▶ God made things in perfect balance!

▶ God put a blanket of air around the Earth to protect us from the heat and cold of space.

People are God's greatest creation.

17

Did You Know?

Adam and Eve

Adam and Eve are unique in many ways. No one lives before them to teach them how things should be done. God is their teacher.

Here are other ways that they are unique:

▶ Adam is the first man; Eve is the first woman.

▶ Adam is first to name the animals.

▶ They are the first parents. Their sons are Cain, Abel, and Seth.

▶ Adam is made from the dust of the earth; Eve is made from Adam's rib.

▶ Adam and Eve take care of the Garden of Eden.

▶ They are the first people to sin against God. They have to leave the beautiful garden.

Read about Adam and Eve on pp. 6-14 of your Picture Bible.

Temptation in the Garden
FROM GENESIS 3

Jealous Brothers

FROM GENESIS 4:1–8

Outside the garden of Eden the land is barren, hot and dry. Weary, alone and frightened, Adam and Eve search until they find a place to make a home.

REMEMBER HOW BEAUTIFUL EDEN WAS? IF ONLY...

YES, IF ONLY WE HAD OBEYED GOD. WE MUST MAKE CERTAIN THAT WE TEACH OUR CHILDREN SO THAT THEY DON'T MAKE THE MISTAKE WE DID!

SO ADAM TEACHES THEIR SONS, CAIN AND ABEL, ABOUT GOD.

HE MADE THE EARTH AND EVERYTHING WE HAVE.

I LIKE TO THINK OF GOD GIVING ME MY LITTLE LAMB.

The Verdict

FROM GENESIS 4:8–26; 5; 6:1–8

In a lonely pasture, Cain killed his brother, Abel. Cain is sure nobody saw the murder. But suddenly the killer is afraid. Did someone see him? Who?

He looks around... and then he hears the voice of God asking: *"Where is Abel, your brother?"*

I—I don't know. Am I my brother's keeper?

God knows I have killed Abel!

Terrified, Cain hears God's verdict—as punishment for murdering Abel, Cain must leave home and forever be a fugitive.

Oh, God! Please! This punishment is more than I can take!

BUT GOD'S SENTENCE WAS CARRIED OUT. CAIN FLED TO A LAND CALLED NOD. THERE HE MARRIED AND BUILT THE FIRST CITY, WHICH HE NAMED FOR HIS SON, ENOCH.

ADAM AND EVE ARE HEARTBROKEN BY THE LOSS OF THEIR TWO SONS.

OUR HOUSE IS SO EMPTY AND STILL. OH, ADAM, WILL WE ALWAYS BE ALONE LIKE THIS?

WE BROUGHT THIS TRAGEDY ON OURSELVES, EVE—AND SO DID CAIN. BUT GOD HAS BEEN GOOD TO US. LET'S ASK HIM TO HELP US NOW...

IN TIME, A THIRD SON IS BORN TO THEM.

WE'LL CALL HIM SETH.

AND WE'LL TEACH HIM TO OBEY GOD THE WAY ABEL DID.

AGAIN ADAM AND EVE'S PRAYERS ARE ANSWERED, FOR SETH LEARNS TO OBEY GOD. TWO OF HIS DESCENDANTS ARE ENOCH WHO "WALKED WITH GOD" AND METHUSELAH WHO DIED AT THE AGE OF 969—THE OLDEST MAN WHO EVER LIVED.

When the Rains Came

FROM GENESIS 6:7–22; 7:1–10

WHEN THE ARK IS COMPLETED, GOD DIRECTS
NOAH AND HIS FAMILY TO ENTER... AND TO
TAKE WITH THEM SEVEN PAIRS OF EACH
KIND OF ANIMAL AND BIRD THAT IS GOOD
TO EAT, AND ONE PAIR OF EACH KIND NOT
USED FOR FOOD.

The Great Flood

FROM GENESIS 7:16–24; 8; 9; 11

WATER FLOWS OVER THE LAND AND RISES ABOVE THE MOUNTAIN-TOPS. ALL THE EARTH IS COVERED... ONLY NOAH'S GREAT ARK SURVIVES. THE FLOOD DESTROYS ALL THAT IS EVIL.

AT LAST THE WATER LEVEL DROPS AND THE ARK RESTS ON THE TOP OF THE MOUNTAINS OF ARARAT.

I WILL SEND OUT A DOVE; IF IT DOES NOT COME BACK WE WILL KNOW IT HAS FOUND LAND.

BUT THE DOVE RETURNS!

NOAH SENDS OUT A DOVE AGAIN, AND IT RETURNS.

AN OLIVE BRANCH! THAT MEANS SOME LAND MUST BE DRY AGAIN.

SEVEN DAYS LATER, NOAH SENDS OUT A DOVE A THIRD TIME. IT DOES NOT RETURN BECAUSE IT HAS FOUND A PLACE TO NEST.

SO, A LITTLE OVER A YEAR AFTER THE FLOOD BEGAN, NOAH STEPS ON DRY LAND ONCE MORE. HE, HIS FAMILY AND THE ANIMALS IN THE ARK ARE THE ONLY CREATURES ON EARTH.

HOW GOOD IT IS TO WALK ON THE GROUND AGAIN!

YES—TO FEEL GRASS UNDER YOUR FEET AND WARM SUNSHINE ON YOUR FACE.

ALL THAT WAS EVIL HAS BEEN DESTROYED. THROUGH US, GOD IS GIVING MANKIND A NEW START. WE MUST OBEY GOD—AND TEACH ALL WHO FOLLOW US TO DO SO.

AS SOON AS NOAH LEAVES THE ARK, HE BUILDS AN ALTAR. HERE HE THANKS GOD FOR HIS CARE AND ASKS GOD'S GUIDANCE IN HELPING NOAH AND HIS FAMILY TO MAKE A NEW START. THEN GOD MAKES A PROMISE TO NOAH AND TO ALL HIS CHILDREN, FOREVER...

WHILE THE EARTH REMAINETH, SEEDTIME AND HARVEST... AND SUMMER AND WINTER, AND DAY AND NIGHT SHALL NOT CEASE...NEITHER SHALL THERE ANY MORE BE A FLOOD TO DESTROY THE EARTH

HOW BEAUTIFUL! SURELY GOD IS GOOD TO US!

YES, AND WHENEVER PEOPLE SEE A RAINBOW IN THE SKY, THEY WILL BE REMINDED OF GOD'S PROMISE THAT NEVER AGAIN WILL A FLOOD DESTROY THE EARTH.

IN THE YEARS AFTER THE FLOOD, NOAH'S SONS—SHEM, HAM AND JAPHETH—AND THEIR FAMILIES MOVE DOWN TO THE RIVER VALLEYS. THEIR FAMILIES GROW LARGER...IN TIME THE MOUNTAINS AND PLAINS ARE DOTTED WITH THE TENTS OF SHEPHERD TRIBESMEN, AND THE RICH RIVER VALLEYS WITH GROWING CITIES.

AS THOSE FROM THE CITIES WORK TOGETHER, THEY BECOME PROUD OF THE THINGS THEY CAN BUILD. THEY EVEN DREAM OF A GREAT TOWER...

WE'LL BUILD IT HIGH ENOUGH TO REACH HEAVEN!

IT WILL MAKE US FAMOUS—AND POWERFUL!

Noah—Man of Righteousness

▶ Read about Noah on pp. 27-34.

Did You Know?

In contrast to the sinful people, God sees only one person on earth who stands out as righteous—Noah. He tries to please God when everyone else chooses to turn away. Here are some interesting facts about Noah:

▶ Noah is 480 years old when God tells him He will destroy the world with water.

▶ Noah preaches for 120 years without one person responding to his message!

▶ Noah is 600 years old when the flood begins.

▶ After the Flood, Noah becomes a farmer.

▶ Noah has a wife, three sons—Shem, Ham, and Japheth, and their wives. These people help Noah build the ark.

▶ There are nine generations from Adam to Noah.

God tells Noah exactly how to build the ark.

After the Flood, Noah offers thanks to God, and God promises never again to destroy the world by water.

Did You Know?

The Ark and the Flood

Here are some interesting facts:

▶ The Bible tells us that the sources of the Flood are: 1) upheavals in the oceans, probably due to earthquakes and volcanoes, and 2) rain falling for 40 days and 40 nights.

▶ God tells Noah to take two of all the clean animals and seven of every unclean animal. Clean animals are those that chew their cud and have a split hoof, like a cow or sheep.

▶ Noah and the animals are on the ark one year and ten days.

▶ The ark lands in the Ararat mountain range in Turkey. The exact mountain of the landing is not known.

▶ The Flood is the biggest catastrophe ever experienced by the earth and its inhabitants.

▶ The ark is 450 feet long (longer than a football field), 75 feet wide, and 45 feet high. It has three decks.

▶ Only eight people—Noah and his family—are saved . . . in the whole world!

The Tower that Crumbled
From Genesis 11

A TOWER THAT WILL REACH TO HEAVEN — HOW BEAUTIFUL IT IS!

IT CAN BE SEEN FOR MILES. IN TIME OF DANGER WE WILL RALLY OUR FORCES AROUND IT. NO ONE IS GOING TO CONQUER AND SCATTER US! WITH THIS TOWER, WE'LL BE INVINCIBLE!

BUT GOD IS DISPLEASED WITH THE PEOPLE'S DESIRE FOR FAME AND POWER. TO STOP THEIR WORK ON THE TOWER, HE CAUSES THE PEOPLE TO SPEAK IN DIFFERENT LANGUAGES.

WHAT KIND OF TALK IS THAT? HOW CAN I WORK WITH A MAN I CAN'T UNDERSTAND?

BECAUSE THEY CANNOT UNDERSTAND ONE ANOTHER, THE BUILDERS ARE CONFUSED. THEY STOP WORKING ON THE TOWER. ONE BY ONE, THE FAMILIES WHO SPEAK THE SAME LANGUAGE MOVE AWAY. THE GIANT TOWER, CALLED BABEL, BEGINS TO CRUMBLE...

SOME OF THE FAMILIES MOVE DOWN THE EUPHRATES RIVER—AND THERE BUILD THE GREAT TRADING CITY OF UR. OTHERS PITCH THEIR TENTS ON THE PLAINS BEYOND. THE BIBLE TRACES THE GENERATIONS FROM NOAH'S SON, SHEM, TO A TRIBAL CHIEFTAIN NAMED TERAH WHO LIVES OUTSIDE UR.

ONE DAY IN TERAH'S CAMP THERE IS GREAT EXCITEMENT—EVERYONE IS GETTING READY FOR A TRIP TO UR.

MAY WE TRADE OUR WOOL FOR ANYTHING WE WANT, FATHER?

YES, ABRAHAM. BUT FIRST YOU MUST HELP ME LOAD OUR SUPPLIES.

LOOK! GREEN BEANS AND MELONS!

WE'LL TRADE SOME OF OUR SUPPLIES FOR FRESH VEGETABLES. THEN YOU, HARAN AND NAHOR MAY GO INTO THE CITY.

A THROW STICK FOR YOUR BAG OF WOOL.

IT'S A DEAL!

IMAGINE THROWING A STICK THAT WILL COME BACK TO YOU.

WHAT IS THAT TOWER?

IT IS A TEMPLE TO THE MOON-GOD.

BACK HOME, ABRAHAM THINKS OFTEN ABOUT HIS VISIT TO UR. AND AS HE GROWS OLDER HE WONDERS ABOUT THE TEMPLE OF THE MOON-GOD.

ONE EVENING ABRAHAM TALKS TO SARAH, THE MOST BEAUTIFUL GIRL IN HIS FATHER'S CAMP.

IT'S ONLY THE MOON, SARAH, NOT SOMETHING TO WORSHIP.

ABRAHAM—BE CAREFUL. MANY PEOPLE HERE WORSHIP THE MOON-GOD. THEY MIGHT HEAR YOU AND DO YOU HARM.

WOULD YOU CARE, SARAH?

YES, ABRAHAM. EVERYONE EXPECTS YOU TO BE HEAD OF OUR TRIBE, SOMEDAY.

SARAH, I LOVE YOU AND WANT YOU TO BE MY WIFE. BUT IT'S ONLY FAIR THAT YOU SHOULD KNOW I DO NOT BELIEVE IN THE MOON-GOD. THERE IS ONLY ONE GOD—THE GOD WHO MADE THE MOON, THE STARS, THE SUN— EVEN US!

I LOVE YOU, ABRAHAM. BUT GIVE ME TIME TO THINK...

A FEW DAYS LATER, A CARAVAN STOPS AT TERAH'S CAMP.

MAY WE CAMP HERE WHILE WE SELL OUR GOODS IN UR?

YOU ARE WELCOME. MY SON, ABRAHAM, WILL SHOW YOUR MEN WHERE TO WATER YOUR CAMELS.

SO YOU COME FROM CANAAN. DO THE PEOPLE THERE WORSHIP THE MOON-GOD, UR?

NO, THEY HAVE THEIR OWN GODS, CALLED BAALS.

BAAL! THE MOON-GOD! EVERY-ONE HAS A DIFFERENT GOD. ABRAHAM, I BELIEVE AS YOU DO—THERE IS ONLY ONE GOD.

DO YOU, SARAH? THEN WE'LL BOTH TRUST IN GOD—NO MATTER WHAT HAPPENS.

IT IS A FESTIVE DAY FOR ALL OF THE TRIBE WHEN ABRAHAM AND SARAH ARE MARRIED. DURING THE CEREMONY SARAH PRAYS TO GOD, ASKING FOR COURAGE TO STAND BY HER HUSBAND—FOR THEY ARE TWO AGAINST MANY WHO BELIEVE IN OTHER GODS.

ONE NIGHT, SEVERAL WEEKS LATER, SARAH WAKENS TO FIND ABRAHAM GONE...

ABRAHAM! ABRAHAM!

The Journey Begins
FROM GENESIS 11

AT LAST THE GREAT DAY ARRIVES. THE FLOCKS... DONKEYS LADEN WITH SUPPLIES...THE FAMILIES...ALL FORM A GREAT CARAVAN THAT PUSHES NORTH ALONG THE EUPHRATES RIVER.

I WONDER WHAT LIES AHEAD, ABRAHAM.

HAVE NO FEAR, SARAH, GOD WILL GUIDE US.

ASSYRIA

HARAN

MEDITERRANEAN SEA

TIGRIS RIVER

EUPHRATES RIVER

DAMASCUS   NORTH

ARABIAN DESERT

MAP OF TERAH'S JOURNEY.

UR

PERSIAN GULF

AFTER A FEW DAYS OUT ABRAHAM CALLS A MEETING OF NAHOR AND LOT.

IT WILL BE COOLER FOR THE FLOCKS IF WE REST BY DAY AND TRAVEL AT NIGHT.

BUT WHAT ABOUT WILD ANIMALS?

I'M TRUSTING THE ONE TRUE GOD TO PROTECT US.

I AGREE WITH UNCLE ABRAHAM.

42

Into the Unknown

FROM GENESIS 11

43

44

45

Raiders of Sodom

FROM GENESIS 12:16–20; 13; 14:1–13

IN THE EGYPTIAN PALACE, SARAH IS INTRODUCED AS ABRAHAM'S SISTER. PHARAOH IS AMAZED BY HER BEAUTY.

GIVE HER BROTHER, ABRAHAM, GIFTS OF SHEEP, OXEN, CAMELS AND SERVANTS. TRULY, HIS SISTER IS A BEAUTIFUL WOMAN!

OH, ABRAHAM, IF I DID NOT LOVE YOU SO MUCH COULD NOT LIVE THIS LIE!

BUT SARAH'S PRESENCE IN PHARAOH'S COURT BRINGS TROUBLE. A PLAGUE BREAKS OUT...

THIS SICKNESS CAME UPON US AT THE TIME THE FOREIGN WOMAN WAS BROUGHT HERE. I HAVE LEARNED SHE IS REALLY ABRAHAM'S WIFE—NOT HIS SISTER. GET RID OF HER!

WHEN PHARAOH LEARNS T TRUTH ABOUT SARAH, HE CALLS FOR HIS SOLDIERS.

BRING ABRAHAM AND SARAH TO ME—NOW!

49

50

A Stranger's Prophecy

FROM GENESIS 15—18; 19:1–10

"LOOK TOWARD HEAVEN, AND COUNT THE STARS, IF THOU BE ABLE TO NUMBER THEM:..SO SHALL THE NUMBER OF THY DESCENDANTS BE."

LATER, WHEN SARAH COMES TO HIM WITH A PLAN, HE LISTENS...

BY THE CUSTOM OF OUR PEOPLE I CAN GIVE YOU HAGAR, MY HANDMAID, AS A WIFE THAT SHE MIGHT HAVE A SON FOR ME.

GOD HAS PROMISED ME AN HEIR— PERHAPS THIS IS RIGHT...

HAGAR HAS A SON, AND HE IS THE PRIDE OF ABRAHAM'S HEART.

MY ISHMAEL IS A PROUD AND DARING ONE!

REMEMBER, HAGAR, HE IS **MY** SON! I ADOPTED HIM!

52

WHILE THEY ARE EATING, ONE OF THE STRANGERS GIVES ABRAHAM SURPRISING NEWS!

YOUR WIFE, SARAH, WILL HAVE A SON.

WHO ARE THESE STRANGERS TO BRING FALSE HOPE TO ABRAHAM? I AM TOO OLD TO HAVE CHILDREN!

AND HOW WOULD THIS AFFECT HAGAR?

IF SARAH HAS A SON, WHAT WILL HAPPEN TO ISHMAEL —AND ME!

WHEN THE STRANGERS LEAVE, ABRAHAM WALKS A WAY WITH THEM.

THAT CITY OF SODOM IS SO WICKED THAT GOD MAY HAVE TO DESTROY IT.

THIS IS A MESSENGER FROM GOD! THEY ARE TALKING ABOUT THE PLACE LOT LIVES!

ABRAHAM PRAYS FOR SODOM, AND GOD PROMISES THAT THE CITY WILL BE SAVED IF THERE ARE TEN GOOD MEN IN IT.

Lost in the Desert

FROM GENESIS 19:11–30; 21:1–16

OUTSIDE LOT'S HOUSE IN SODOM, THE MOB GOES WILD. RIOTERS HOWL FOR REVENGE AGAINST LOT AND THE STRANGERS WHO RESCUED HIM.

COME ON— WE'LL BREAK DOWN THE DOOR!

AS THE MEN PUSH AGAINST LOT'S DOOR, THE ANGELS STRIKE THE RIOTERS BLIND.

HELP! I CAN'T SEE!

MY EYES— WHO HIT ME?

INSIDE LOT'S HOUSE...

RUN FOR YOUR LIVES! THE LORD HAS SENT US TO DESTROY THIS WICKED CITY!

MY FAMILY— I MUST SAVE THEM!

BUT LOT'S SONS-IN-LAW ONLY LAUGH WHEN HE TRIES TO WARN THEM. THEY REFUSE TO LEAVE THE DOOMED CITY, SO, EARLY THE NEXT MORNING, THE TWO ANGELS LEAD LOT, HIS WIFE AND THEIR TWO DAUGHTERS AWAY. SUDDENLY ALL SODOM BURSTS INTO FLAME!

DON'T LOOK BACK AT THE CITY—OR YOU WILL ALSO DIE!

I DON'T CARE WHAT GOD SAYS—I WANT TO GO BACK!

LOT'S WIFE STOPS...LOOKS BACK LONGINGLY... AND IS TURNED INTO A PILLAR OF SALT...SO ONLY LOT AND HIS TWO DAUGHTERS ESCAPE GOD'S PUNISHMENT.

NEXT MORNING, ABRAHAM GOES TO THE HILLTOP TO WORSHIP—AND SEES THE SMOULDERING RUINS OF THE WICKED CITY...

AS SURELY AS NIGHT FOLLOWS DAY, DESTRUCTION FOLLOWS SIN. O GOD, HELP ME TO LEAD MY PEOPLE IN THE PATHS OF RIGHTEOUSNESS!

EAGER TO LEAVE THE RUINS OF SODOM, ABRAHAM MOVES TO BEER-SHEBA, NEAR THE DESERT. HERE, SARAH'S SON IS BORN.

ABRAHAM HAS NAMED HIS SECOND SON, ISAAC.

WHAT WILL BECOME OF ISHMAEL, HIS FIRST SON? HE MIGHT HAVE BEEN OUR RULER AFTER ABRAHAM, BUT NOW THE BABY, ISAAC, WILL RULE OUR PEOPLE.

I'M AFRAID THERE WILL BE TROUBLE.

SARAH AND HAGAR BECOME MORE JEALOUS DAY BY DAY. THEN AT THE BABY ISAAC'S FIRST FEAST...

SEE HOW CLUMSY LITTLE ISAAC IS!

ISHMAEL! BE QUIET!

SARAH IS ANGRY! WHAT WILL SHE DO?

HAGAR'S SON CAN'T MAKE FUN OF MINE! ABRAHAM, YOU MUST SEND ISHMAEL AND HAGAR AWAY, BEFORE THEY CAUSE TROUBLE IN THE TRIBE.

NIGHT AFTER NIGHT, ABRAHAM SEEKS GOD'S ANSWER TO HIS PROBLEM. FINALLY, HE KNOWS WHAT HE MUST DO.

Test of Faith

FROM GENESIS 21:17–21; 22:1–10

DEAD TIRED AND CHOKING WITH THIRST, HAGAR TURNS HER BACK ON HER SON, ISHMAEL... SHE CANNOT WATCH HIM DYING. SUDDENLY SHE HEARS A VOICE. IT'S GOD SAYING: "LIFT UP THE LAD, FOR I WILL MAKE HIM A GREAT NATION".

HAGAR STARTS TOWARD HER SON... AND SEES A SPRING NEARBY.

WATER! WE WILL NOT DIE! O ISHMAEL, GOD HAS SAVED US!

61

62

Abraham—Man of Faith

Many times Abraham demonstrates his faith in God by doing exactly what God asks him to do without question. Here are some examples:

▶ God asks Abraham to leave his home and go to an unknown land. *Abraham leaves with his whole family and goes almost 600 miles to Haran (page 41).*

▶ Abraham wants an heir. God promises him as many descendants as there are stars. *He believes God, even though* *it doesn't happen right away. At age 100, God gives Abraham Isaac. (page 51).*

There are 8,000 stars visible from earth. But at any one time, we can only see about 2,000.

▶ God asks Abraham to sacrifice his son. *Abraham prepares to do that, but God supplies a ram at the last minute (page 62).*

Abraham lives 175 years. Isaac lives 180 years.

Abraham is thought of as the father of the Hebrews.

Did You Know?   **A Bride Is Chosen**

On pp. 67-71, we read about Abraham sending his servant, Eliezer, to find a bride for his son, Isaac. In Bible times in the East, parents select the bride for their sons. This story helps us understand how it is done.

1. **Abraham sends Eliezer to select a bride and meet her family.**

2. **Eliezer meets with Rebekah's brother, the family's representative.**

3. **Eliezer is offered food but refuses to eat until the negotiation is complete.**

4. **Eliezer gets permission for the bride to marry and then a dowry amount is set. He gives many gifts to Rebekah's family, showing Abraham's great wealth.**

• • • • • • • • • • • • • • • • • •

A dowry is a gift given to the bride's father to make up for the loss of his daughter's help.

• • • • • • • • • • • • • • • • • •

5. **The marriage agreement is sealed by everyone eating food together.**

• • • • • • • • • • • • • • • • • •

Some gifts are given to the bride. Rebekah's father gives her a nurse and maids to attend her.

• • • • • • • • • • • • • • • • • •

6. **The bride goes to meet her husband and they are married.**

The bride becomes part of the groom's family in Old Testament times.

WITH JOYOUS HEARTS, ABRAHAM AND ISAAC GIVE THANKS TO GOD. AND ABRAHAM HEARS GOD'S PROMISE: "THROUGH YOU, ALL NATIONS OF THE EARTH SHALL BE BLESSED."

ON THE WAY HOME, ISAAC WALKS AHEAD—AND ALONE. THROUGH HIS MIND FLASH SCENES OF THE DAY. HE CAN STILL FEEL THE ROPES THAT TIED HIM ON THE ALTAR...SEE HIS FATHER'S DAGGER...FEEL THE JOY OF KNOWING HE WOULD NOT BE KILLED.

SARAH RUSHES OUT OF THE CAMP TO GREET THEM.

ISAAC, MY SON, WHAT HAPPENED? YOU LEFT HERE A BOY—YOU HAVE RETURNED A MAN— LIKE YOUR FATHER, STRONG, TALL, WISE.

FROM MY FATHER I LEARNED THE COST OF FAITH... AND FROM GOD, THE REWARD.

IN THE YEARS THAT FOLLOW, THE TRIBE OF ABRAHAM PROSPERS. THEN ONE DAY, SAD NEWS SPREADS THROUGHOUT THE CAMP...SARAH IS VERY SICK.

ONE EVENING, ABRAHAM APPEARS AT THE DOOR OF HIS TENT... THE CAMP GROWS QUIET... AND LIKE A MAN IN A DREAM, HE TELLS HIS PEOPLE, SARAH, HIS WIFE, IS DEAD.

SARAH IS BURIED IN A CAVE AT MACHPELAH, AND THE WHOLE TRIBE MOURNS HER DEATH.

ISAAC IS GOING ALONE INTO THE WILDERNESS TO MOURN FOR HIS MOTHER.

IT IS WELL. HE MUST CONQUER HIS GRIEF.

ONE DAY, ABRAHAM CALLS HIS MOST TRUSTED SERVANT TO HIM.

BEFORE I DIE, I WANT TO SEE MY SON HAPPILY MARRIED— TO A WOMAN OF MY OWN PEOPLE. GO TO HARAN AND BRING BACK A WIFE FOR ISAAC.

ABRAHAM'S SERVANT GATHERS A LONG CARAVAN. HE LEADS IT ACROSS THE DESERT AND FINALLY REACHES THE CITY OF HARAN, WHERE ABRAHAM'S RELATIVES LIVE.

WHAT A BIG CITY! HOW WILL I EVER FIND THE RIGHT WIFE FOR THE MAN WHO WILL ONE DAY BE CHIEF OF OUR TRIBE?

A Bride for Isaac

FROM GENESIS 24:11–67; 25:7–8

WHEN THE GIRL HAS FINISHED WATERING THE CAMELS, THE SERVANT GIVES HER EARRINGS AND GOLD BRACELETS.

WHAT IS YOUR NAME? DO YOU THINK THERE IS ROOM FOR ME TO STAY IN YOUR FATHER'S HOUSE?

HOW BEAUTIFUL THESE PRESENTS ARE! MY NAME IS REBEKAH, AND WE HAVE ROOM FOR YOU IN OUR HOUSE. WAIT...

REBEKAH RUNS TO TELL HER FAMILY. WHEN SHE SHOWS THE PRESENTS, LABAN, HER BROTHER, GOES OUT TO MEET ABRAHAM'S SERVANT.

COME! MY FATHER HAS ROOM FOR YOU AND YOUR CARAVAN.

ABRAHAM'S SERVANT TELLS WHO HE IS AND EXPLAINS THAT GOD HAS CHOSEN REBEKAH TO BE THE BRIDE OF ISAAC, SON AND HEIR OF ABRAHAM, HER GREAT UNCLE.

TAKE REBEKAH TO BE THE WIFE OF MY UNCLE'S SON— AS THE LORD HAS SPOKEN.

EARLY THE NEXT MORNING, THE CARAVAN GETS READY TO RETURN TO ABRAHAM'S CAMP. REBEKAH SAYS GOOD-BY TO HER FAMILY AND THE CARAVAN BEGINS ITS LONG JOURNEY.

DAYS LATER, THE CARAVAN NEARS ABRAHAM'S CAMP. REBEKAH WONDERS...

WHAT WILL ISAAC BE LIKE? TALL AND STRONG LIKE A CHIEF'S SON? I WONDER IF HE WILL LOVE ME...

WHO IS THE MAN COMING TO MEET US?

IT IS ISAAC!

HE IS HANDSOME!

IS THIS WOMAN TO BE MY WIFE?

WHEN ISAAC SEES REBEKAH, HE FALLS IN LOVE WITH HER AT ONCE AND TAKES HER TO HIS FATHER FOR HIS BLESSING.

MAY GOD WHO HAS GUIDED ME, GUIDE YOU, MY CHILDREN. SERVE HIM ALWAYS.

THE WHOLE CAMP REJOICES WHEN ISAAC AND REBEKAH ARE MARRIED. "LONG LIFE AND HAPPINESS," SHOUT THE PEOPLE WHO KNOW THAT SOMEDAY ISAAC WILL BE THEIR CHIEFTAIN.

YEARS LATER, THEY REJOICE AGAIN, WHEN TWIN SONS, JACOB AND ESAU, ARE BORN TO ISAAC AND REBEKAH.

MORE YEARS PASS AND ABRAHAM GROWS OLDER. HE BECOMES FEEBLE AND FINALLY TOO SICK TO MOVE. THE END IS NEAR AND THE PEOPLE DREAD THE NEWS ISAAC BRINGS ONE DAY...

MY FATHER IS DEAD!

OUR SORROW IS GREAT...

YES, BUT WE SALUTE YOU, ISAAC, OUR NEW CHIEF!

IN HIS FIRST MOMENTS AS CHIEF OF THE TRIBE, ISAAC THINKS OF HIS BROTHER...

TAKE THE NEWS OF MY FATHER'S DEATH TO HIS FIRST SON, ISHMAEL.

ISHMAEL! WHAT IF HE TAKES REVENGE ON ISAAC?

TRADERS FROM THE WILDERNESS SAY ISHMAEL IS A MIGHTY HUNTER— HIS ARROWS NEVER MISS!

ISAAC WOULD BE NO MATCH FOR SUCH A ONE!

The Scheming Brother

FROM GENESIS 25:9–33

THE WHOLE TRIBE MOURNS THE DEATH OF ITS GREAT LEADER, ABRAHAM. THROUGHOUT THE CAMP THERE IS A STIR OF UNEASINESS. BEHIND ISAAC'S BACK MEN WHISPER, "WILL ISHMAEL COME?" ONE DAY, A GREAT CLOUD OF DUST RISES IN THE DISTANCE...

IT'S ISHMAEL! WITH A BAND OF RIDERS!

BREATHLESSLY, THE WHOLE CAMP LOOKS ON AS ISAAC GOES OUT TO MEET HIS BROTHER.

ISHMAEL— MY BROTHER!

THAT SAME DAY THE TRIBE OF ABRAHAM JOURNEYS TO THE BURIAL CAVE OF MACHPELAH—TO PLACE THE BODY OF ITS GREAT CHIEFTAIN BESIDE HIS WIFE, SARAH. BUT IN THE MIDST OF THEIR GRIEF, THE PEOPLE ANXIOUSLY WATCH ISHMAEL...

BUT ISHMAEL, LIKE ISAAC, HAS KNOWN THE LOVING CARE OF GOD. THE OLDER BROTHER HAS NO THOUGHTS OF REVENGE.

IS IT WELL WITH YOU AND YOUR PEOPLE, ISHMAEL?

I HAVE TWELVE SONS. MY TRIBE IS POWERFUL. THE SONS OF ABRAHAM WILL LIVE IN PEACE, MY BROTHER.

TIME AND AGAIN GOD HAD TESTED ABRAHAM'S FAITH... AND BY FAITH ABRAHAM HAD OBEYED. TIME AND AGAIN, TOO, GOD HAD PROMISED TO MAKE ABRAHAM THE FOUNDER OF GREAT NATIONS...AND THROUGH HIS SONS THE PROMISE WAS FULFILLED.

UNDER ISAAC'S PEACEFUL LEADERSHIP, THE TRIBE CONTINUES TO GROW. THE PEOPLE ARE LOYAL, EVEN WHEN ISAAC MOVES THEM FROM PLACE TO PLACE TO AVOID WAR WITH NEIGHBORING TRIBES OVER WATER HOLES THAT ARE RIGHTFULLY HIS. BUT ISAAC FAILS TO SEE THE CONFLICT BETWEEN HIS OWN SONS.

WHICH ONE WILL RULE OUR TRIBE AFTER ISAAC?

ESAU—IT IS HIS BIRTHRIGHT BECAUSE HE WAS BORN FIRST.

Cry of Revenge

FROM GENESIS 25:32–34; 26; 27:1–41

ISAAC HAS GROWN OLD. HIS EYESIGHT IS FAILING. NOW HE DECIDES IT IS TIME TO GIVE HIS ELDEST SON THE BLESSING WHICH WILL INCLUDE RULING THE TRIBE.

YOU CALLED ME, FATHER?

YES, ESAU. I AM OLD AND TIRED—AND I DON'T KNOW HOW SOON I SHALL DIE. BRING ME SOME CHOICE VENISON AND I WILL GIVE YOU THE BLESSING THAT SEALS YOUR BIRTHRIGHT.

THE NEWS REBEKAH OVERHEARS SENDS HER RUNNING THROUGH THE CAMP...

FIND JACOB! TELL HIM TO COME TO HIS MOTHER'S TENT— AT ONCE! HURRY!

LISTEN, JACOB! YOUR FATHER IS GETTING READY TO GIVE ESAU THE BLESSING. YOU MUST GET THAT BLESSING, OR THE BIRTHRIGHT YOU GOT FROM ESAU MEANS NOTHING.

BUT WHAT CAN I DO?

BEFORE YOU AND YOUR BROTHER WERE BORN, THE LORD SPOKE TO ME AND SAID: "THE ELDER SHALL SERVE THE YOUNGER." BUT ESAU WILL SERVE YOU ONLY IF YOU ARE CHIEF OF THE TRIBE.

MY SKIN IS SMOOTH, BUT ESAU IS HAIRY. FATHER WILL TOUCH ME AND KNOW I AM NOT ESAU. WHAT CAN WE DO?

I HAVE THOUGHT OF THAT, TOO. HERE, PUT ON ESAU'S ROBE—THESE SKINS ON YOUR ARMS AND NECK WILL MAKE YOU FEEL LIKE ESAU.

BUT WHAT IF...

76

77

NO SOONER IS THE BLESSING GIVEN, THAN JACOB RUSHES OUT OF HIS FATHER'S TENT.

MOTHER! THE BLESSING IS MINE! BUT WHAT WILL ESAU SAY?

NO MATTER WHAT ESAU SAYS, THE BLESSING IS YOURS. NOT EVEN YOUR FATHER CAN TAKE IT BACK NOW!

BUT WHILE JACOB AND HIS MOTHER ARE REJOICING, ESAU RETURNS.

A New Start

FROM GENESIS 27:42–46; 28; 29:1–25

WITH ESAU'S THREAT TO KILL JACOB RINGING IN HER EARS, THE SERVANT GIRL RUNS TO REBEKAH'S TENT.

ESAU IS GOING TO KILL JACOB!

ESAU IS UPSET—TELL NO ONE WHAT YOU HAVE HEARD. FIND JACOB AND TELL HIM TO COME TO ME— AT ONCE!

YOU MUST GO AWAY UNTIL YOUR BROTHER'S ANGER COOLS. GO TO MY BROTHER, LABAN, IN HARAN. I WILL SEND FOR YOU WHEN IT IS SAFE TO RETURN.

WHAT WILL I TELL MY FATHER?

ONCE AGAIN, REBEKAH PAVES THE WAY FOR HER FAVORITE SON.

ISAAC, ESAU'S WIVES ARE A GREAT TROUBLE TO ME. LIFE WILL NOT BE WORTH LIVING FOR ME IF JACOB MARRIES A WOMAN OF THIS COUNTRY. IF ONLY HE COULD MARRY A GIRL FROM MY PEOPLE—REMEMBER HOW YOUR FATHER'S SERVANT FOUND ME AT MY FATHER'S HOUSE IN HARAN AND BROUGHT ME TO YOU?

ISAAC'S THOUGHTS GO BACK OVER THE YEARS TO THE DAY HE FIRST SAW REBEKAH. HE ALSO KNOWS THERE WILL BE TROUBLE BETWEEN HIS SONS. HE SENDS FOR JACOB.

ASHAMED, BUT FRIGHTENED BY ESAU'S ANGER, JACOB COMES TO HIS FATHER.

GO TO THY MOTHER'S BROTHER, LABAN, AND FIND A WIFE FROM AMONG HIS FAMILY. GOD BLESS YOU, MY SON.

A FEW HOURS LATER—AT THE EDGE OF CAMP...

GOOD-BY, MY SON. I'LL SEND WORD WHEN IT IS SAFE TO RETURN.

MY FATHER IS OLD—I MAY NEVER SEE HIM AGAIN. ESAU WANTS TO KILL ME. OH, MOTHER, YOU ARE THE ONLY ONE I WILL BE ABLE TO COME BACK TO!

ONE PUNISHMENT FOR THEIR DECEIT IS THAT REBEKAH AND JACOB NEVER SEE EACH OTHER AGAIN.

TRAVELING FARTHER AND FARTHER FROM HIS FAMILY AND FRIENDS, JACOB IS TORTURED BY LONELINESS. HE ESPECIALLY MISSES HIS MOTHER, WHO HAS ALWAYS PROTECTED AND ADVISED HIM. HE IS HAUNTED BY THE MEMORY OF HOW HE TRICKED HIS FATHER AND BROTHER.

AS NIGHT APPROACHES...

IT'S GETTING DARK...I'LL HAVE TO STOP HERE TONIGHT.

JACOB SOON FALLS ASLEEP...AND HE DREAMS OF A SHINING LADDER, REACHING UP TO HEAVEN. ON THE LADDER ARE ANGELS, GOING UP AND DOWN AS IF BRINGING HELP FROM GOD. AND JACOB HEARS GOD SPEAK TO HIM, PROMISING TO TAKE CARE OF HIM AND BRING HIM SAFELY HOME AGAIN.

THE NEXT MORNING JACOB AWAKENS, STILL AWED BY THE DREAM HE HAD.

SURELY GOD IS IN THIS PLACE—AND THIS IS THE GATE OF HEAVEN.

JACOB REALIZES THE WRONG HE HAS DONE. BUT HE KNOWS THAT GOD WILL HELP HIM IF HE OBEYS HIM. QUICKLY HE TURNS A STONE ON END FOR AN ALTAR AND WORSHIPS GOD. HE CALLS THE PLACE BETH-EL, WHICH MEANS "THE HOUSE OF GOD."

IF GOD WILL GO WITH ME, I'LL BE GOD'S MAN.

JACOB GOES ON HIS WAY A STRONGER, NOBLER YOUNG MAN SO HE IS EAGER TO PUT BEHIND HIM THE DISHONESTY OF HIS PAST AND GIVE EVIDENCE OF GOD'S LOVE AND CARE.

84

FROM GENESIS 29:26—32:6

SO JACOB MARRIES RACHEL AND BEGINS HIS SECOND SEVEN YEARS OF WORK FOR LABAN. UNDER JACOB'S CARE THE FLOCKS CONTINUE TO INCREASE. AT THE END OF THE SEVEN YEARS JACOB THREATENS TO LEAVE, BUT LABAN MAKES ANOTHER BARGAIN: JACOB CAN HAVE ALL OF THE SPECKLED OR SPOTTED ANIMALS. SO, JACOB STAYS; AND IN A FEW YEARS HIS FLOCKS OUTNUMBER LABAN'S. LABAN BECOMES ANGRY...

ONE DAY JACOB CALLS HIS WIVES TO HIM.

I CAN SEE THAT TROUBLE IS RISING IN THE TRIBE. IT IS BETTER. IF WE LEAVE WHILE YOUR FATHER IS AWAY. HELP ME PACK, AND WE WILL GO AT ONCE.

THE CAMEL TRAIN IS QUICKLY PACKED, THE FLOCKS HERDED TOGETHER; SOON THE CARAVAN IS ON ITS WAY.

LABAN MAY FOLLOW— KEEP WATCH AND TELL ME IF YOU SEE HIM COMING.

AS THEY TRAVEL, JACOB GUARDS THE CAMEL ON WHICH HIS BELOVED RACHEL AND HER ONLY SON, JOSEPH, ARE RIDING. LEAH AND JACOB'S OTHER TEN SONS WATCH WITH JEALOUS EYES. WITHOUT REALIZING IT, JACOB IS SOWING SEEDS OF TROUBLE FOR THE SON HE LOVES THE BEST...

88

Journey to Hebron

FROM GENESIS 32:7—33; 35:1–20

JACOB IS FRIGHTENED...
BUT HE IS ALSO SHREWD. HE DIVIDES HIS CARAVAN
INTO TWO SECTIONS, AND SENDS SERVANTS AHEAD
WITH PRESENTS FOR ESAU.

IF ESAU ATTACKS ONE GROUP, THE OTHER CAN ESCAPE.

THAT NIGHT JACOB PRAYS— CONFESSING HIS SINS, ADMITTING HIS FEAR, AND ASKING GOD'S HELP. BUT STILL HE CANNOT SLEEP.

MY FAMILY WOULD BE SAFER ON THE OTHER SIDE OF THE RIVER.

SO, IN THE MIDDLE OF THE NIGHT, HE MOVES HIS FAMILY...

YOU WILL BE SAFER ON THE OTHER SIDE, RACHEL.

I WISH YOU WOULD STAY WITH US.

BUT JACOB NEEDS TO BE ALONE... AND LATER THAT NIGHT AS HE PRAYS, HE FEELS HIMSELF WRESTLING WITH A MYSTERIOUS STRANGER. IT IS A FIERCE STRUGGLE, BUT JACOB DOES NOT GIVE UP UNTIL THE STRANGER BLESSES HIM: "THY NAME SHALL BE CALLED NO MORE JACOB, BUT ISRAEL: FOR AS A PRINCE HAST THOU POWER WITH GOD."

THE NEXT MORNING JACOB FINDS HIMSELF LAME FROM WRESTLING WITH THE ANGEL. BUT JACOB IS HAPPY...FOR HE KNOWS HIS EVIL NATURE HAS BEEN CONQUERED AND THAT HE HAS BEEN BLESSED BY GOD. JACOB GOES CONFIDENTLY TO MEET HIS BROTHER.

JACOB, MY BROTHER! I AM HAPPY TO SEE YOU AGAIN!

ESAU! HOW GLAD I AM. YOU DO NOT HATE ME ANY MORE!

PROUDLY JACOB PRESENTS HIS FAMILY...

AND THIS IS MY WIFE, RACHEL, AND MY SON, JOSEPH.

IT IS GOOD TO SEE MY BROTHER'S FAMILY. GOD HAS BLESSED YOU MUCH.

AFTER FEASTING TOGETHER, THE BROTHERS SAY GOOD-BY. JACOB HEADS TOWARD HIS FATHER'S HOME IN HEBRON.

FAREWELL, AND GREET MY FATHER FOR ME.

I WILL TELL HIM ALL IS WELL WITH YOU. GOOD-BY, AND GOD BLESS YOU, ESAU.

SOME TIME LATER ON THE WAY, JACOB STOPS AT BETH-EL.

THIS STONE, RACHEL, MARKS THE PLACE WHERE I SAW ANGELS COMING TO ME FROM HEAVEN, AND WHERE GOD PROMISED TO TAKE CARE OF ME. HE HAS, RACHEL...MORE THAN I DESERVE.

GOD HAS BEEN GOOD TO US, JACOB. AND I PRAY THAT HE WILL TAKE CARE OF OUR SON, JOSEPH— AND THE CHILD WHO IS SOON TO BE BORN.

FARTHER ALONG ON THE JOURNEY— NOT FAR FROM BETHLEHEM— RACHEL'S CHILD IS BORN...

IT'S A BOY, BUT OH, MY MASTER, YOUR WIFE, RACHEL, IS DEAD!

JACOB BURIES HIS BELOVED WIFE, RACHEL. THEN HE AND HIS FAMILY CONTINUE SADLY ON THEIR JOURNEY...STOPPING NOW AND THEN TO REST AND FEED THE FLOCKS. AS THEY TRAVEL ON, JACOB WONDERS...

RACHEL AND MY MOTHER ARE DEAD. WILL I GET TO MY FATHER WHILE HE IS STILL ALIVE?

Into the Pit

FROM GENESIS 35:27–29; 37:1–26

JACOB'S HAND TREMBLES AS HE SHADES HIS EYES AND LOOKS TOWARD THE DISTANT CITY OF HEBRON.

IS THAT WHERE MY GRANDFATHER, ISAAC, LIVES?

YES, JOSEPH. I PRAY WE ARE NOT TOO LATE... HE IS VERY OLD.

JACOB'S PRAYERS ARE ANSWERED. AT THE SIGHT OF HIS BLIND AND AGED FATHER, HE FALLS TO HIS KNEES.

O FATHER, I AM YOUR SON, JACOB— THANK GOD, I AM WITH YOU AGAIN.

JACOB, MY SON! I HAVE PRAYED FOR YOUR RETURN. DO YOU HAVE CHILDREN NOW?

PROUDLY JACOB PRESENTS HIS 12 SONS TO THEIR GRANDFATHER, ISAAC.

FATHER, THESE ARE JOSEPH AND BENJAMIN, THE SONS OF MY BELOVED RACHEL.

BE STRONG, MY CHILDREN, AND OBEY GOD ALWAYS.

Wrestling with a Stranger

▶ Read about Jacob on pp. 72-120.

Jacob is a deceiver. He tricks his brother out of the birthright and deceives his father out of the family blessing. Esau is so angry he threatens to kill Jacob. But two things happened to change Jacob:

▶ Jacob dreams of a ladder to heaven with angels going up and down. The Lord promises him the ground where he is sleeping, many children, and that He will be with Jacob whereever he goes. Jacob calls the place Bethel, meaning "house of God." (See p. 82.)

IF GOD WILL GO WITH ME, I'LL BE GOD'S MAN.

▶ Jacob wrestles all night with a stranger. Needing to have God's blessing as he faces angry Esau, Jacob refuses to let the stranger go. When morning comes, God changes Jacob's name to Israel, and he becomes the father of the Israelite nation. (See p. 90.)

▶ Jacob has twelve sons for whom the twelve tribes of Israel are named.

Did You Know?

God Turns Bad into Good . . .

▶ Read about Joseph on pp. 97-122.

Sometimes circumstances seem bad when actually they are opportunities for God to show us His power and love. Joseph faces several things that seem bad, but God turns them around for good.

▶ **Joseph is sold as a slave by his brothers. . . .**
He becomes the manager of Potiphar's household. Potiphar is captain of the king's guard (p. 97).

▶ **Joseph is falsely accused and thrown into prison. . . .**
He finds favor and is put in charge of all the prisoners (p. 100).

▶ **Even though Joseph is in prison, he is called before Pharaoh to interpret a dream. . . .**
Pharaoh makes him ruler over all of Egypt (p. 103).

▶ **The brothers who hated Joseph now come to him for food. . . .**
Joseph forgives them and gives them all the food they need (p. 113).

Joseph stays true to God.

WHEN ISAAC DIES, JACOB TAKES OVER AS HEAD OF THE TRIBE. WORD IS SENT TO ESAU, WHO COMES TO HELP JACOB BURY THEIR FATHER. AS SOON AS ESAU LEAVES, JACOB CALLS HIS SONS TO HIM...

THERE IS NOT ENOUGH PASTURE LAND FOR ALL OF OUR FLOCKS. WE WILL TAKE SOME OF THEM TO SHECHEM.

MAY I GO WITH MY BROTHERS TO TEND THE FLOCKS?

NO, JOSEPH, STAY HERE WITH ME. I HAVE SOMETHING FOR YOU.

SEE HOW FATHER FAVORS JOSEPH!

HE ALWAYS HAS! NOW HE MAY TRAIN HIM TO RULE THE TRIBE.

I'LL NEVER TAKE ORDERS FROM JOSEPH!

WHEN THE OLDER SONS ARE GONE...

HERE, MASTER JOSEPH, IS THE COAT YOUR FATHER HAD MADE FOR YOU.

FOR ME! WHY IT'S JUST LIKE A CHIEFTAIN'S ROBE!

96

Slave Train to Egypt

FROM GENESIS 37:27–36; 39:1–20

THROWN INTO A DEEP PIT BY HIS JEALOUS BROTHERS, JOSEPH WAITS HELPLESSLY WHILE THEY DECIDE HIS FATE.

SEE THAT CARAVAN COMING? WE COULD SELL THEM JOSEPH AS A SLAVE. THAT WOULD GET RID OF HIM!

O THE BROTHERS PULL JOSEPH OUT OF HE PIT AND DRAG HIM TO THE CARAVAN.

THE BOY IS OUR SLAVE. WHAT WILL YOU GIVE US FOR HIM?

HE'S A HANDSOME ONE—SHOULD BRING A GOOD PRICE IN EGYPT.

HE LOOKS SOFT—I'LL GIVE YOU 20 SHEKELS.

BUT I'MMM—

KEEP STILL, SLAVE!

IT'S A DEAL— TAKE HIM!

98

99

BUT JOSEPH'S SUCCESS ALSO LEADS TO TROUBLE. POTIPHAR'S WIFE FALLS IN LOVE WITH THE HANDSOME, YOUNG SLAVE. ONE DAY WHILE POTIPHAR IS AWAY...

JOSEPH, COME, SIT BESIDE ME. TELL ME WHERE YOU CAME FROM AND WHY YOU ARE IN EGYPT.

THANK YOU, BUT I HAVE WORK TO FINISH BEFORE POTIPHAR RETURNS.

MUST YOU ALWAYS THINK OF POTIPHAR?

HE IS MY MASTER— I WILL NOT BE UNTRUE TO HIM OR DISOBEY MY GOD.

NO MAN CAN SCORN ME—AND LIVE!

SHE BIDES HER TIME...WHEN POTIPHAR RETURNS SHE GREETS HIM WITH TEARS IN HER EYES, AND A LIE ON HER LIPS.

YOUR HEBREW SLAVE TRIED TO KISS ME! I SCREAMED AND HE LEFT...BUT HE DROPPED HIS ROBE. HERE— SEE IT!

I'LL THROW HIM IN PRISON FOR THIS!

BEFORE THE SUN SETS THAT DAY, JOSEPH IS CHAINED AND THROWN INTO THE KING'S PRISON.

HO— WHAT A HANDSOME PRISONER WE HAVE WITH US!

WHEN HE'S BEEN HERE AS LONG AS I HAVE, HE'LL FORGET WHAT IT'S LIKE TO WEAR SUCH FINE, CLEAN CLOTHES.

The King's Dream

FROM GENESIS 39:21–23; 40—42:1–6

ALSELY ACCUSED, JOSEPH **FACES** HIS FIRST NIGHT IN PRISON. BUT E IS NOT AFRAID, AN**D HE** IS NOT ALONE BECAUSE GOD IS WITH HIM. OSEPH PRAYS... AS HE HAS DONE EVERY OTHER NIGHT IN HIS LIFE.

WHAT GOD CAN SAVE HIM NOW?

LEAVE HIM ALONE! HE IS BRAVER THAN THE REST OF US.

ONE LONG, HOT DAY FOLLOWS ANOTHER. THE PRISONERS QUARREL OVER FOOD—WATER— THE BEST PLACE TO SLEEP. ONE DAY A FIGHT BREAKS OUT...

STOP IT! FIGHTING WON'T HELP US.

EVEN IN PRISON GOD IS WITH JOSEPH. WHEN THE KEEPER OF THE JAIL LEARNS JOSEPH IS A LEADER, HE PUTS JOSEPH IN CHARGE OF THE OTHER PRISONERS.

ONE DAY THE KING'S BAKER AND BUTLER ARE THROWN INTO PRISON FOR OFFENDING THE KING. BOTH MEN HAVE DREAMS THAT TROUBLE THEM, AND THEY COME TO JOSEPH FOR HELP.

WHAT DO YOU THINK MY DREAM MEANT?

IN THREE DAYS YOU WILL BE THE KING'S BUTLER AGAIN. WHEN THAT TIME COMES, PLEASE SAY A GOOD WORD FOR ME.

NOW TELL ME WHAT MY DREAM MEANS.

I'M SORRY, BUT THE DREAM SHOWS YOU WILL BE HANGED, IN JUST THREE DAYS.

JOSEPH'S WORDS COME TRUE. THREE DAYS LATER, ONE MAN DIES, AND THE OTHER RETURNS TO SERVE THE KING. BUT HE FORGETS HIS PROMISE. TWO YEARS GO BY...

YOU CALLED, O KING?

YES. IS THERE NO ONE IN MY WHOLE KINGDOM WHO CAN TELL ME WHAT MY DREAM MEANS? I MUST FIND OUT...

O KING, I KNOW A HEBREW PRISONER WHO CAN TELL THE MEANING OF DREAMS. HE TOLD MINE!

BRING HIM TO ME—AT ONCE!

FROM THE THRONE ROOM, JOSEPH GOES TO HIS OWN ROOM AND KNEELS IN PRAYER, THANKING GOD FOR PROTECTION AND GUIDANCE.

JOSEPH ORDERS THE PEOPLE TO START PREPARING FOR THE FAMINE. HE BECOMES FAMOUS, AND ALL REJOICE WHEN HE MARRIES THE BEAUTIFUL DAUGHTER OF THE PRIEST OF ON.

I AM PROUD TO BE YOUR WIFE, JOSEPH. YOU HAVE DONE SO MUCH FOR OUR PEOPLE.

THERE IS MORE TO BE DONE, MY DEAR. THE YEARS OF PLENTY WILL PASS QUICKLY.

ALL TOO SOON, THE FAMINE BEGINS. AS IT CONTINUES, PEOPLE FROM OTHER COUNTRIES COME TO EGYPT SEEKING FOOD. ONE DAY TRIBESMEN FROM CANAAN ENTER JOSEPH'S CITY...

IN ORDER TO BUY GRAIN, THEY APPEAR BEFORE THE GOVERNOR OF EGYPT. THEY BOW BEFORE HIM...

MY BROTHERS! THEY DO NOT RECOGNIZE ME AFTER ALL THESE YEARS!

104

Trouble in Egypt
FROM GENESIS 42:6–38

THE TEN SONS OF JACOB STAND BEFORE THE GOVERNOR OF EGYPT—NOT KNOWING THAT HE IS JOSEPH, THE BROTHER THEY SOLD INTO SLAVERY YEARS BEFORE. BUT JOSEPH RECOGNIZES HIS HALF-BROTHERS—AND DECIDES TO FIND OUT WHETHER THEY HAVE LEARNED TO BE KIND AND MERCIFUL.

YOU ARE SPIES!

NO, MY LORD! WE ARE TEN OF THE SONS OF THE GREAT CHIEFTAIN, JACOB. HE SENT US TO BUY GRAIN.

TEN SONS? HOW MANY MORE SONS DOES YOUR FATHER HAVE?

HE HAD TWELVE—THE YOUNGEST, BENJAMIN, IS HOME WITH OUR FATHER. THE OTHER ONE DIED LONG AGO!

I STILL SAY YOU ARE SPIES. GUARDS—TAKE THEM TO PRISON!

106

The Stolen Cup

FROM GENESIS 43:1—44:12

THEY ENTER THE COURTYARD OF THE GOVERNOR... WHO THEY DO NOT KNOW IS THEIR BROTHER JOSEPH.

WE ARE THE SONS OF JACOB COME AGAIN FOR GRAIN. WHEN WE RETURNED HOME FROM BUYING FOOD, WE FOUND MONEY IN OUR SACKS. WE HAVE BROUGHT THAT MONEY WITH US—AND MORE TO BUY MORE GRAIN.

MY MASTER KNOWS YOU HAVE COME. WAIT HERE—

SIMEON!

O BENJAMIN, THANK GOD YOU CAME!

YOU ARE ALL RIGHT?

YES, BUT I WAS AFRAID YOU'D NEVER COME. THE PRISON WAS DARK AND LONELY. ALL I COULD THINK OF WAS THE EVIL I HAD DONE IN MY LIFE.

FORGET THE PAST, SIMEON. WE ARE ELEVEN BROTHERS AND WE WILL STICK TOGETHER.

THEN—TO THEIR SURPRISE—THE BROTHERS ARE LED INTO A GREAT BANQUET HALL. THE GOVERNOR OF EGYPT STANDS WAITING...

IS YOUR FATHER WELL?

YES, YOUR EXCELLENCY

AND IS THIS YOUR YOUNGEST BROTHER?

YES—THIS IS BENJAMIN!

THE SIGHT OF HIS OWN BROTHER, BENJAMIN, REMINDS JOSEPH OF THEIR MOTHER WHO DIED WHEN BENJAMIN WAS BORN. SUDDENLY, HE CANNOT FACE HIS HALF BROTHERS—HE TURNS AND LEAVES THE ROOM.

WHAT HAPPENED?

ALONE, JOSEPH CONQUERS THE GRIEF THAT OVERCAME HIM.

HE RETURNS TO THE BANQUET HALL TO CONTINUE THE PLAN TO TEST HIS BROTHERS. THEY ARE SEATED—AND THE FOOD IS SERVED. BUT EVEN THIS PRESENTS A MYSTERY.

DO YOU NOTICE— WE ARE SEATED ACCORDING TO AGE?

I TELL YOU— THIS MAN KNOWS TOO MUCH ABOUT US. WHAT IS HE UP TO?

BUT EVEN AS THEY WONDER, THE GOVERNOR HAS THE BROTHERS SERVED — GIVING THE LARGEST PORTION TO BENJAMIN. IT IS A SIGN OF GREAT HONOR.

DO YOU SEE THAT?

AT LEAST BENJAMIN IS SAFE!

THE BANQUET ENDS; THE NEXT MORNING THE BROTHERS BUY THEIR GRAIN AND LEAVE. BUT THEY ARE HARDLY OUT OF THE CITY BEFORE A CHARIOT OVERTAKES THEM.

STOP! ONE OF YOU HAS STOLEN MY MASTER'S SILVER CUP!

YOUR MASTER'S CUP? WE ARE INNOCENT! SEARCH US IF YOU WILL.

IF THE CUP IS FOUND, THE MAN IN WHOSE SACK IT IS HIDDEN SHALL BECOME MY MASTER'S SLAVE!

ONE BY ONE THE SACKS ARE SEARCHED... AT LAST THE OFFICER OPENS BENJAMIN'S...

THE CUP!

LOADED WITH SUPPLIES AND GIFTS THE HAPPY CARAVAN SETS OUT FOR HOME. WHEN THEY APPROACH JACOB'S CAMP, SOME OF THE BROTHERS RUN AHEAD TO TELL THE GOOD NEWS.

South into Egypt

FROM GENESIS 45:27–28; 47; 48; 50:1–15

119

FOR SEVENTEEN YEARS JACOB AND HIS SONS LIVE HAPPILY IN EGYPT. THEN ONE DAY A MESSENGER BRINGS SAD NEWS TO JOSEPH...

SIR, YOUR FATHER IS VERY ILL. HE WANTS YOU AND YOUR SONS TO COME— RIGHT AWAY!

THEY HURRY TO JACOB'S BEDSIDE.

BRING YOUR SONS TO ME SO I CAN BLESS THEM BEFORE I DIE.

MAY GOD, WHO HAS GUIDED ME ALL MY LIFE, BLESS MY GRANDSONS.

THEN JACOB CALLS ALL OF HIS SONS TO HIM AND BLESSES THEM. JACOB DIES AND HIS SONS CARRY THE OLD CHIEFTAIN'S BODY BACK TO HIS HOMELAND OF CANAAN.

AFTER JACOB'S FUNERAL, JOSEPH WALKS AWAY FROM THE CAMP ALONE. HIS BROTHERS WATCH HIM SUSPICIOUSLY...

JOSEPH WAS GOOD TO US WHILE OUR FATHER LIVED, BUT NOW...

HE MAY GET EVEN. THERE'S ONLY ONE THING TO DO...

BECAUSE OF THE WICKEDNESS OF HIS OLDER SONS, JACOB GIVES THE FAMILY BIRTHRIGHT TO JOSEPH AND HIS SONS.

Death Sentence

FROM GENESIS 50:15–26;
EXODUS 1:1—2:1–2

FOLLOWING THE BURIAL OF THEIR FATHER, JOSEPH AND HIS BROTHERS GO BACK TO EGYPT. BUT THE BROTHERS ARE AFRAID THAT JOSEPH MAY NOW TAKE REVENGE FOR THE EVIL THEY DID TO HIM.

WE HAVE ONLY ONE COURSE TO TAKE— BUT LET'S WAIT UNTIL WE REACH EGYPT.

YES, OUR FAMILIES ARE THERE.

IN EGYPT THE BROTHERS WASTE NO TIME...

TAKE THIS MESSAGE TO OUR BROTHER, JOSEPH.

JOSEPH WEEPS WHEN HE HEARS THE WORDS OF THE MESSENGER.

BRING MY BROTHERS TO ME— IS IT POSSIBLE THAT EVEN YET THEY HAVE NOT LEARNED THAT I HAVE FORGIVEN THEM?

123

RE STRONG.

...THEM HARDER
...DAY, BUT THERE ARE
...E HEBREWS THAN BEFORE.
THE KING WILL NOT BE
HAPPY ABOUT THIS...

WHEN THE KING HEARS THE REPORT...

I'LL TAKE CARE OF THE SLAVES! THROW EVERY HEBREW BOY BABY IN THE RIVER!

THE CRUEL ORDER IS CARRIED OUT. HEBREW MOTHERS AND FATHERS RISK THEIR LIVES TO PROTECT THEIR SONS...BUT THE KING'S MEN NEVER GIVE UP THEIR SEARCH.

NIGHT AFTER NIGHT ONE HEBREW FATHER HURRIES HOME FROM WORK—AFRAID THAT THE SOLDIERS HAVE VISITED HIS HOME.

O GOD, HELP ME SAVE OUR BOY FROM THE EGYPTIANS.

ry of a Slave

ROM EXODUS 2:3–11

128

e Fiery Bush

м Exodus 2:11—3:4

SES JUMPS FROM HIS CHARIOT TO
ESTIGATE...AND FINDS AN EGYPTIAN GUARD BEATING
A HEBREW SLAVE.

SUDDEN ANGER MOSES STRIKES
OUT HARD—

LOOK! HE
KILLED THE
GUARD!

THE NEXT DAY MOSES RETURNS. WHEN HE SEES TWO HEBREWS FIGHTING, HE TRIES TO STOP THEM.

WHY DO YOU FIGHT AMONG YOURSELVES?

WHO MADE YOU A JUDGE OVER US? ARE YOU GOING TO KILL ME AS YOU DID THAT EGYPTIAN?

IF PHARAOH HEARS OF THIS HE WILL ACCUSE ME OF BEING A TRAITOR. THERE IS ONLY ONE THING FOR ME TO DO, AND I MUST DO IT NOW...

LATER THAT DAY IN THE PALACE...

PRINCE MOSES KILLED AN EGYPTIAN GUARD FOR BEATING A HEBREW SLAVE!

FIND THE TRAITOR—AND KILL HIM!

BUT PHARAOH'S ORDERS ARE TOO LATE...MOSES HAS A HEAD START ON THE SOLDIERS WHO CHASE HIM. HE ESCAPES— AND AFTER LONG, HARD RIDING REACHES THE LAND OF MIDIAN.

131

MOSES STAYS WEEKS AND THEN MONTHS. HE MARRIES ZIPPORAH AND IN TIME THEY HAVE TWO SONS.

GERSHOM HANDLES HIS SLING VERY WELL.

HE WILL MAKE A GOOD SHEPHERD— LIKE HIS FATHER.

YEAR AFTER YEAR THE FLOCKS OF JETHRO INCREASE. BUT ONE YEAR THE GRASSES DRY UP AND MOSES LEADS HIS SHEEP TO PASTURES NEAR THE MOUNTAIN OF SINAI.

BUT MOSES CANNOT FORGET THE HEBREW PEOPLE IN EGYPT.

I WONDER IF PHARAOH IS STILL ALIVE... AND WHAT HAS BECOME OF MY SISTER MIRIAM AND MY BROTHER AARON?

HE WONDERS, TOO, ABOUT THE HEBREW SLAVES STILL STRUGGLING UNDER THE WHIPS OF EGYPTIAN RULERS. ONE DAY HE LOOKS UP TO SEE A STRANGE SIGHT ON MOUNT SINAI.

A BUSH ON FIRE— YET IT IS NOT DESTROYED!

HE STEPS CLOSER—THEN STOPS. A VOICE FROM THE FIERY BUSH CALLS OUT "MOSES!"

Moses, God's Leader

Did You Know?

Moses is a great man of God—prophet, leader, and lawgiver to God's people, the Israelites. Because Moses is God's spokesman, God entrusts him with special information that he explains to the people.

▶ **The Tabernacle:** God gives Moses instructions to build a tent for worshiping Him in the wilderness. It becomes the center of the Israelite camp and reminds them that worshiping God is very important (p. 163).

▶ **The Law:** God gives Moses laws to teach His people how to live. The Ten Commandments are part of this Law (p. 157).

▶ **The Priesthood:** God instructs Moses to separate Aaron's family for priestly service. They perform special duties in the tabernacle that no one else is allowed to do.

Moses writes the first five books of the Bible. These books are referred to as the Pentateuch.

Countdown to Freedom

▶ Turn to pp. 137-143 in your Picture Bible for the story.

God uses plagues to convince Pharaoh to let the Israelites leave Egypt. But because they are his slaves, Pharaoh doesn't want to let them go. God finally steps in with plague number ten and Pharaoh is convinced that God is serious. He lets the Israelites go.

The plague countdown:
1. Water to blood
2. Frogs
3. Lice
4. Flies
5. Diseased cattle
6. Boils on people and animals
7. Hail
8. Locusts
9. Darkness for three days
10. Death of the firstborn son

▶ The Egyptians worship the Nile River. When the water turns to blood, all of the fish die and the river stinks.

A locust is a grasshopper that travels in destructive swarms and devours vegetation.

▶ The plague of lice could also include gnats, maggots, sand flies, and fleas.

▶ The death angel passes over the Hebrew homes where blood is brushed on the frame of the front door. Jews today still celebrate this deliverance as Passover.

Plague of Death

WHEN MOSES AND AARON DEMAND THE RELEASE OF THE HEBREW SLAVES, PHARAOH IS FURIOUS—AND MAKES THE SLAVES WORK HARDER THAN BEFORE. IN ANGER THEY TURN AGAINST MOSES. MOSES SEEKS GOD'S HELP AND IS TOLD TO VISIT PHARAOH AGAIN.

SHOW ME HOW POWERFUL YOUR GOD IS.

WHEN THIS ROD STRIKES THE GROUND, IT WILL BECOME A SERPENT.

AARON'S WORDS COME TRUE, BUT PHARAOH ONLY LAUGHS.

YOU ARE CLEVER, BUT MY MAGICIANS CAN DO THE SAME THING.

PHARAOH CALLS FOR HIS OWN MAGICIANS. THEY TOO THROW DOWN THEIR RODS—WHICH BECOME SERPENTS.

SEE?

137

BUT WHILE PHARAOH WATCHES, THE SERPENT OF AARON DEVOURS THE SERPENTS OF THE EGYPTIAN MAGICIANS. PHARAOH IS STUNNED... BUT HE REFUSES TO ADMIT THAT MOSES' GOD IS MORE POWERFUL THAN THE GODS OF EGYPT.

AGAIN MOSES SEEKS GOD'S HELP... AND AGAIN GOD TELLS HIM WHAT TO DO. IN THE MORNING MOSES AND AARON MEET PHARAOH ON THE BANK OF THE RIVER NILE.

WHAT ARE _YOU_ DOING HERE?

BECAUSE YOU WILL NOT LET THE HEBREWS GO, THE RIVER WILL BE TURNED TO BLOOD.

AT MOSES' COMMAND, AARON STRIKES THE WATER WITH HIS ROD AND THE WATER TURNS RED.

I DON'T DARE BATHE IN THAT BLOODY STREAM!

WHEN WOMEN COME TO WASH THEIR CLOTHES IN THE RIVER, THEY ARE TURNED BACK. MEN HAVE TO DIG WELLS TO GET DRINKING WATER. FINALLY THE RIVER IS CLEAR AGAIN, BUT STILL PHARAOH WILL NOT LISTEN TO MOSES' PLEA. AND SO GOD SENDS A DIFFERENT PLAGUE...

143

THE NEXT DAY THE GREAT EXODUS FROM EGYPT IS ON ITS WAY. JOYFULLY THE HEBREWS MARCH TOWARD THE LAND GOD HAS PROMISED THEM WILL BE THEIR HOME. THEY ARE GUIDED BY A BRIGHT CLOUD BY DAY...

AND A PILLAR OF FIRE BY NIGHT.

BUT IN THEIR RUSH FOR FREEDOM THEY DO NOT FORGET TO TAKE WITH THEM THE BODY OF THEIR GREAT LEADER, JOSEPH.

HE WAS A GREAT MAN IN EGYPT, BUT HE ASKED TO BE BURIED IN HIS HOMELAND.

AFTER SEVERAL DAYS OF TRAVEL, THEY REACH THE RED SEA...

THE SEA IS IN FRONT OF US AND THE MOUNTAINS ALL AROUND.

WHAT WILL WE DO NOW? WHERE CAN WE GO?

144

Crossing the Sea

FROM EXODUS 14:10—16:10

PHARAOH AND HIS ARMY LOOK AT THE HEBREWS CAMPED BESIDE THE RED SEA.

TRAPPED—JUST AS I SAID!

GOOD! THEY'LL SOON SEE WHO IS MIGHTIER—PHARAOH OR THE GOD THEY WORSHIP!

AS MOSES SPEAKS THE CLOUD THAT LEADS THEM MOVES TO THE BACK OF THE CAMP.

LOOK! THE CLOUD IS HIDING US FROM THE EGYPTIANS!

AT THE SAME TIME IN THE HEBREW CAMP...

I'D RATHER SERVE THE EGYPTIANS THAN DIE THIS WAY!

FEAR NOT, STAND STILL, AND SEE THE SALVATION OF THE LORD. THE EGYPTIANS WHOM YOU SEE TODAY, YOU SHALL SEE NO MORE.

THEN MOSES HOLDS OUT HIS HAND, AS GOD HAD TOLD HIM. A STRONG EAST WIND BLOWS ALL NIGHT AND ROLLS BACK THE WATERS OF THE SEA...

AWED BY THE SIGHT, THE HEBREWS RUSH JOYFULLY ACROSS THE PATH IN THE SEA.

147

PHARAOH CHARGES, BUT THE HEBREW CAMP IS EMPTY! THE EGYPTIANS RACE OUT ACROSS THE SEA FLOOR, BUT SAND CLOGS THEIR CHARIOT WHEELS...

IN TERROR THEY TRY TO TURN BACK... BUT THE WIND DIES, AND THE WATERS RETURN. ALL OF PHARAOH'S MEN ARE CAUGHT IN THE RUSHING SEA.

SAFE ON THE OTHER SIDE, THE HEBREWS LOOK BACK...

GOD HAS SAVED US!

I'LL NEVER AGAIN DOUBT THAT MOSES WAS SENT BY GOD TO SAVE US FROM THE EGYPTIANS.

JOYFULLY THE HEBREWS CELEBRATE GOD'S DELIVERANCE. THE TRIBES DESCENDED FROM JACOB (ISRAEL) ARE A FREE PEOPLE—READY TO FORM A NEW NATION. MIRIAM, MOSES' SISTER, LEADS THE WOMEN'S CHORUS SINGING PRAISES TO GOD.

THE LORD IS MY STRENGTH AND SONG: HE IS MY SALVATION.

SING TO THE LORD.

FROM THE RED SEA, THE ISRAELITES MARCH ACROSS THE DESERT. BUT AFTER DAYS OF TRAVEL THEY FORGET WHAT GOD HAS DONE FOR THEM. AND THEY BEGIN TO COMPLAIN...

I'M THIRSTY.

THREE DAYS AND NO WATER IN SIGHT.

Attacked!

FROM EXODUS 16:11–17

THAT EVENING GREAT FLOCKS OF QUAIL DROP INTO THE CAMP.

BIRDS! THOUSANDS OF THEM!

FOOD— ENOUGH FOR EVERYONE!

MOSES WAS RIGHT. GOD SENT THE QUAIL TO FEED US. GOD IS LEADING US!

YES—ONLY GOD COULD SAVE US FROM STARVING. NEVER AGAIN WILL I DOUBT GOD'S POWER AND GUIDANCE.

150

BUT THE NEXT MORNING...

UGH! IT HAS SPOILED!

I SEE NOW—MOSES WARNED US. WE MUST HAVE FAITH THAT GOD WILL TAKE CARE OF US.

ON THE SIXTH DAY OF THE WEEK, THE PEOPLE GATHER FOOD FOR THAT DAY AND THE SABBATH. THE FOOD KEPT FOR THE SABBATH DOES NOT SPOIL...NEITHER DOES IT APPEAR ON THE GROUND ON THE SABBATH.

WITH RENEWED FAITH IN GOD, THE ISRAELITES CONTINLE THEIR JOURNEY. AS THEY TRAVEL TOWARD MOUNT SINAI, WHERE MOSES WAS CALLED BY GOD TO SET THEM FREE FROM SLAVERY, MOSES SENDS HIS WIFE AND TWO SONS ON AHEAD TO VISIT THEIR OLD HOME.

TELL YOUR FATHER, JETHRO, WHAT GOD HAS DONE FOR OUR PEOPLE!

FARTHER ON...WHILE THE ISRAELITES CAMP IN A PEACEFUL VALLEY...FIERCE TRIBESMEN WATCH FROM THE HILLS...

THIS WILL BE EASY—A SURPRISE ATTACK, AND THE CAMP IS OURS!

153

The Mountain Trembles

FROM EXODUS 17:12—19:20

HIGH ON THE HILL, AARON AND HUR ARE HOLDING UP MOSES' TIRED ARMS. WHEN THE ISRAELITE SOLDIERS SEE THE ROD THEY TAKE COURAGE AND RENEW THE FIGHT. GOD GIVES THEM THE VICTORY.

AT SUNSET JOSHUA'S MEN RETURN VICTORIOUS.

THEN MOSES BUILDS AN ALTAR AND LEADS HIS PEOPLE IN A PRAYER OF THANKSGIVING TO GOD.

FRESH FROM THEIR FIRST MILITARY VICTORY, THE ISRAELITES EAGERLY PUSH ON.

ONLY A FEW WEEKS AGO WE WERE SLAVES IN EGYPT. NOW WE ARE FREE MEN — STRONG ENOUGH TO DEFEND OURSELVES!

WHEN WE GET TO THE PROMISED LAND — WE'LL BUILD A NATION — MIGHTIER THAN ALL EGYPT!

WHEN THEY REACH THE WILDERNESS OF MOUNT SINAI, MOSES SETS UP CAMP. ONE DAY A MESSENGER BRINGS HIM GOOD NEWS...

YOUR FATHER-IN-LAW, JETHRO, YOUR WIFE AND SONS ARE ON THEIR WAY TO SEE YOU.

MOSES GOES OUT AT ONCE TO MEET THEM...

HOW GLAD I AM TO SEE YOU!

I HAVE BEEN HEARING THE WONDERFUL THINGS GOD HAS DONE FOR YOU AND YOUR PEOPLE.

PROUDLY, MOSES SHOWS JETHRO AROUND THE CAMP. AS THE DAYS GO BY, JETHRO MAKES SOME KEEN OBSERVATIONS...

THIS IS WRONG. I MUST SPEAK TO MOSES AT ONCE.

Commandments of God

FROM EXODUS 20—32:19

WHILE THE PEOPLE OF ISRAEL STAND BEFORE MOUNT SINAI, GOD SPEAKS FROM THE MOUNTAIN AND GIVES THEM THE TEN COMMANDMENTS:

I AM THE LORD YOUR GOD... YOU MUST HAVE NO OTHER GODS BEFORE ME.

YOU MUST NOT MAKE ANY IDOLS.

YOU MUST NOT USE THE NAME OF THE LORD YOUR GOD WRONGLY.

REMEMBER THE SABBATH DAY, TO KEEP IT HOLY.

HONOR YOUR FATHER AND YOUR MOTHER.

YOU MUST NOT KILL.

YOU MUST NOT COMMIT ADULTERY.

YOU MUST NOT STEAL.

YOU MUST NOT BEAR FALSE WITNESS...

YOU MUST NOT COVET... ANYTHING THAT IS YOUR NEIGHBOR'S.

GOD GIVES MOSES MORE LAWS, AND WHEN THESE ARE WRITTEN DOWN, MOSES BUILDS AN ALTAR. HE AND HIS PEOPLE MAKE AN AGREEMENT, OR COVENANT, WITH GOD. "ALL THAT THE LORD HATH SAID WILL WE DO," THE PEOPLE PROMISE.

LATER, GOD CALLS MOSES TO COME AGAIN TO MOUNT SINA JOSHUA GOES PART WAY WITH HIM. DAYS PASS, AND MOSE DOES NOT RETURN.

WHEN IS MOSES COMING BACK?

CAN WE GO LOOK FOR HIM?

WE DON'T KNOW—BUT YOU MUST NOT FOLLOW HIM UP THE MOUNTAIN. HE IS ALONE WITH GOD.

WHO KNOWS —MAYBE MOSES ISN'T COMING BACK...

IF HE DOESN'T, WHAT WILL WE DO?

LET'S ASK AARON TO MAKE US A STATUE THAT WE CAN WORSHIP.

YES— WE WANT A GO WE CAN SEE.

FEELING LOST WITHOUT THEIR LEADER, THE PEOPLE FORGET GOD'S COMMANDMENTS AND THEIR PROMISE TO WORSHIP HIM ONLY. THEY BRING THEIR JEWELRY TO AARON WHO MELTS IT AND MAKES A GOLDEN STATUE OF A CALF.

BACK IN CAMP, THE PEOPLE PRAY FOR MOSES' SAFE RETURN. BUT WHEN THEY SEE HIM COMING DOWN THE MOUNTAIN, THEY ARE AFRAID...

IT'S MOSES! BUT LOOK AT HIS FACE—IT HAS A BRIGHTNESS LIKE THE SUNLIGHT!

THE GLORY OF HAVING BEEN WITH GOD SHINES ON MOSES' FACE. HE COVERS HIS FACE WITH A VEIL SO THAT THE PEOPLE WILL NOT BE FRIGHTENED.

COME—DO NOT BE AFRAID. GOD HAS FORGIVEN YOU.

AND HE HAS GIVEN ME PLANS FOR A TENT-HOUSE OF WORSHIP. BRING YOUR OFFERINGS AND WE WILL ALL WORK TOGETHER TO MAKE IT.

THE PEOPLE GLADLY BRING JEWELRY, CLOTH, SKINS, RARE METALS AND WOOD SO THAT GOD'S HOUSE WILL BE BEAUTIFUL.

The Tabernacle

FROM EXODUS 25—40:18–38;
LEVITICUS 1—10:2

AFTER MANY WEEKS OF CAREFUL, LOVING WORK THE HOUSE OF GOD, THE TABERNACLE, IS READY...JOYOUSLY THE PEOPLE WATCH AS MOSES CARRIES THE SACRED ARK CONTAINING THE TEN COMMANDMENTS INTO THE TABERNACLE. HE PLACES IT IN A SPECIAL ROOM CALLED THE HOLY OF HOLIES. THEN A CLOUD COVERS THE TABERNACLE AND THE GLORY OF THE LORD FILLS IT.

NOW THE ISRAELITES ARE NO LONGER A MOB OF FLEEING SLAVES. IN THE ONE YEAR SINCE THEY LEFT EGYPT, THEY HAVE BECOME A NATION WITH LAWS, JUDGES AND A PLACE OF WORSHIP.

Traveling with the Israelites

With over two million people leaving Egypt, Moses has his hands full. Yet he proves to be an able leader with God's help. Here are some of the things that happen along the way:

▶ The Red Sea parts. The Israelites cross on dry land (p. 147).

▶ Bitter water is made sweet (p. 149).

▶ The Israelites run out of food. God provides manna (p. 151).

▶ God gives them victory over an attack by enemy raiders (p. 152).

When Moses is delayed, the Israelites worship a gold calf (p. 158).

Did You Know?

The Journey Continues . . .

▶ People complain about the manna. God sends quail (p. 170).

▶ Some people rebel against Moses. God sends an earthquake (p. 181).

▶ The Israelites have no water. Moses strikes the rock and water flows out (p. 183).

▶ Because of the Israelites' grumbling, God sends snakes. Many are bitten, but God provides help (p. 184).

WHAT IS IT? IT LOOKS LIKE FROST!

IT IS MANNA-FOOD THAT GOD HAS SENT YOU

▶ Many times Moses prays to God for the people, and God forgives them. But when they refuse to take Canaan, God makes them return to wander in the desert (p. 177).

Because the Israelites rebel against God, they have to roam for forty years before they enter the Promise Land.

BIRDS! THOUSANDS OF THEM!

FOOD-ENOUGH FOR EVERYONE!

ire in Camp

EXCITEMENT SPREADS THROUGH THE CAMP AS THE PEOPLE TALK MORE AND MORE ABOUT THE PROMISED LAND TO WHICH GOD IS LEADING THEM. ONE DAY THE BLAST OF TWO GREAT SILVER TRUMPETS FILLS THE AIR...

THAT IS A SIGNAL FOR ALL OF THE PEOPLE TO COME TO THE TABERNACLE. SOMETHING IMPORTANT MUST BE HAPPENING.

THE PEOPLE DROP WHAT THEY ARE DOING, AND HURRY TO THE TABERNACLE.

DOES THIS MEAN WE ARE GOING TO MOVE?

I DON'T KNOW. WE'LL HAVE TO WAIT AND SEE. OUR ORDERS COME FROM GOD.

WHEN EVERYONE HAS GATHERED...

LOOK! THE CLOUD IS LIFTING!

THE SIGN HAS BEEN GIVEN! EAGERLY THE PEOPLE LINE UP FOR THE MARCH TOWARD THE PROMISED LAND! LEADING THEM IS THE SACRED ARK, CARRIED BY THE PRIESTS.

167

YOU'RE RIGHT, MIRIAM. IT'S TIME WE HAVE A TALK WITH OUR BROTHER.

IN ANGER, THEY GO TO MOSES...

WE'RE TIRED OF HAVING YOU RUN EVERYTHING, MOSES. DO YOU THINK YOU ARE THE ONLY ONE WHO CAN SPEAK FOR GOD? DIDN'T GOD CALL AARON TO BE THE HIGH PRIEST? AND DON'T FORGET, I AM A PROPHETESS, TOO!

BEFORE MOSES CAN ANSWER, GOD CALLS THE THREE OF THEM TO THE TABERNACLE.

THEN GOD SPEAKS FROM A CLOUD, AND TELLS THEM THAT HE HAS CHOSEN MOSES TO LEAD THE PEOPLE OF ISRAEL. WHEN THE CLOUD DISAPPEARS, MIRIAM AND AARON GET THE SHOCK OF THEIR LIVES.

Spies Sent Out

FROM NUMBERS 12:11—14:10

IN A FIT OF JEALOUSY, MIRIAM AND AARON ACCUSE THEIR BROTHER, MOSES, OF ACTING AS IF HE WERE GOD'S ONLY SPOKESMAN. GOD ANSWERS THEIR ANGRY WORDS AND TELLS MIRIAM AND AARON THAT MOSES IS HIS CHOSEN LEADER. WHEN GOD FINISHES SPEAKING, MIRIAM DISCOVERS THAT SHE HAS LEPROSY—THE DISEASE MOST DREADED BY THE ISRAELITES.

OH! NO! WHY DID I SPEAK AGAINST MOSES? HELP ME! HELP ME!

WE WERE WRONG, MOSES. BUT DO NOT HOLD IT AGAINST US—PLEASE! CAN'T YOU HELP MIRIAM?

ONLY GOD CAN HEAL HER, AARON. BUT I WILL PRAY FOR OUR SISTER.

HEAL HER NOW, O GOD, I BEG OF THEE.

MIRIAM IS HEALED, BUT SHE IS BANISHED FROM THE CAMP FOR SEVEN DAYS.

ON THE SEVENTH DAY MIRIAM RETURNS, AND AARON, AS HIGH PRIEST, ACCEPTS HER BACK INTO THE CAMP.

I HAVE LEARNED MY LESSON, AARON.

SO HAVE I. LET US NEVER AGAIN DOUBT OR QUESTION GOD'S WISDOM.

176

THIS IS A MASSACRE! LET'S GET OUT OF HERE!

IF WE GET BACK ALIVE, I'LL OBEY EVERY WORD MOSES SAYS.

THE BATTLE IS SOON OVER — THE DEFEATED ISRAELITES LIMP BACK TO CAMP.

WHAT HAPPENED?

WE DIDN'T HAVE A CHANCE. THE ENEMY CAME AT US FROM EVERY DIRECTION. OUR LEADERS WERE THE FIRST TO RUN.

THE PEOPLE SEE THE RESULTS OF DISOBEDIENCE — AND FOR A TIME THEY GLADLY FOLLOW MOSES.

BUT THEN A MAN NAMED KORAH AND SOME OF THE OTHER HELPERS IN THE TABERNACLE GROW JEALOUS OF MOSES' LEADERSHIP.

WE ARE AS GOOD AS MOSES! WHY SHOULD HE TELL US WHAT TO DO?

LET'S TELL MOSES WE'LL RUN OUR OWN AFFAIRS!

KORAH AND HIS FOLLOWERS GO TO MOSES... AND MOSES CALLS ALL THE PEOPLE TOGETHER.

TOMORROW THE LORD WILL SHOW US WHO HE HAS CHOSEN TO LEAD OUR PEOPLE!

erpents in the Wilderness

FROM NUMBERS 16:5—21:9, 21–35

ORAH AND SOME OF HIS FRIENDS LED REVOLT AGAINST MOSES AND MOSES ROMISED THEM THAT ON THE FOLLOWING AY GOD WOULD POINT OUT HIS CHOSEN EADER. THE MOMENT HAS COME...

DEPART FROM KORAH AND THE MEN WHO WOULD LEAD YOU TO EVIL, LEST YOU LOSE YOUR LIVES. IF GOD HAS CHOSEN ME TO LEAD YOU, THE EARTH WILL OPEN AND SWALLOW THEM UP...

AS MOSES SPEAKS, THERE IS A GREAT EARTHQUAKE, AND THE TENTS OF KORAH AND HIS FOLLOWERS FALL INTO A DEEP CRACK IN THE EARTH

BUT MOSES IS STILL SO ANGRY WITH HIS PEOPLE THAT HE DISREGARDS GOD'S COMMAND AND STRIKES THE ROCK—TWICE—INSTEAD OF SPEAKING TO IT. WATER GUSHES OUT, AND THE PEOPLE DRINK HAPPILY.

BUT GOD IS DISPLEASED. HOW CAN MOSES AND AARON TEACH THE PEOPLE TO OBEY GOD IF THEY THEMSELVES DO NOT FOLLOW GOD'S INSTRUCTIONS? BECAUSE OF THE BAD EXAMPLE THEY HAVE SET, GOD TELLS THEM THAT NEITHER ONE SHALL ENTER THE PROMISED LAND.

THE ISRAELITES TRAVEL ON. WHEN THEY COME TO MOUNT HOR, GOD TELLS MOSES THAT AARON WILL SOON DIE, AND THAT HE SHOULD TAKE AARON AND HIS SON, ELEAZAR, TO THE MOUNTAINTOP.

ELEAZAR WILL TAKE YOUR PLACE AS HIGH PRIEST, AARON. I WILL PUT YOUR ROBES ON HIM.

AARON DIES ON MOUNT HOR, AND THE ISRAELITES MOURN FOR THIRTY DAYS. THEN THEY MOVE ON. A CLOUD LEADS THEM BY DAY, AND A PILLAR OF FIRE BY NIGHT.

BUT THE PEOPLE SOON FORGET GOD'S CARE... AND AGAIN THEY COMPLAIN...

THERE'S NOT ENOUGH WATER— I'M ALWAYS THIRSTY.

HAS NOT GOD ALWAYS GIVEN US WATER WHEN WE NEEDED IT?

YES, BUT—THE FOOD— I'M SICK OF THIS STUFF THAT MUST BE GATHERED EVERY DAY AND MADE INTO BREAD. I WANT FOOD LIKE WE HAD IN EGYPT— MELONS, FRUIT...

IN EGYPT YOU WERE BEATEN AND MADE TO WORK LIKE SLAVES. AND YOU CRIED FOR FREEDOM.

AND _YOU_ SAID GOD WOULD GIVE US FREEDOM! DO YOU CALL _THIS_ FREEDOM—WANDERING AROUND IN THE WILDERNESS?

SUDDENLY—AS PUNISHMENT FOR THEIR GRUMBLING—THE CAMP BECOMES ALIVE WITH POISONOUS SNAKES.

HELP! I'VE BEEN BITTEN!

HELP ME—OR I'LL DIE!

OSES, WE HAVE SINNED—GAINST GOD AND AGAINST OU. FORGIVE US—AND TAKE AWAY THESE SERPENTS. PLEASE!

I WILL ASK GOD TO HELP YOU.

MOSES PRAYS AND GOD DIRECTS HIM TO MAKE A SERPENT OF BRASS AND PUT IT ON A POLE.

LISTEN TO ME, ALL YOU WHO HAVE BEEN BITTEN BY THE SNAKES. GOD HAS SAID THAT IF YOU LOOK AT THIS BRASS SERPENT, YOU WILL BE WELL AGAIN.

186

187

New Leader

OM NUMBERS 21:33—27:18;

UTERONOMY 34; JOSHUA 1

OLDLY THE GIANT KING OG OF BASHAN
TS OUT TO TEACH THE ISRAELITES A
SSON IN WARFARE. BUT HE SOON FINDS
IS NO MATCH FOR JOSHUA. OG'S ARMY
BEATEN. HE TRIES TO ESCAPE...

AFTER HIM, MEN! CATCH HIM!

THE KING IS CAPTURED, AND THE ISRAELITES TAKE THE COUNTRY.

AFTER CONQUERING THE AMORITES AND BASHAN, THE ISRAELITES SET UP THEIR TENTS ON THE PLAINS OF MOAB.

MEDITERRANEAN SEA

SEA OF GALILEE

BASHAN

CANAAN

JORDAN RIVER

RIVER JABBOK

JERICHO

PLAINS OF MOAB

AMORITES

AMMONITES

DEAD SEA

RIVER ARNON

MOAB

BROOK ZERED

190

THE AGED LEADER CLIMBS MOUNT NEBO AND GAZES DOWN ON THE LAND GOD HAS PROMISED HIS PEOPLE AND THERE—ALONE WITH GOD—HE DIES.

BACK IN CAMP JOSHUA PRAYS TO GOD FOR HELP, AND THE LORD ANSWERS: BE NOT AFRAID, FOR THE LORD THY GOD IS WITH THEE.

THE ISRAELITES MOURN THIRTY DAYS FOR MOSES. THEN, JOSHUA CALLS A MEETING.

THE CAMPAIGNS AHEAD WILL BE HARD AND DANGEROUS. BUT I'LL SEEK GOD'S GUIDANCE IN EVERYTHING WE DO.

AND WE WILL FOLLOW YOU AS WE DID MOSES!

THREE DAYS FROM NOW WE WILL CROSS THE JORDAN RIVER. THEN WE MUST CAPTURE THE CITY OF JERICHO—BUT FIRST WE NEED TO LEARN ALL WE CAN ABOUT IT.

191

iege of Jericho

OM JOSHUA 4:1—6:20

S IF HELD BACK BY A GIANT HAND, THE WATERS OF THE ORDAN STOP FLOWING WHILE THE ISRAELITES CROSS VER INTO THE PROMISED LAND. WHEN ALL HAVE CROSSED, OSHUA ORDERS A MAN FROM EACH OF THE TRIBES TO RING A LARGE STONE FROM THE RIVER BED.

CARRY THESE STONES TO CAMP. THEY WILL REMIND US OF HOW GOD STOPPED THE JORDAN SO THAT WE MIGHT CROSS OVER SAFELY.

THEN JOSHUA SETS UP 12 OTHER STONES IN THE MIDDLE OF THE JORDAN — AT THE PLACE WHERE THE PRIESTS HOLD THE ARK. AFTER THAT HE COMMANDS THE PRIESTS TO CARRY THE ARK ACROSS. WHEN THEY REACH THE BANK THE FLOOD WATERS OF THE JORDAN RUSH FORTH...

THE ISRAELITES SET UP THEIR FIRST CAMP AT GILGAL—AND HERE THEY CELEBRATE THEIR FIRST PASSOVER FEAST IN THE PROMISED LAND.

AND HERE, TOO, THEY FIND FRUIT AND GRAIN.

LOOK! FOOD— ENOUGH FOR EVERYONE!

THANK GOD— THIS IS TRULY A WONDERFUL LAND.

NOW THAT THE PEOPLE CAN FIND FOOD FOR THEMSELVES, GOD NO LONGER SENDS THE MANNA WHICH HE HAS FURNISHED THEM SINCE THEY LEFT EGYPT FORTY YEARS AGO.

WHILE THE REST OF THE CAMP IS ENJOYING THE NEW LAND, JOSHUA SCOUTS THE AREA IN PREPARATION FOR THE ATTACK ON JERICHO. SUDDENLY HE LOOKS UP AND SEES A MAN WITH A SWORD!

IS HE GOING TO TRY TO KILL ME?

BUT JOSHUA IS NO COWARD— BRAVELY HE FACES THE STRANGER.

ARE YOU FRIEND— OR ENEMY?

I AM THE CAPTAIN OF THE LORD'S ARMY!

199

200

ONCE EACH DAY FOR SIX DAYS THE ISRAELITES HAVE MARCHED AROUND THE CITY OF JERICHO. NOW, ON THE SEVENTH DAY, JOSHUA ORDERS THEM TO MARCH AROUND SEVEN TIMES. THE PRIESTS BLOW THEIR TRUMPETS—THE MARCHERS SHOUT—AND THE WALLS OF THE MIGHTY CITY FALL FLAT.

JERICHO IS OURS!

202

JOSHUA'S MEN LOSE NO TIME IN APPROACHING IT.

GREETINGS! WE'RE GOING TO AI—IS IT A BIG CITY?

I'D SAY ABOUT 12,000, AND THAT INCLUDES A SMALL ARMY.

THE SCOUTS RETURN TO CAMP, EAG[...] TO GIVE THEIR GOOD NEWS TO JOSH[...]

THE ARMY OF AI IS SMALL. WE CAN TAKE THE CITY AND LEAVE MOST OF O[...] TROOPS HERE T[...] REST.

JOSHUA TAKES THE ADVICE OF HIS SCOUTS AND SENDS ONLY 3,000 MEN TO TAKE AI.

BUT AT THE GATES OF THE CITY...

HO, LOOK AT THE[...] RUN. THEY'R[...] AFRAID TO FIGHT.

SO THESE ARE THE BRAVE ISRAELITES WHO TOOK JERICHO!

205

206

207

209

JOSHUA MARCHES HIS SOLDIERS ALL NIGHT— AND CATCHES THE ENEMY FORCES AROUND GIBEON BY SURPRISE.

DON'T LET A MAN ESCAPE!

FLEEING FROM THE ISRAELITES, THE ENEMY IS CAUGHT IN A TERRIBLE HAILSTORM.

JOSHUA IS AFRAID THE ENEMY WILL ESCAPE DURING THE NIGHT SO HE COMMANDS THE SUN AND MOON TO STAND STILL...

AND DAYLIGHT LASTS UNTIL JOSHUA WINS THE VICTORY. THE PEOPLE OF GIBEON ARE SAVED, BUT THE PRICE OF THEIR TRICK ALLIANCE IS THAT THEY MUST WORK AS SERVANTS FOR THE ISRAELITES.

UNDER JOSHUA THE ISRAELITES CONQUER ALL OF THE CITIES OF SOUTHERN CANAAN. THEN THEY GO BACK TO THEIR CAMP AT GILGAL.

PRAISE THE LORD. PEACE AT LAST!

213

Battle in the Storm

FROM JUDGES 4—5

AGAIN THE ISRAELITES FORGET ALL THAT GOD HAS DONE FOR THEM AND TURN TO WORSHIP THE IDOLS OF THEIR NEIGHBORS. SOON THEY BECOME SO WEAK AND AFRAID THEY CAN'T EVEN PROTECT THEIR OWN FIELDS FROM CANAANITE RAIDERS.

STOP! THAT'S MY GRAIN!

IT'S OURS NOW—SO, WHAT ARE YOU GOING TO DO ABOUT IT?

YEARS AGO OUR GREAT LEADER, JOSHUA, CONQUERED THE CANAANITES. NOW THEY ARE CONQUERING US!

WHAT'S THE MATTER WITH OUR LEADERS? WE'LL STARVE IF KING JABIN'S MEN KEEP STEALING OUR GRAIN.

ONE FIELD AFTER ANOTHER IS RAIDED UNTIL AT LAST THE FARMERS HAVE A MEETING.

SOMETHING MUST BE DONE—AT ONCE—TO STOP THOSE CANAANITES.

LET'S GO IN A BODY TO SEE DEBORAH.

I'LL GO, BUT BECAUSE YOU DID NOT HAVE THE FAITH TO LEAD BY YOURSELF, BARAK, YOU WILL NOT GET THE CREDIT FOR THE VICTORY. GOD WILL DELIVER JABIN'S GENERAL, SISERA, INTO THE HAND OF A WOMAN.

AFTER A QUICK MARCH, THE ISRAELITES REACH MOUNT TABOR. DEBORAH'S PROPHECY COMES TRUE—THE CANAANITE ARMY COMES TO MEET THEM.

HAVE FAITH— FOR THIS IS THE DAY THE LORD WILL DELIVER US!

DEBORAH GIVES THE SIGNAL...AND BARAK CHARGES DOWN THE MOUNTAIN AT THE HEAD OF HIS TROOPS. ABOVE THEM LIGHTNING FLASHES...

A CLOUDBURST TURNS THE PLAIN INTO A SEA OF MUD. THE IRON CHARIOTS OF THE CANAANITE SINK INTO THE MIRE. TRAPPED, THEY ARE AT THE MERCY OF THE ISRAELITES, WHO ATTACK WITH SPEED AND COURAGE.

THE CANAANITES RETREAT.

TO THE RIVER!

WHEN SISERA, GENERAL OF THE CANAANITE FORCES, SEES THAT THEY HAVE BEEN DEFEATED, HE TRIES TO ESCAPE TO A DISTANT CITY. ON THE WAY HE STOPS TO REST IN WHAT HE THINKS IS A FRIENDLY TENT. BUT THE WOMAN WHO LIVES THERE, NAMED JAEL, IS LOYAL TO ISRAEL AND KILLS SISERA WHILE HE IS ASLEEP.

BUT THE KISHON RIVER IS ALREADY OVERFLOWING ITS BANKS... AND THE CANAANITES WHO TRY TO SWIM TO SAFETY SINK UNDER THE WEIGHT OF THEIR HEAVY ARMOR.

WHEN DEBORAH LEARNS THAT THE CANAANITES HAVE BEEN DEFEATED, SHE SINGS A SONG OF VICTORY...

I WILL SING UNTO THE LORD; I WILL SING PRAISES TO THE LORD GOD OF ISRAEL.

THE PEOPLE REJOICE AND SING THEIR PRAISES, TOO. AND FOR FORTY YEARS THERE IS PEACE IN ISRAEL. FAMILIES WORK IN THEIR FIELDS AND HARVEST THEIR CROPS. BUT IN TIME THEY AGAIN FORGET GOD, AND FIND THEMSELVES IN MORE TROUBLE THAN EVER BEFORE.

Chosen by God

FROM JUDGES 6—7

IN THE YEARS OF PLENTY THAT FOLLOW DEBORAH'S VICTORY OVER THE CANAANITES, THE ISRAELITES AGAIN FORGET GOD. ONE BY ONE THEY JOIN THEIR NEIGHBORS IN WORSHIPING THE IDOL, BAAL. AT LAST ONLY A FEW MEN IN ALL ISRAEL REMEMBER THAT IT WAS GOD WHO HAD RESCUED THEM FROM THEIR ENEMIES.

ROVING BANDS OF DESERT TRIBESMEN BEGIN TO TERRORIZE THE ISRAELITE VILLAGES, AND RAID THE FIELDS.

RUN FOR YOUR LIVES!

IF THEY FIND WHERE I HID MY GRAIN, WE'LL STARVE.

EN THE RAID IS OVER...

IT'S GONE—
MY GRAIN,
IT'S GONE!

FOR SEVEN LONG YEARS THE ISRAELITES SUFFER AT THE HANDS OF THE DESERT TRIBESMEN. THEY HIDE OUT IN CAVES, THRESH THEIR GRAIN IN SECRET PLACES...BUT ALWAYS THE RAIDERS RETURN.

THEN EVEN MORE FRIGHTENING NEWS COMES...

THE MIDIANITES ARE COMING AGAIN. AND WITH THEM GREAT HORDES FROM THE EAST.

LIKE GRASSHOPPERS THE ENEMY SWARMS OVER THE ISRAELITE FIELDS...STEALING GRAIN, CATTLE, AND SHEEP.

E DAY A YOUNG RAELITE IS CRETLY RESHING G GRAIN EN A RANGER PEARS FORE HIM.

WHO ARE YOU? AND WHAT DO YOU WANT?

GOD HAS CHOSEN YOU, GIDEON, TO SAVE YOUR PEOPLE.

ME? I'M ONLY A POOR FARMER—HOW CAN I SAVE ISRAEL? GIVE ME A SIGN THAT YOU ARE THE ANGEL OF GOD.

GIDEON PREPARES SOME FOOD AND BRINGS IT TO THE STRANGER.

PUT THE FOOD ON THE ROCK.

THE STRANGER TOUCHES THE FOOD WITH HIS STAFF. INSTANTLY, A FIRE BURSTS FORTH AND CONSUMES IT.

I HAVE SEEN THE ANGEL OF THE LORD— FACE TO FACE!

WHEN THE ANGEL DISAPPEARS, GOD SPEAKS TO GIDEON AND TELLS HIM WHAT TO DO.

THAT NIGHT GIDEON AND HIS SERVANT BREAK DOWN THE ALTAR OF BAAL.

AND WHEN THEY HAVE FINISHED, HE BUILDS AN ALTAR TO GOD.

GIDEON CALLS THE LEADERS OF ISRAEL TOGETHER.

WITH GOD'S HELP WE CAN DRIVE THE MIDIANITES FROM OUR LAND. ARE YOU WITH ME?

YES!

YES!

WITH AN ARMY OF 32,000 MEN GIDEON MARCHES TO THE HILLS SURROUNDING THE MIDIANITE CAMP.

WHAT A CAMP! THEY HAVE MORE CAMELS THAN THERE ARE SANDS ON THE SHORE.

DON'T WORRY. GOD HAS TOLD ME HOW WE CAN DEFEAT THEM.

GIDEON SPEAKS TO HIS ARMY...

IF ANY OF YOU ARE AFRAID TO FIGHT, LEAVE US NOW AND GO HOME.

ALL BUT 10,000 MEN LEAVE.

GIDEON WATCHES THE MEN WHO ARE LEFT AS THEY DRINK FROM THE BROOK. MOST OF THEM ARE CARELESS AND PUT THEIR FACES DOWN INTO THE WATER. BUT SOME KEEP THEIR HEADS UP, THEIR EYES ALERT—ON THE WATCH FOR DANGER. GIDEON CHOOSES THOSE WHO ARE ALERT— AND SENDS THE REST HOME.

ONLY THREE HUNDRED MEN ARE LEFT OUT OF GIDEON'S ARMY OF 32,000 MEN. NOW THE ISRAELITES KNOW BEYOND ALL DOUBT THAT ONLY WITH GOD'S HELP CAN THEY DEFEAT THE ENEMY.

HIDE YOUR TORCHES IN THESE PITCHERS. SPREAD OUT ON THREE SIDES OF THE CAMP. LISTEN FOR MY SIGNAL ON THE TRUMPET.

WE'RE READY.

AT GIDEON'S SIGNAL, THE MEN BLOW THEIR TRUMPETS, SMASH THEIR PITCHERS, WAVE THEIR TORCHES, GIVE THE BATTLE CRY...

THE SWORD OF THE LORD AND OF GIDEON!

AND CHARGE DOWN THE HILL— THREE HUNDRED AGAINST THOUSANDS!

Philistine Raiders

FROM JUDGES 7:22–25; 8:28

WE'VE BEEN ATTACKED!

THE STILLNESS OF THE NIGHT IS SUDDENLY BROKEN BY THE BLARE OF 300 TRUMPETS AND CRASH OF BROKEN PITCHERS. STARTLED FROM THEIR SLEEP, THE MIDIANITES RUSH OUT TO FIND THEIR CAMP ABLAZE WITH FLAMING TORCHES. IN THEIR PANIC THEY EVEN ATTACK ONE ANOTHER...BUT GIDEON AND HIS 300 ISRAELITES SURROUND THEM

WHERE'S MY SWORD— MY SHIELD?

THE MIDIANITES THINK THEY HAVE BEEN ATTACKED BY A GIANT ARMY...AND IN TERROR MANY TRY TO ESCAPE TO THE RIVER.

TAKE WORD TO THE TRIBE OF EPHRAIM TO HOLD THE FORDS OF THE JORDAN.

SOME OF THE MIDIANITES REACH THE JORDAN RIVER — BUT THEY ARE CAPTURED BY ISRAELITE SOLDIERS FROM EPHRAIM WAITING IN AMBUSH

IN THE NORTH, GIDEON CHASES THE ENEMY ACROSS THE JORDAN...AND AT LAST ALL OF THE MIDIANITE FORCES ARE DEFEATED.

The Roller-Coaster Ride of the Israelites

The Book of Judges tells us about a rocky time in Israel's history. In fact, many people call this the roller-coaster period. When Joshua dies, the Israelites turn from God and fight with each other and their neighbors. When things get bad, they cry out to God and He sends a judge to straighten things out. When the judge dies, Israel forgets about God, and the whole cycle repeats. Israel goes up and down, just like a roller-coaster!

God Delivers

Israel Disobeys God

Ask for God's Help

Consequences of Sin

Israel Disobeys God

Here are interesting facts about some of the judges:

▶ **Ehud** (Judges 3:12-30) is a left-handed Benjamite who stabs the King of Moab with a dagger he has hidden under his clothes.

▶ **Shamgar** (Judges 3:31) slays 600 Philistines with a pointed stick used to urge oxen along.

Why was Israel weak? See p. 213.

▶ **Deborah** (Judges 4-5) was a prophetess and judge who urges Barak to attack the Canaanite army. God sends a cloudburst that immobilizes the enemies' 900 chariots of iron. Read the story on pp. 214-217.

Did You Know?

Who was the woman that killed the mighty Sisera? See p. 217.

▶ **Gideon** (Judges 6–8) defeats the 32,000-man Midianite army with 300 men. See pp. 219-224 for the details.

▶ **Jephthah** (Judges 10:6–12:7) makes a vow to God that if God gives him victory over his enemies, he will sacrifice the first thing that comes out of his house. Little does Jephthah realize that the sacrifice will be so great!

▶ **Samson's** (Judges 13–16) great strength allows him to kill 1,000 Philistines with the jawbone of a donkey and single-handedly carry the gates of a city to a nearby hill! Read his story on pp. 227-246.

• • • • • • • • • • • • • • • • • • • •

Samson takes a Nazirite vow from birth. For anyone who takes this vow, it means:
• you can't eat grapes or drink wine.
• you can't cut your hair.
• you can't touch anything dead.

• • • • • • • • • • • • • • • • • • • •

Samson kills more Philistines at his death than when he is alive. How could he do this? See pp. 244-246 for the story.

• • • • • • • • • • • • • • • • • • • •

God always punishes sin . . . but He is ready at any moment to forgive when you tell Him truthfully that you are sorry for any wrong that you've done.

• • • • • • • • • • • • • • • • • • • •

ttacked by a Lion

OM JUDGES 13:2—14:5

HE PHILISTINE RAIDERS STRIKE IME AND AGAIN T THE ISRAELITE ILLAGES, CARRYING FF GRAIN, CATTLE— VEN CHILDREN TO VORK AS SLAVES. UT ONE ISRAELITE OTHER AND FATHER VAIT EAGERLY FOR STRANGE AND VONDERFUL ROMISE TO COME RUE. ONE DAY HEY TELL THEIR OUNG SON, SAMSON, BOUT IT.

BEFORE YOU WERE BORN, AN ANGEL OF GOD TOLD US THAT SOME DAY YOU WOULD BE THE LEADER OF OUR PEOPLE AND SAVE US FROM THE WICKED PHILISTINES.

I WOULD SAVE OUR PEOPLE? HOW?

WE DON'T KNOW HOW, SON, BUT IF YOU TRUST IN GOD, HE WILL SHOW YOU THE WAY. BUT YOU MUST KEEP A PROMISE YOUR MOTHER MADE TO GOD.

A PROMISE? WHAT IS IT?

TO SET YOU APART AS ONE DEDICATED TO GOD, YOU WILL NEVER CUT YOUR HAIR—OR TOUCH STRONG DRINK.

227

SAMSON KEEPS HIS MOTHER'S PROMISE TO GOD. AND AS THE YEARS PASS AND THE PHILISTINES CONTINUE TO ROB AND PLUNDER THE ISRAELITES, HE DREAMS OF THE DAY WHEN HE CAN SAVE HIS PEOPLE. ONE DAY AFTER A RAID, HE STORMS ANGRILY INTO A MEETING OF THE ELDERS.

THEY KILLED MY COUSIN WITH THIS SPEAR! IT HAS AN IRON HEAD...

YES, THE PHILISTINES KNOW HOW TO MAKE IRON SPEARS, BUT WE DON'T. HOW CAN WE FIGHT THEM WITH WOODEN SPEARS?

SOME DAY I'LL FIGHT THEM, AND WHEN I DO...

HE SNAPPED THAT SPEAR AS IF IT WERE A TWIG.

IF HE IS THAT STRONG NOW, WHAT WILL HE BE LIKE WHEN HE IS A MAN?

AS SAMSON GROWS, HIS STRENGTH GROWS UNTIL AT LAST HE IS THE STRONGEST MAN IN ALL THE TRIBE OF DAN. SOME OF THE PEOPLE WATCH ANXIOUSLY AS HE SETS OUT ONE DAY SEEKING ADVENTURE IN A PHILISTINE VILLAGE.

I HOPE HE DOESN'T GET INTO ANY TROUBLE.

NO MAN IN HIS RIGHT MIND WOULD RISK A FIGHT WITH SAMSON.

NO—NO ONE MAN, BUT A WHOLE VILLAGE MIGHT. AND THAT COULD MEAN TROUBLE FOR US, TOO.

ON THE DAY SAMSON SETS OUT FOR HIS WEDDING, HE STOPS TO EXAMINE THE BODY OF THE LION HE HAD KILLED--AND FINDS THAT BEES HAVE MADE HONEY IN THE CARCASS.

FOOD FROM A LION-- HONEY FROM THE STRONG. GIVES ME AN IDEA FOR A RIDDLE TO TRY ON THE WEDDING GUESTS.

IN TIMNATH HE IS GREETED BY A GROUP OF YOUNG MEN.

I AM YOUR BEST MAN, AND I HAVE BROUGHT 29 OF MY FRIENDS TO BE YOUR GUESTS.

GOOD! NOW WIL YOU TRY TO GUESS MY RIDDLE. IF YO DO, I'LL GIVE EACH OF YOU SHIRT AND A ROE IF YOU CAN'T, EACH OF YOU WILL GIVE ME SHIRT AND ROBE

WE'LL TAKE YOU UP ON THAT-- WHAT'S THE RIDDLE?

OUT OF THE EATER CAME FOOD; OUT OF THE STRONG CAME SWEETNESS. YOU HAVE A WEEK TO GUESS THE ANSWER.

BUT AS THE WEEK GOES BY, NEITHER THE BEST MAN NOR ANY OF HIS FRIENDS CAN GUESS SAMSON'S RIDDLE.

WHAT WILL WE DO? I CAN'T AFFORD TO GIVE HIM A SHIRT AND ROBE.

NEITHER CAN I. WE'LL HAVE TO GET THE ANSWER FROM HIS WIFE. AFTER ALL, SHE IS A PHILISTINE.

GET THE ANSWER FROM SAMSON, O WE'LL SET FIRE TO YOUR FATHER' HOUSE WITH YO IN IT!

NO! NO! GIVE ME TIME.

Fire!

FROM JUDGES 14:19—15:12

SAMSON IS FURIOUS! HE HAS LOST THE WAGER OF THIRTY ROBES TO THE PHILISTINES WHO FORCED HIS WIFE TO TELL THEM THE ANSWER TO HIS RIDDLE. HE LEAVES HIS WEDDING FEAST AND ENTERS ANOTHER CITY...

AH! ENOUGH PHILISTINE TO PAY MY DEBT--AND ALL OF THEM HANDSOM DRESSED, TOO.

WHO HIT ME?

WHAT'S HAPPENING?

PHILISTINES TRICKED ME, SO PHILISTINES WILL PAY THE DEBT.

STILL IN A RAGE, SAMSON RETUR TO THE WEDDING FEAST...

HERE THE DEBT IS PAID! AND B' THE LIVES OF YOUR OWN COUNTRYME

232

The Gaza Trap

FROM JUDGES 15:13—16:2

WHEN THE PHILISTINE ARMY DEMANDS THAT THE TRIBE OF JUDAH TURN SAMSON OVER TO THEM, THE TRIBAL LEADERS AGREE. "IT'S YOU," THEY TELL SAMSON, "OR EVERY MAN, WOMAN AND CHILD IN JUDAH." SO SAMSON SURRENDERS...

THAT OUGHT TO DO IT. THE ROPES ARE NEW, AND THE KNOTS ARE TIGHT. HE'S HELPLESS-- LET'S GO.

O GOD, BE WITH ME WHEN I FACE MY ENEMY.

IT'S A GREAT MOMENT FOR THE PHILISTINES WHEN SAMSON IS BOUND AND DELIVERED INTO THEIR HANDS.

I WONDER HOW THE STRONG MAN FEELS NOW?

I'D LIKE TO BE THE FIRST ONE TO GET EVEN WITH HIM.

NOT I-- I DON'T TRUST ROPES TO HOLD SAMSON.

WAIT TILL WE SHOW THE MIGHTY MAN OF JUDAH TO THE PEOPLE BACK HOME.

THAT JAWBONE-- IT'S JUST WHAT I NEED!

235

SUDDENLY, SAMSON BURSTS THE ROPES...
AND SEIZES THE JAWBONE OF AN ASS.

NOW WHAT ARE YOU GOING TO SHOW THE PEOPLE BACK HOME?

WITH DEADLY AIM SAMSON STRIKES DOWN ONE PHILISTINE SOLDIER AFTER ANOTHER. THOSE WHO CAN, RUN FOR THEIR LIVES. IN A SHORT WHILE THE ONE-MAN ATTACK IS OVER...

THEN, WEARY AND THIRSTY, SAMSON PRAYS TO GOD.

LORD, YOU GAVE ME THE VICTORY. DON'T LET ME NOW DIE OF THIRST.

237

The Big Bribe

FROM JUDGES 16:3–5

DO YOU THINK HE'S GOING TO TELL *US* WHAT IT IS?

NO--BUT HE'LL TELL THE RIGHT PERSON. I HEAR HE IS IN LOVE WITH DELILAH...

DELILAH? SHE'S A PHILISTINE.

RIGHT. SHE'LL GET SAMSON TO TELL HER HIS SECRET-- THEN SHE'LL TELL US.

WILL SHE? WHAT IF SHE IS IN LOVE WITH SAMSON?

SHE'S ALS[O] IN LOVE WIT[H] MONEY. COM[E] ON--LET'S GO TO SEE HER.

SO THE PHILISTINE RULERS VISIT DELILAH...

IF YOU FIND OUT SAMSON'S SECRET FOR US, WE'LL *EACH* GIVE YOU ELEVEN HUNDRED PIECES OF SILVER.

PAYABLE ON THE DATE SAMSON IS IN OUR HANDS.

HMM...ELEVEN HUNDRED TIMES FIVE-- HOW CAN I REFUSE?

WATCH OUT--HE'S FREE! RUN FOR YOUR LIVES!

SAMSON TRICKED ME!

DELILAH KEEPS TRYING TO LEARN THE SECRET OF SAMSON'S STRENGTH. SHE BINDS HIM IN DIFFERENT WAYS, BUT EACH TIME HE BREAKS FREE. AT LAST...

YOU DON'T LOVE ME, SAMSON! IF YOU DID, YOU'D TELL ME THE TRUTH.

I DO LOVE YOU, AND TO PROVE IT, I'LL TELL YOU MY SECRET. WHEN I WAS DEDICATED TO GOD A PROMISE WAS MADE NEVER TO CUT MY HAIR. IF I BREAK THAT PROMISE, GOD WILL TAKE AWAY MY STRENGTH. I'LL BE AS WEAK AS ANY MAN.

AT LAST DELILAH HAS THE REAL SECRET. SHE CALLS THE PHILISTINES AND PLANS TO TRAP SAMSON THAT NIGHT.

HAVE YOUR CHAINS READY-- AND TELL YOUR MASTERS TO BRING THE MONEY THEY PROMISED ME.

THAT EVENING SAMSON CALLS ON DELILAH. WHEN HE FALLS ASLEEP...

NOW'S YOUR CHANCE.

I'VE NEVER SEEN SUCH LONG HAIR-- BUT I STILL DON'T SEE HOW THIS WILL TAKE HIS STRENGTH AWAY.

SAMSON! WAKE UP-- THE PHILISTINES ARE HERE.

Samson's Victory

FROM JUDGES 16:21–30

BETRAYED BY DELILAH, SAMSON IS CAPTURED BY THE PHILISTINES, BLINDED, AND MADE TO GRIND GRAIN IN THE PRISON AT GAZA. BUT—UNNOTICED BY HIS CAPTORS—HIS HAIR BEGINS TO GROW...

O GOD, GIVE ME ONE MORE CHANCE TO FREE MY PEOPLE FROM THE SLAVERY OF THE PHILISTINES!

OUTSIDE THE PRISON WALLS, THE PHILISTINES PREPARE FOR A GREAT FESTIVAL TO DAGON, THEIR GOD.

BRING YOUR GIFTS TO DAGON WHO DELIVERED SAMSON INTO OUR HANDS.

DURING THE FEAST...

WHAT CAN WE DO TO PLEASE THE CROWD?

I HAVE IT—BRING SAMSON OUT AN LET THE PEOPLE HAVE THEIR FUN WITH HIM.

244

245

O GOD, JUST ONCE MORE, GIVE ME THE STRENGTH I NEED.

AND NOW, LET ME DIE WITH THE PHILISTINES.

USING ALL HIS MIGHTY STRENGTH, SAMSON PUSHES AGAINST THE PILLARS—AND THE GIANT TEMPLE TO THE HEATHEN GOD, DAGON, CRASHES TO THE GROUND. CRUSHED BENEATH IT ARE THE PHILISTINES WHO HAD MADE SLAVES OF SAMSON'S PEOPLE...

BUT THE FIGHT IS NOT YET OVER...AND IN THE MIDST OF THESE TROUBLESOME TIMES THERE COMES A WOMAN FROM A FOREIGN LAND WHO GIVES ISRAEL A VICTORIOUS KING.

Naomi's Strategy

FROM RUTH 2:6—3:18

AND WHEN THE MEAL IS OVER AND RUTH HAS GONE BACK TO WORK—

DROP SOME GRAIN ON PURPOSE FOR HER TO PICK UP. AND SEE THAT NO HARM COMES TO HER!

HAVE NO FEAR, BOAZ. SHE WILL BE SAFE—AND SHE WILL FIND ALL THE GRAIN SHE NEEDS.

THAT EVENING—

LOOK AT ALL THE GRAIN I FOUND! OH, NAOMI, YOUR GOD IS GOOD TO US.

I THOUGHT WHEN MY HUSBAND AND SONS DIED THAT GOD HAD FORGOTTEN ME. NOW I KNOW HOW MUCH HE LOVES ME, FOR HE HAS GIVEN ME A DAUGHTER-IN-LAW WHO CARES FOR ME AS A DAUGHTER. BUT—NOW—TELL ME ABOUT THE DAY. IN WHOSE FIELD DID YOU GLEAN?

HIS NAME WAS BOAZ—HE WAS VERY KIND.

AND VERY HANDSOME, TOO.

BOAZ? HE IS A RELATIVE OF MY HUSBAND'S FAMILY. GOD BLESS HIM FOR BEING KIND TO YOU.

ALL THROUGH THE HARVEST SEASON RUTH GLEANS IN BOAZ' FIELD AND TAKES CARE OF NAOMI. ONE EVENING...

I BELIEVE BOAZ LOVES YOU, BUT HE DOESN'T KNOW HOW YOU FEEL. WE ISRAELITES HAVE A CUSTOM ABOUT THE RIGHTS OF RELATIVES IN MARRIAGE. TONIGHT BOAZ WILL STAY AT THE THRESHING FLOOR TO GUARD HIS GRAIN. IF YOU DO AS I SAY—

I LOVE BOAZ, AND I'LL DO WHAT YOU TELL ME.

248

A Joyful Wedding

FROM RUTH 4

NEXT MORNING BOAZ WATCHES FOR THE RELATIVE WHO HAS FIRST RIGHT TO BUY THE LAND THAT BELONGED TO **NAOMI'S** DEAD HUSBAND—AND TO MARRY RUTH.

GOOD MORNING! WILL YOU STOP AND DISCUSS A MATTER THAT IS IMPORTANT TO BOTH OF US?

GOOD MORNING TO YOU, BOAZ. WHAT IS THE PROBLEM?

WHEN THE MAN IS SEATED BOAZ INVITES THE ELDERS OF THE CITY TO JOIN THEM

THE LAND THAT BELONGED TO NAOMI'S HUSBAND IS FOR SALE. ONE OF US MUST BUY IT TO KEEP IT IN THE FAMILY. YOU ARE THE CLOSEST RELATIVE... WILL YOU BUY THE LAND?

YES, I WILL BUY IT!

251

THE NEWS OF RUTH AND BOAZ' COMING MARRIAGE SPREADS RAPIDLY THROUGHOUT ALL BETHLEHEM, FOR BOAZ IS A WELL-TO-DO LANDOWNER. AT THE WEDDING THERE IS FEASTING, MUSIC AND LAUGHTER...

ARE YOU HAPPY, MY DEAR?

HAPPIER THAN I EVER DREAMED I COULD BE. GOD HAS BEEN GOOD TO ME.

AFTER HER MARRIAGE, RUTH MOVES INTO THE BIG HOUSE OF BOAZ. LATER, WHEN A SON IS BORN TO RUTH, NAOMI PROUDLY CARES FOR THE CHILD. HE IS NAMED OBED, WHICH MEANS "SERVANT."

OH, RUTH, I THANK GOD FOR THE DAY YOU LEFT MOAB TO COME WITH ME TO BETHLEHEM. FOR NOW I HAVE A GRANDSON TO SERVE ME IN MY OLD AGE.

I THANK HIM, TOO, NAOMI— FOR TRULY YOUR PEOPLE HAVE BECOME MY PEOPLE—AND YOUR GOD MY GOD...

AND MY PRAYER IS THAT OBED WILL SERVE GOD AND HIS PEOPLE.

RUTH'S PRAYER COMES TRUE— FOR HER SON BECOMES THE GRANDFATHER OF DAVID, ISRAEL'S GREATEST KING, WHO FREES HIS PEOPLE FROM THEIR ENEMIES...

252

all in the Night

ᴿᴼᴹ **1 Sᴀᴍᴜᴇʟ 1:1—3:17**

HUNDREDS OF YEARS HAVE PASSED SINCE THE ISRAELITES SETTLED IN THE PROMISED LAND OF CANAAN. DURING THAT TIME THEY OFTEN TURNED FROM GOD TO WORSHIP HEATHEN IDOLS. AS A RESULT THEY HAVE BECOME WEAK— ALMOST SLAVES OF THEIR ENEMIES, THE PHILISTINES. TO SOME IT SEEMS THAT GOD HAS FORGOTTEN HIS PROMISE TO MAKE ISRAEL STRONG.

THE BOOK OF **1 SAMUEL** BEGINS...

T THE TABERNACLE AT SHILOH, ELI, THE ᴳH PRIEST, WATCHES THE FAITHFUL COME ᴼ WORSHIP. HE NOTICES A WOMAN AND ᴜᴅDENLY HE BECOMES ANGRY...

SHE ACTS AS IF SHE'S DRUNK! HOW DARE SHE INSULT GOD!

ᴺGRILY HE ᴄᴜSES HER...

NO! NO! I AM NOT DRUNK, I AM UNHAPPY; AND IN MY SORROW I HAVE POURED OUT MY HEART TO GOD, ASKING HIM TO HELP ME.

GO IN PEACE, HANNAH, AND MAY GOD GRANT THEE THY PRAYER.

HANNAH IS SO HAPPY THAT SHE RUSHES OUT OF THE TABERNACLE TO FIND HER HUSBAND.

OH, ELKANAH, I PRAYED TO GOD FOR A SON—AND ELI BLESSED ME AND ASKED GOD TO GIVE ME WHAT I PRAYED FOR.

A SON? I, TOO, PRAY THAT GOD WILL GRANT YOUR PRAYER.

GOD ANSWERS HANNAH'S PRAYER—AND WHEN THE BOY IS OLD ENOUGH TO LEAVE HIS MOTHER, SHE BRINGS HIM TO ELI.

WHEN I ASKED GOD FOR A SON, I PROMISED THAT HE WOULD SERVE THE LORD ALL HIS LIFE. SO I HAVE BROUGHT HIM HERE TO BE TRAINED IN GOD'S HOUSE. HIS NAME IS SAMUEL.

GOD BLESS YOU, HANNAH. LEAVE THE BOY WITH ME AND I WILL TEACH HIM TO BE A SERVANT OF THE LORD.

SAMUEL STAYS WITH ELI AND EAGERLY LEARNS WHAT GOD EXPECTS OF THOSE WHO SERVE HIM. EACH YEAR WHEN HANNAH AND HER HUSBAND COME TO WORSHIP, SHE BRINGS SAMUEL A NEW COAT.

IT'S JUST LIKE A PRIEST'S ROBE. THANK YOU, MOTHER.

OLD ELI IS PROUD OF SAMUEL—BUT HE IS BROKENHEARTED WHEN HE THINKS OF HIS OWN TWO SONS. AS PRIESTS, THEY HAVE SINNED AGAINST GOD AND CHEATED THE PEOPLE. ELI KNOWS THAT HE, TOO, IS GUILTY BECAUSE HE HAS DONE NOTHING TO STOP THEM.

256

IF WE DON'T, WE'LL BE SLAVES TO THE ISRAELITES WHO HAVE BEEN _OUR_ SLAVES ...COME ON, LET'S TAKE THE ADVANTAGE AND STRIKE FIRST!

THE PHILISTINES ATTACK! BUT THE ISRAELITES, BELIEVING IN THE POWER OF THE ARK, COUNTER ATTACK WITH SUDDEN FURY.

CAPTURE THE ARK—AND THEY'LL GIVE UP.

HE ARK IS CAPTURED, AND THE ISRAELITES FLEE IN TERROR. A MESSENGER TAKES THE NEWS O ELI...

THE BATTLE IS LOST—YOUR SONS ARE DEAD—AND THE PHILISTINES HAVE CAPTURED THE ARK.

THE ARK! CAPTURED?

AT THE NEWS, ELI FALLS AND BREAKS HIS NECK. MEANWHILE THE PHILISTINES TRIUMPHANTLY CARRY THE ARK HOME AND PLACE IT IN THE TEMPLE OF THEIR GOD, DAGON.

BUT IN THE MORNING...

The Turning Point

FROM 1 SAMUEL 5:3—7:10

WITH SHOUTS OF TRIUMPH THE PHILISTINES PLACE THE SACRED ARK OF GOD IN THEIR HEATHEN TEMPLE. TO THEM IT IS A SIGN THAT THE PHILISTINE GOD, DAGON, HAS CONQUERED THE GOD OF ISRAEL. BUT THE NEXT MORNING THE IDOL LIES ON ITS FACE BEFORE THE ARK. PRIESTS REPLACE THE IDOL, AND ON THE FOLLOWING MORNING...

LOOK! OUR GREAT GOD, DAGON, LIES BROKEN BEFORE THE ARK OF THE ISRAELITES!

SO THE ARK IS TAKEN FROM ONE PHILISTINE CITY TO ANOTHER...AND IN EACH CITY A PLAGUE BREAKS OUT...

NOT A FAMILY HAS ESCAPED THIS STRANGE ILLNESS.

OUR FIELDS ARE OVER RUN WITH MICE. I TELL YOU—A CURSE HAS BEEN PUT UPON THIS CITY.

THE PHILISTINES SOON REALIZE THAT THEIR TROUBLES BEGAN WHEN THEY CAPTURED THE HOLY ARK OF ISRAEL. FINALLY THEY RETURN THE ARK TO ISRAEL, BUT ISRAEL IS WORSHIPING IDOLS. THE ARK IS PLACED IN A HOUSE AND ALMOST FORGOTTEN.

259

260

Samuel Prays for a King

FROM 1 SAMUEL 7:10—9:20

THE PHILISTINE ARMY PREPARES FOR A RUSH ATTACK ON THE ISRAELITES GATHERED AT MIZPEH. ON THE HILLTOP SAMUEL OFFERS A SACRIFICE AND PRAYS TO GOD FOR HELP.

THIS TIME WE'LL TEACH THEM A LESSON THEY WON'T FORGET.

BUT WHEN THE PHILISTINES ARE WITHIN BATTLE RANGE, A SUDDEN STORM BREAKS...

WE CAN FIGHT THE ISRAELITES, BUT WE CAN'T FIGHT THE GOD OF THUNDER AND LIGHTNING!

GOD HAS ANSWERED OUR PRAYER.

LET'S GO AFTER THEM.

THE PHILISTINE DEFEAT IS A TURNING POINT IN ISRAEL'S HISTORY—NEVER AGAIN DO THE PHILISTINES INVADE ISRAEL WHILE SAMUEL IS ITS LEADER. TO REMIND HIS PEOPLE THAT IT WAS GOD WHO HELPED THEM WIN THEIR VICTORY, SAMUEL ERECTS A STONE WHICH HE CALLS EBENEZER (STONE OF HELP).

FOR YEARS SAMUEL JUDGES THE PEOPLE OF ISRAEL, AND THERE IS PEACE. BUT AS HE GROWS OLD THE TRIBAL LEADERS BECOME WORRIED...

SAMUEL, YOU ARE GROWING OLD, AND YOUR SONS ARE NOT WORTHY TO TAKE YOUR PLACE AS JUDGE OF ISRAEL. GIVE US A KING LIKE OTHER NATIONS HAVE.

I WILL PRAY TO GOD ABOUT YOUR REQUEST.

LATER—

THE LORD HAS TOLD ME TO WARN YOU WHAT A KING WILL DO—HE WILL SEND YOUR SONS TO BATTLE, YOUR DAUGHTERS WILL BECOME HIS SERVANTS, AND YOUR BEST CROPS WILL BE USED TO FEED HIS COURT.

MAYBE SO, BUT WE STILL WANT A KING!

Test for a King

FROM 1 SAMUEL 9:20—11:7

THE YOUNG FARMER, SAUL, IS STUNNED WHEN SAMUEL TELLS HIM THAT GREAT THINGS ARE IN STORE FOR HIM. THEY WORSHIP GOD TOGETHER, THEN SAMUEL INVITES SAUL TO A SPECIAL FEAST.

WHY SHOULD THIS YOUNG MAN BE SO HIGHLY HONORED?

SAMUEL MAKES NO EXPLANATION TO HIS GUESTS, BUT EARLY THE NEXT MORNING HE ACCOMPANIES SAUL AND HIS SERVANT AS THEY LEAVE THE CITY.

SEND YOUR SERVANT ON AHEAD, SAUL. I HAVE A MESSAGE FOR YOU FROM GOD.

THE LORD HAS ANOINTED YOU TO RULE OVER HIS PEOPLE. CALL ON THE LORD, AND HE WILL BE WITH YOU.

SURPRISED—AND A LITTLE FRIGHTENED—AT ALL THAT HAS HAPPENED TO HIM, SAUL STARTS HOME. BUT ON THE WAY THE SPIRIT OF GOD COMES TO HIM. HOWEVER, WHEN HE REACHES HOME, HE DOES NOT TELL ANYONE THAT HE HAS BEEN ANOINTED KING!

WHEN SAMUEL CALLS THE PEOPLE TO MIZPEH, SAUL GOES, TOO. BEFORE ALL ISRAEL SAMUEL MAKES A SURPRISING ANNOUNCEMENT.

GOD HAS CHOSEN SAUL TO RULE OVER YOU.

WHERE **IS** HE?

SEARCH IS QUICKLY MADE, AND SAUL—WHO IS AWED BY THE THOUGHT OF BEING KING—IS FOUND HIDING.

WHEN HE IS BROUGHT FORTH, THE PEOPLE SHOUT: LONG LIVE THE KING!

AT MIZPEH THE PEOPLE SHOUTED THEIR PRAISES TO SAUL—BUT AFTER HE RETURNS HOME, SOME COMPLAIN.

FINE THING—THERE GOES OUR KING—BACK TO THE FARM.

HE'LL BE NO HELP TO US.

265

266

Prophet, Priest, and Judge

▶ Read about Samuel on pp. 253-296.

Samuel is one of greatest leaders of Israel. Called as a small boy, Samuel dedicates his life to serving God. Here are some of the things he does:

▶ Samuel grows up in the Tabernacle, learning how to be a priest (p. 254).

▶ Samuel is a man who prays (Psalm 99:6).

▶ He may have written some books of the Bible, such as Judges and Ruth.

▶ He prays for Israel's deliverance from the Philistines and erects a stone to remind the people of God's help (p. 261).

▶ He anoints Saul to be the first king (p. 264).

▶ He is a true prophet of God (p. 255).

▶ He is the last major judge in Israel, traveling from town to town (1 Samuel 7:15-17).

He anoints David to be king (p. 278).

267

Israel's First King— Saul

From the beginning, Saul looks like a good candidate for king. But as time goes by, things change and his life seems in a downward spin.

Looking for lost donkeys when he is chosen king (p. 263).

Saul is a humble Benjamite farmer, a head taller than other men (p. 264).

Found hiding in the baggage at his coronation (p. 265).

His army is crushed; his sons are killed (p. 305).

Wins the people's confidence (p. 269).

Falls on his own sword and dies (p. 305).

Big Mistake #3
He visits a witch (p. 300).

Big mistake #1
Offers sacrifices as a priest, then makes excuses for doing so (p. 272).

Jealous of David and tries to kill him (p. 289).

Big mistake #2
Disobeys God, lies to Samuel, and is rejected as king (p. 274).

By Order of the King

FROM 1 SAMUEL 11—13:9

WHEN WORD COMES THAT THE AMMONITES HAVE SURROUNDED AN ISRAELITE CITY, SAUL FACES HIS FIRST TEST AS KING. TO HIS AMAZEMENT—AND ANGER—HE DISCOVERS THAT SOME OF HIS PEOPLE ARE AFRAID TO FIGHT! HE ACTS AT ONCE...

BY ORDER OF THE KING WE ARE TO KILL THE OXEN OF ANY MAN WHO REFUSES TO DEFEND HIS COUNTRY!

ER—I'LL JOIN THE ARMY RIGHT NOW!

AN ARMY IS QUICKLY FORMED, AND SAUL ATTACKS AT DAWN. CAUGHT BY SURPRISE, THE AMMONITES ARE DEFEATED.

PROUD OF THEIR VICTORY, THE ISRAELITES SHOUT THEIR PRAISES TO SAUL.

SURE, THEY'RE **ALL** FOR YOU TODAY. BUT WHAT ABOUT THE MEN WHO DIDN'T WANT YOU TO BE KING? THEY SHOULD BE KILLED.

NO! NO MAN SHALL BE PUT TO DEATH FOR THAT.

NOW THAT ISRAEL HAS A KING, SAMUEL PREPARES TO WITHDRAW FROM HIS POSITION AS JUDGE OF ISRAEL. BUT BEFORE HE DOES, HE CALLS THE PEOPLE TOGETHER AND SPEAKS TO THEM AS THE PROPHET OF GOD.

OBEY THE LORD AND SERVE YOUR KING, AND ALL WILL BE WELL WITH YOU. BUT IF YOU RETURN TO ANY OF YOUR WICKED WAYS, YOU SHALL BE DESTROYED — BOTH YOU AND YOUR KING!

SPURRED ON BY HIS VICTORY OVER THE AMMONITES, SAUL FORMS A STANDING ARMY AND PREPARES TO WIN HIS PEOPLE'S FREEDOM FROM THE PHILISTINES. HIS SON, JONATHAN, MAKES A SUCCESSFUL ATTACK ON A PHILISTINE GARRISON—AND AGAIN ISRAEL CHEERS.

BUT WHEN WORD REACHES THE MAIN ARMY OF THE PHILISTINES...

TAKE THIRTY THOUSAND CHARIOTS, SIX THOUSAND HORSEMEN AND ALL OUR INFANTRY—SET UP A CAMP AT MICHMASH. FROM THERE WE CAN SEND OUT RAIDING PARTIES THAT WILL DRAW SAUL FROM HIS STRONGHOLD AT GILGAL.

IN SPITE OF FORMER VICTORIES MANY OF THE ISRAELITES LOSE COURAGE WHEN THEY SEE THE SIZE OF THE ENEMY FORCES.

THE PHILISTINES OUTNUMBER US BY THOUSANDS. I'M HIDING OUT UNTIL THIS IS OVER.

THERE'S A PIT DOWN THE VALLEY— I'LL HIDE THERE.

EVEN IN THE CAMP OF KING SAUL, THE SOLDIERS ARE AFRAID.

A RAID ON A PHILISTINE GARRISON IS ONE THING—FIGHTING THE WHOLE PHILISTINE ARMY IS ANOTHER.

THE MEN ARE LOSING THEIR NERVE. WE CAN'T WAIT MUCH LONGER FOR SAMUEL TO COME AND OFFER THE SACRIFICE TO GOD.

YOU'RE RIGHT. WE'LL WAIT NO LONGER. I'LL MAKE THE OFFERING!

271

The King Disobeys

FROM 1 SAMUEL 13:10—15:14

THE ISRAELITES WATCH WITH GROWING TERROR AS THE PHILISTINE ARMY SETS UP CAMP AT MICHMASH. SAUL, AFRAID THAT HIS PEOPLE WILL PANIC, LOSES FAITH IN GOD'S GUIDANCE. INSTEAD OF WAITING FOR SAMUEL TO OFFER THE SACRIFICE, HE MAKES THE OFFERING HIMSELF. HE NO SOONER FINISHES THAN HE SEES SAMUEL COMING...

I WAS AFRAID MY PEOPLE WOULD FLEE BEFORE YOU GOT HERE, SO I OFFERED THE SACRIFICE.

YOU HAVE DISOBEYED GOD. YOU CANNO DO THAT AND HOLD YOUR KINGDOM!

MEANTIME—INSTEAD OF MAKING AN OPEN ATTACK, THE PHILISTINES SEND OUT RAIDING PARTIES TO DRAW SAUL FROM CAMP—BUT SAUL WILL NOT COME OUT. HIS SON, PRINCE JONATHAN, DECIDES TO TAKE ACTION...

LET'S ATTACK THE PHILISTINE GARRISON BY OURSELVES.

I'M WITH YOU!

272

...CRETLY JONATHAN AND HIS ARMOR-BEARER ...VE CAMP. WHEN THEY REACH THE FOOT OF ...E CLIFF THAT LEADS TO THE PHILISTINE ...RRISON, THE ENEMY DARES THEM TO COME ... AND FIGHT. BOLDLY, JONATHAN AND HIS ...END SCALE THE CLIFF...

FOLLOW ME, FOR WITH THE LORD THERE IS NO NEED FOR LARGE NUMBERS.

AT THE TOP THEY ATTACK WITH SUCH DARING THAT THE PHILISTINES FLEE IN PANIC. IN THEIR CONFUSION, THE PHILISTINES EVEN ATTACK ONE ANOTHER.

WHEN SAUL LEARNS THE PHILISTINES ARE RETREATING, AND DISCOVERS THAT IT IS JONATHAN WHO HAS ATTACKED THEM, HE LEADS HIS ARMY AGAINST THE ENEMY AND DRIVES THEM BACK TO THEIR OWN COUNTRY.

AFTER THIS VICTORY, SAUL ATTACKS THE OTHER ENEMIES OF ISRAEL AND DRIVES THEM AWAY. BUT THE RAIDS OF THE DESERT TRIBE OF THE AMALEKITES CONTINUE —

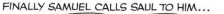

FINALLY SAMUEL CALLS SAUL TO HIM...

THE LORD WANTS YOU TO DESTROY THE AMALEKITES WHO HAVE BEEN ENEMIES OF ISRAEL EVER SINCE OUR PEOPLE LEFT EGYPT. BRING NOTHING AWAY WITH YOU, FOR THIS IS NOT A WAR TO GAIN WEALTH.

SAUL ATTACKS THE AMALEKITES AND DRIVES THEM BACK TOWARD EGYPT, BUT HE BRINGS THE BEST OF THE SHEEP AND OXEN HOME WITH HIM.

AT GILGAL, HE COMES FACE TO FACE WITH SAMUEL...

I HAVE OBEYED THE COMMANDMENT OF GOD AND DESTROYED THE AMALEKITES.

IF YOU HAVE OBEYED GOD, THEN WHAT IS THE MEANING OF THIS NOISE OF SHEEP AND CATTLE THAT I HEAR?

Mysterious Visit

OM 1 SAMUEL 15:15—16:11

SAUL HAS BEEN COMMANDED BY SAMUEL TO BRING HOME NO SPOILS FROM HIS VICTORY. BUT HE CANNOT RESIST THE FAT SHEEP AND CATTLE. HE BRINGS THEM HOME—AND IS CAUGHT RED-HANDED BY SAMUEL.

MY PEOPLE TOOK ONLY THE BEST TO SACRIFICE TO GOD.

D OBEY IS BETTER THAN D SACRIFICE. THIS IS THE ECOND TIME YOU HAVE ISOBEYED GOD. AND ECAUSE YOU HAVE ONE SO, THE LORD ILL TAKE YOUR INGDOM FROM YOU.

NO—MY PEOPLE —I...

AT FIRST SAUL TRIES TO LAY THE BLAME ON HIS PEOPLE, BUT FINALLY HE ADMITS HE HAS SINNED AGAINST GOD. SAMUEL PRAYS WITH SAUL—THEN GOES HOME, NEVER AGAIN TO VISIT THE KING.

SEVEN OF JESSE'S SONS APPEAR BEFORE SAMUEL—BUT NOT ONE OF THEM IS CHOSEN.

HAVE I SEEN ALL OF YOUR SONS?

NO, THE YOUNGEST, DAVID, IS TENDING THE SHEEP. I'LL SEND ONE OF MY SONS AND A SERVANT FOR HIM.

WONDER WHY SAMUEL INSISTS UPON SEEING DAVID?

THE WHOLE THING IS A MYSTERY.

JESSE'S SON FINDS HIS BROTHER IN THE FIELDS OUTSIDE BETHLEHEM.

THERE'S DAVID.

LOOK—A LION—AND DAVID DOESN'T SEE IT!

The Chosen One

FROM 1 SAMUEL 16:12–19

WHEN SAMUEL, THE PROPHET OF GOD, ASKS TO SEE ALL OF JESSE'S SONS, JESSE HAS TO SEND FOR HIS YOUNGEST, DAVID, WHO IS AWAY TENDING SHEEP. THE MESSENGERS REACH THE FIELDS IN TIME TO SEE A LION ABOUT TO SPRING ON THE YOUNG SHEPHERD. DAVID'S KEEN EARS HEAR A SWISH IN THE TALL GRASS. HE WHIRLS...

A LION!

DAVID! THE LION—YOU KILLED IT!

I KILLED A B A FEW DAYS NOTHING'S GOIN HURT MY FATH SHEEP IF I C HELP IT.

YOU'RE A BRAVE SHEPHERD, DAVID. BUT HURRY HOME—SAMUEL WANTS TO SEE YOU. I'VE BROUGHT A MAN TO STAY WITH THE SHEEP.

ME? BUT WHY?

ON THE HIKE BACK TO THE CITY, DAVID CONTINUES TO WONDER. BUT WHEN SAMUEL SEES THE YOUNG SHEPHERD BOY, HE KNOWS HIS SEARCH HAS ENDED, FOR HE HEARS GOD SAY: *"THIS IS MY CHOSEN ONE."*

FORE JESSE AND HIS SONS, SAMUEL BLESSES VID AND ANOINTS HIS HEAD WITH OIL.

THE LORD BLESS YOU, FOR YOU WILL BE THE NEXT KING OF ISRAEL.

DAVID DOES NOT KNOW WHEN HE WILL BE MADE KING. BUT AS HE GOES BACK TO HIS SHEEP HE HAS A SPECIAL FEELING OF GOD'S PRESENCE WITH HIM.

THE LORD IS MY STRENGTH. WHAT HAVE I TO FEAR?

Giant's Challenge

AMUEL 16:23—17:26

TWICE KING SAUL DELIBERATELY DISOBEYS GOD. THE PROPHET, SAMUEL, HAS TOLD HIM THAT HIS KINGDOM WILL BE TAKEN FROM HIM. SAUL IS AFRAID—AND AT TIMES

HIS MIND BECOMES UNBALANCED. WHEN HIS ADVISORS TELL HIM ABOUT DAVID, A YOUNG SHEPHERD, WHO SINGS AND PLAYS A HARP, SAUL SENDS FOR HIM. DAVID ARRIVES AT THE PALACE...

THE KING IS VERY ILL TODAY—SO HE MAY BE DANGEROUS. NEVER TAKE YOUR EYES OFF HIM.

JIETLY DAVID ENTERS HE KING'S ROOM AND EGINS TO PLAY...SAUL TARES AT HIM WILDLY... JT DAVID CONTINUES O PLAY AND SING OF S FAITH IN GOD.

AT LAST KING SAUL RELAXES AND FALLS QUIETLY ASLEEP. AFTER THAT DAVID IS OFTEN CALLED TO THE PALACE. HIS MUSIC QUIETS SAUL'S TORTURED MIND—AND IN TIME THE KING SEEMS WELL AGAIN.

AND WHEN WORD COMES THAT THE PHILISTINES ARE PREPARING FOR AN ATTACK, SAUL LEADS HIS ARMY AGAINST THEM. DAVID'S THREE OLDEST BROTHERS JOIN THE KING'S FORCES.

ONE EVENING DAVID COMES FROM THE FIELDS TO FIND H[IS] FATHER BUSY PACKING FOOD

THIS IS FOR YOUR BROTHER[S] I WANT YOU TO TAKE IT T[O] THE[M]

I'LL LEAVE RIGHT AWAY. WHAT'S THE LATEST NEWS FROM THE FRONT?

NOT GOOD, AND I'M WORRIED.

WHEN DAVID REACHES THE ISRAELITE CAMP, HE FINDS THE SOLDIERS STRANGELY QUIET.

WHAT'S THE MATTER?

The Challenge Is Met

FROM 1 SAMUEL 17:28–48

WHEN DAVID REACHES THE ISRAELITE CAMP, HE FINDS THAT NO ISRAELITE SOLDIER IS BRAVE ENOUGH TO ACCEPT THE PHILISTINE GIANT'S CHALLENGE TO FIGHT. DAVID IS ANGRY—BUT SO IS ELIAB, HIS BIG BROTHER...

WHAT ARE **YOU** DOING HERE? WHY AREN'T YOU HOME WHERE YOU BELONG —TAKING CARE OF THE SHEEP?

FATHER SENT ME HERE WITH FOOD FOR YOU—NOW **YOU** TELL ME WHY NO ONE HAS ACCEPTED GOLIATH'S CHALLENGE TO FIGHT?

EVER SINCE THE PROPHET SAMUEL CHOSE DAVID INSTEAD OF HIM, ELIAB HAS BEEN FILLED WITH JEALOUSY...NOW IT BURSTS INTO THE OPEN.

YOU'RE JUST A SHOW-OFF.

I'M NOT AFRAID. I'LL FIGHT THE GIANT.

MEANWHILE IN KING SAUL'S TENT

EVERY DAY THAT GIANT DEFIES US I HAVE OFFERED A HANDSOME REWARD —EVEN MY DAUGHTER IN MARRIAGE— BUT NOT ONE SOLDIER IN MY WHOLE ARMY WILL ACCEPT THE CHALLENGE.

O KING—
THERE IS
NE OUTSIDE
HO ACCEPTS,
BUT—

BRING HIM
HERE AT
ONCE!

DAVID ENTERS—BUT SAUL DOES NOT
REMEMBER THE SHEPHERD WHO
PLAYED FOR HIM.

A SHEPHERD BOY!
YOU CAN'T FIGHT
A GIANT!

HE LORD
HO HELPED
E KILL A LION
ND A BEAR
ILL HELP
ME NOW.

MAYBE YOU'RE RIGHT—
AT LEAST YOU HAVE
COURAGE. GO, AND THE
LORD BE WITH THEE.
YOU CAN WEAR MY
OWN ARMOR.

I CAN'T WEAR THIS—
I'M NOT USED TO FIGHTING
IN ARMOR. BESIDES, MY
PLAN IS NOT TO DEFEND
MYSELF, BUT TO ATTACK!

The Jealous King

FROM 1 SAMUEL 17:48—18:9

FOR FORTY DAYS THE PHILISTINE GIANT, GOLIATH, CHALLENGES THE ISRAELITES TO FIGHT. BUT NOT ONE SOLDIER IN ALL OF KING SAUL'S ARMY IS BRAVE ENOUGH TO ACCEPT THE CHALLENGE, UNTIL DAVID, THE YOUNG SHEPHERD, OFFERS TO MEET THE GIANT WITH ONLY A STAFF, A SLING—AND HIS FAITH IN GOD! EVEN WHILE DAVID WHIRLS HIS SLING, THE GIANT LAUGHS, BUT THE STONE HITS ITS MARK...AND THE GIANT FALLS!

GOLIATH'S DEAD!

IN TERROR, THE PHILISTINES FLEE FOR THEIR LIVES. SPURRED ON BY THIS SUDDEN TURN OF EVENTS, THE EXCITED ISRAELITES CHASE THE PHILISTINES BACK TO THEIR OWN LAND.

WHEN THE ARMY RETURNS, SAUL'S GENERAL, ABNER, TAKES DAVID TO SEE THE KING.

YOU SAVED ISRAEL, DAVID. FROM NOW ON YOU WILL LIVE IN THE PALACE. PRINCE JONATHAN WILL TAKE YOU BACK WITH HIM.

DAVID AND JONATHAN BECOME TRUE FRIENDS— AND MAKE A PACT OF FRIENDSHIP.

DAVID, I'M PROUD TO BE THE FRIEND OF THE BRAVEST MAN IN ISRAEL. I WANT TO GIVE YOU MY ROBE AND ARMOR AS A SIGN THAT I WILL BE LOYAL TO YOU—FOREVER!

THANK YOU, JONATHAN. GOD IS MY WITNESS THAT I WILL BE YOUR FRIEND UNTIL DEATH.

289

Jonathan Defends David

FROM 1 SAMUEL 19:22—20:33

I'LL KILL HIM MYSELF! DAVID MAY BE A HERO TO THE PEOPLE, BUT HE WON'T LIVE TO TAKE MY KINGDOM FROM ME!

THREE TIMES SAUL SENDS MEN TO RAMAH TO CAPTURE DAVID. BUT EACH TIME THE MEN FAIL. IN A FIT OF RAGE, SAUL SETS OUT...

—BUT ON THE WAY A STRANGE THING HAPPENS...

GOD TAKES CONTROL OF SAUL. AND WHEN SAUL REACHES RAMAH HE FALLS TO THE GROUND AND LIES THERE FOR A DAY AND A NIGHT.

WHILE SAUL IS IN RAMAH, DAVID HURRIES BACK TO THE PALACE T SEE HIS FRIEND, PRINCE JONATHA

INSIDE THE PALACE DAVID SEEKS OUT HIS FRIEND.

DAVID! WHAT BRINGS YOU BACK HERE?

I MUST KNOW WHY YOUR FATHER WANTS TO KILL ME. COME—LET'S GO WHERE WE CAN TALK WITHOUT BEING HEARD.

MY FATHER MEANS YOU NO HARM, DAVID. HE WOULD TELL ME IF HE DID.

NO, JONATHAN. HE WOULD NOT TELL YOU BECAUSE YOU ARE MY FRIEND.

TOMORROW STARTS THE KING'S FEAST OF THE NEW MOON—BUT I WON'T ATTEND. IF YOUR FATHER ASKS ABOUT ME, TELL HIM I HAVE GONE TO BETHLEHEM TO SEE MY FAMILY. IF HE IS NOT ANGRY, THEN ALL IS WELL. BUT IF HE IS—REMEMBER THE AGREEMENT WE MADE BEFORE GOD TO BE FRIENDS, ALWAYS.

I'LL FIND OUT THE TRUTH. NOW, LET'S GO OUT IN THE FIELD WHERE WE CAN SET UP A SECRET PLAN FOR ME TO LET YOU KNOW HOW MY FATHER FEELS.

Trapped in a Cave

FROM 1 SAMUEL 21:13—24:5

FORCED TO FLEE FOR HIS LIFE FROM KING SAUL, DAVID TRIES TO FIND SAFETY IN ENEMY COUNTRY. BUT SOME OF THE PHILISTINES REMEMBER DAVID AND WARN THEIR KING AGAINST HIM. TO FOOL THEM, DAVID PRETENDS HE IS CRAZY.

THIS IS DAVID, THE ISRAELITE WHO KILLED GOLIATH.

HE'S MAD! TAKE THAT CRAZY MAN OUT OF MY SIGHT!

DAVID RETURNS TO ISRAEL...AND THE NEWS OF HIS WHEREABOUTS SPREADS QUICKLY AMONG HIS FRIENDS.

KING SAUL HAS ORDERED US TO FIGHT **AGAINST** YOU— BUT WE WANT TO FIGHT **FOR** YOU.

GOOD. THAT MAKES FOUR HUNDRED MEN ON OUR SIDE.

BUT NEWS ABOUT DAVID ALSO REACHES SAUL.

THE PRIESTS AT NOB ARE HELPING DAVID. ONE OF THEM GAVE HIM GOLIATH'S SWORD. I SAW THE WHOLE THING WITH MY OWN EYES.

BRING THE PRIESTS TO ME—I'LL MAKE AN EXAMPLE OF TRAITORS WHO HELP DAVID.

THE PRIESTS OF NOB PLEAD INNOCENT TO THE CHARGE OF PLOTTING AGAINST SAUL—BUT HE WILL NOT LISTEN!

YOU HELPED MY ENEMY—AND FOR THIS YOU WILL DIE!

IN HIS INSANE DESIRE FOR REVENGE, SAUL ORDERS THE DEATH OF NOT ONLY THE PRIESTS OF NOB, BUT OF EVERY MAN, WOMAN AND CHILD IN THEIR CITY. ONLY ONE MAN ESCAPES, ABIATHAR...

...WHO CARRIES THE TRAGIC NEWS TO DAVID.

GOD FORGIVE ME. I AM PARTLY TO BLAME. I ASKED FOR HELP, AND YOUR FATHER GAVE IT. STAY WITH ME—FOR NOW SAUL SEEKS YOUR LIFE AS WELL AS MINE.

REPORTS OF DAVID'S MOVEMENTS ARE AGAIN BROUGHT TO SAUL—AND THIS TIME THE JEALOUS KING SETS OUT WITH THREE THOUSAND MEN.

AFTER A TIME SAUL LEAVES THE CAVE—AND DAVID CALLS AFTER HIM.

MY LORD THE KING.

DAVID!

WHY DO YOU KEEP HUNTING ME? I MEAN YOU NO HARM. SEE THIS PIECE OF CLOTH? I CUT IT FROM YOUR ROBE. I COULD HAVE KILLED YOU, BUT I DIDN'T.

I AM ASHAMED. YOU ARE A BETTER MAN THAN I AM, DAVID. I WILL GO NOW AND LEAVE YOU ALONE.

SAUL LEADS HIS ARMY AWAY ...BUT A SHORT TIME LATER DAVID LEARNS THAT SAUL HAS FORCED MICHAL DAVID'S WIFE, TO MARRY ANOTHER MAN. DAVID KNOWS NOW THAT SAUL IS STILL ANGRY AND THAT HE WILL NEVER BE SAFE AS LONG AS SAUL LIVES. WORD COMES, TOO, THAT HIS OLD FRIEND, SAMUEL, THE PROPHET, IS DEAD

David's Dilemma

FROM 1 SAMUEL 26:6—28:2

KING SAUL AND HIS ARMY ARE CAMPED IN THE VALLEY—PREPARING TO ATTACK DAVID. BUT DAVID IS WARNED, AND IN THE DARK OF NIGHT HE AND HIS YOUNG NEPHEW, ABISHAI, STEAL PAST THE SLEEPING GUARDS IN SEARCH OF THE KING. ONE FALSE MOVE AND THE WHOLE CAMP WILL BE AROUSED...

STEALTHILY THEY CREEP UP BESIDE THE SLEEPING KING.

GOD HAS PUT YOUR ENEMY IN OUR HANDS. I'LL PIN HIM TO THE GROUND WITH ONE BLOW.

NO! THE LORD ANOINTED SAUL KING OF ISRAEL, AND THE LORD WILL DECIDE WHEN AND HOW SAUL IS TO DIE.

SO—FOR THE FIRST TIME SINCE THEY JOINED DAVID—HIS FOLLOWERS HAVE A SETTLED PLACE IN WHICH TO LIVE.

IT'S GOOD, ABIGAIL, TO SEE MY MEN RAISING THEIR FAMILIES IN PEACE.

AND I'M SO GLAD YOUR LIFE IS NO LONGER IN DANGER.

...VID REASONS ...AT THE ...ILISTINES ...OW OF HIS ...OUBLE WITH ...UL AND THAT ...IS TIME THEY ...LL ACCEPT HIM. ...ND HE IS RIGHT. ...NG ACHISH OF ...E PHILISTINES ...GLAD TO HAVE ...VID'S SIX ...UNDRED ...ARRIORS ON ...S SIDE. HE ...EN GIVES THEM ...E CITY OF ...KLAG TO ...E IN.

...E DAY DAVID SEES KING ...HISH RIDING INTO THE CITY.

...VONDER WHAT ...BRINGS HIM ...HERE?

I PRAY HIS VISIT IS A FRIENDLY ONE.

DAVID GOES OUT TO WELCOME THE KING.

GREETINGS, DAVID. WE ARE PLANNING AN ATTACK ON YOUR OLD ENEMY, KING SAUL, AND WE EXPECT YOU TO HELP US.

HOW CAN I FIGHT MY OWN PEOPLE? KING SAUL AND PRINCE JONATHAN WILL BE LEADING THE ISRAELITES!

299

At the Witch's House

FROM 1 SAMUEL 28:5–11; 29

DAVID IS ON THE SPOT! KING ACHISH HAS ORDERED HIM TO JOIN THE ATTACK ON KING SAUL AND HIS OWN PEOPLE. IF HE REFUSES, THE PHILISTINES WILL TURN ON HIM. SO—AGAINST HIS WILL—HE JOINS THE MARCH AGAINST ISRAEL.

O GOD—HELP ME SO THAT I WILL NOT HAVE TO FIGHT SAUL AND JONATHAN.

UNKNOWN TO DAVID, SOME OF THE PHILISTINE LEADERS ARE HOPING TO KEEP HIM OUT OF THE FIGHT—FOR ANOTHER REASON. THAT NIGHT THEY GO TO KING ACHISH'S TENT.

I DON'T LIKE HAVING DAVID AND HIS MEN BRINGING UP THE REAR. REMEMBER, DAVID IS AN ISRAELITE.

AND HE COULD CUT US TO PIECES WHILE WE'RE BUSY AT THE FRONT.

I THINK DAVID IS LOYAL TO ME. BUT, IF YOU WISH, I'LL SEND HIM HOME.

ACHISH CALLS FOR DAVID.

I FIND NO FAULT IN YOU, DAVID, BUT THE OTHERS DON'T TRUST YOU. YOU'D BETTER RETURN HOME AS SOON AS IT IS LIGHT.

DAVID'S PRAYER HAS BEEN ANSWERED. AT DAWN HE LEADS HIS SOLDIERS OUT OF THE CAMP AND BACK TOWARD THEIR CITY OF ZIKLAG. THE PHILISTINES MARCH ON...

WHEN SAUL SEES THE POWERFUL PHILISTINE ARMY, HE IS AFRAID. FRANTICALLY HE CALLS UPON GOD FOR HELP—BUT GOD DOES NOT ANSWER. TERRIFIED, HE CALLS FOR A SERVANT.

A Voice from the Dead

FROM 1 SAMUEL 28:11–25; 31:1–6; 30:1–3

SAUL IS TERRIFIED BY THE SIGHT OF THE APPROACHING PHILISTINE ARMY. IN DESPERATION, HE DISGUISES HIMSELF AND STEALS THROUGH THE NIGHT TO SEEK THE ADVICE OF A WITCH.

CALL UP THE SPIRIT OF THE PROPHET SAMUEL.

FOR A MOMENT ALL IS STILL...THE WOMAN CALLS FOR THE SPIRIT OF SAMUEL. SUDDENLY SHE CRIES OUT IN TERROR...

THEN SAUL HEARS THE VOICE OF SAMUEL: BECAUSE YOU DISOBEYED GOD, THE LORD WILL DELIVER ISRAEL INTO THE HANDS OF THE PHILISTINES. TOMORROW YOU AND YOUR SONS WILL BE DEAD.

NEXT MORNING THE PHILISTINES ATTACK. ...AEL, UNDER A WEAK AND FRIGHTENED ...G, RETREATS IN PANIC.

THE ENEMY IS EVERYWHERE! WE CAN'T STOP THEM!

MY SONS— WHERE ARE THEY?

DRAW YOUR SWORD AND KILL ME. I WOULD RATHER DIE BY YOUR HAND THAN BE CAPTURED BY THE PHILISTINES.

KILL MY KING? I CAN'T— I CAN'T!

DEAD, SIR.

DEAD! AND I AM BADLY WOUNDED.

SO SAUL DRAWS HIS OWN SWORD— AND FALLS UPON IT.

WHEN THE PEOPLE OF ISRAEL LEARN THAT THEIR KING IS DEAD AND THE ARMY HAS FLED, THEY DESERT THEIR CITIES, LEAVING THEM TO THE CONQUERING PHILISTINES. SO— SAMUEL'S PROPHECY COMES TRUE!

MEANTIME, DAVID AND HIS MEN RIDE TOWARD ZIKLAG...

LOOK! WHAT'S THAT RED GLOW AGAINST THE SKY?

On the Robber's Trail

FROM 1 SAMUEL 30:1–11

DAVID AND HIS MEN RETURN TO FIND THEIR CITY OF ZIKLAG IN SMOLDERING RUINS.

IN VAIN THEY SEARCH THROUGH THE RUBBLE AND ASHES FOR THEIR FAMILIE

DAVID AND HIS FOLLOWERS ARE ON THE TRAIL OF THE ROBBERS WHO SACKED THEIR CITY AND CARRIED THEIR WOMEN AND CHILDREN OFF INTO SLAVERY. ON THE WAY THEY FIND A MAN LYING BESIDE THE ROAD.

HE'S SICK —AND STARVING.

GIVE HIM FOOD AND WATER. AS SOON AS HE IS ABLE TO TALK, WE'LL QUESTION HIM.

WHO ARE YOU? AND WHY WERE YOU LEFT HERE— SICK AND WITHOUT FOOD AND WATER?

I'M A SLAVE. I WAS WITH THE AMALEKITES WHEN THEY BURNED ZIKLAG. BUT WHEN I BECAME SICK MY MASTER LEFT ME HERE TO DIE. THAT WAS THREE DAYS AGO.

SO IT WAS THE AMALEKITES WHO RAIDED ZIKLAG? DO YOU KNOW WHERE THEY ARE NOW?

I'LL TAKE YOU TO THEIR CAMP—IF YOU PROMISE NOT TO TURN ME OVER TO MY MASTER. HE'D KILL ME.

DAVID PROMISES. AND, TRUE TO HIS WORD, TH SLAVE GUIDES DAVID TO THE AMALEKITE CAM WHERE THE SOLDIERS ARE CELEBRATING THEIR VICTORY.

WE'LL SOON END **THAT** PARTY!

DAVID MAKES A LIGHTNING ATTACK—THE AMALEKITES RALLY THEIR FORCES, BUT THEY ARE NO MATCH FOR COURAGEOUS MEN FIGHTING FOR THEIR WIVES AND CHILDREN.

WHEN THE BATTLE IS OVER...

OH, DAVID, I KNEW **YOU** WOULD COME!

THANK GOD, ABIGAIL, YOU ARE SAFE!

THE AMALEKITE WHO LEFT HIS SLAVE TO DIE PAID DEARLY FOR HIS CRUELTY, FOR BY THIS ACT HE AND MOST OF HIS COUNTRYMEN LOST THEIR LIVES. BUT DAVID, WHO OBEYED GOD, RESCUES ALL OF THE ISRAELITE WOMEN AND CHILDREN. AND WHEN HE DIVIDES THE SPOIL OF BATTLE HE SHARES IT NOT ONLY WITH HIS MEN, BUT WITH LEADERS OF THE TOWNS OF JUDAH.

TRIUMPHANTLY DAVID AND HIS MEN BRING THEIR FAMILIES AND POSSESSIONS BACK TO THE BURNED CITY. THEY TALK EAGERLY OF HOW THEY WILL REBUILD THEIR HOMES AND ONCE AGAIN LIVE IN PEACE. BUT DAVID'S THOUGHTS ARE FAR AWAY...

YOU LOOK WORRIED, DAVID.

YES, I KEEP WONDERING HOW THE BATTLE BETWEEN THE PHILISTINES AND KING SAUL CAME OUT.

TWO DAYS LATER...

WHO ARE YOU — AND WHAT DO YOU WANT?

I WAS WITH SAUL IN THE BATTLE WITH THE PHILISTINES — AND I HAVE GOOD NEWS FOR DAVID.

Rival Kings

FROM 2 SAMUEL 1:2—2:9

THE BOOKS OF 2 SAMUEL AND 1 CHRONICLES RECORD THE SAME PERIOD OF HISTORY—THE REIGN OF DAVID, ISRAEL'S GREATEST KING. 2 SAMUEL PRESENTS IT THROUGH THE EYES OF THE PROPHETS, WHILE 1 CHRONICLES RELATES IT FROM THE VIEWPOINT OF THE PRIESTS.

SOON AFTER DAVID AND HIS MEN RETURN TO ZIKLAG, A MESSENGER COMES WITH NEWS FOR DAVID.

WHO ARE YOU—AND WHAT BRINGS YOU HERE?

I COME FROM THE BATTLE BETWEEN THE PHILISTINES AND ISRAEL. YOUR OLD ENEMY, KING SAUL, IS DEAD—SO IS CROWN PRINCE JONATHAN!

HOW DO YOU KNOW THIS?

I DO NOT KNOW HOW JONATHAN DIED, BUT I FOUND THE KING ON THE BATTLEFIELD. HE WAS INJURED, AND HE ASKED ME TO KILL HIM. I DID— AND HERE ARE HIS CROWN AND BRACELETS TO PROVE IT!

DAVID DOES NOT KNOW THAT THE MAN IS TELLING A LIE, WITH THE HOPE OF RECEIVING A REWARD. FOR A MOMENT HE IS LOST IN GRIEF—THEN HE TURNS IN ANGER UPON THE MAN WHO BROUGHT THE NEWS.

EVEN IF THE KING ASKED YOU TO KILL HIM, YOU HAD NO RIGHT TO TAKE THE LIFE OF THE MAN CHOSEN BY GOD TO BE KING OF ISRAEL. FOR THIS CRIME YOU WILL PAY—WITH YOUR LIFE!

THEN, BEFORE ALL OF HIS FAITHFUL FOLLOWERS, DAVID SINGS A MEMORIAL SONG FOR JONATHAN AND THE KING.

Song of the Bow

... HOW ARE THE MIGHTY FALLEN! ...
THE BOW OF JONATHAN TURNED
   NOT BACK,
AND THE SWORD OF SAUL
   RETURNED NOT EMPTY....
IN THEIR DEATH THEY WERE NOT
   DIVIDED:
THEY WERE SWIFTER THAN EAGLES,
THEY WERE STRONGER THAN LIONS....
I AM DISTRESSED FOR YOU, MY
   BROTHER JONATHAN:
VERY PLEASANT HAVE YOU BEEN
   TO ME:
YOUR LOVE TO ME WAS WONDERFUL,
PASSING THE LOVE OF WOMEN.
HOW ARE THE MIGHTY FALLEN,
AND THE WEAPONS OF WAR
   PERISHED!

SO THE MAN WHO LIED TO WIN FAVOR WITH DAVID LOSES NOT ONLY THE FAVOR—BUT HIS LIFE!

NOW THAT SAUL IS DEAD, DAVID KNOWS THAT HE CAN RETURN TO HIS HOMELAND. BUT BEFORE HE MAKES ANY PLANS, HE PRAYS TO GOD.

LORD, SHALL I RETURN NOW TO MY OWN PEOPLE IN JUDAH?

GOD TELLS DAVID TO RETURN—AND WHEN HE DOES, THE PEOPLE OF JUDAH WELCOME THEIR HERO, AND MAKE HIM KING OF THEIR TRIBE.

GOD BLESS KING DAVID!

LONG LIVE THE KING!

BUT DAVID'S TROUBLES ARE NOT OVER...FOR ACROSS THE JORDAN RIVER SAUL'S YOUNGEST SON, ISHBOSHETH, HAS BEEN CROWNED KING OF THE OTHER TRIBES OF ISRAEL...

The Road to Becoming a King

As a boy, David never dreams that one day he will be king over Israel. But God has plans for this talented shepherd boy. . . .

▶ David grows up in Bethlehem. He is the youngest of Jesse's eight sons. As he watches his father's sheep, he writes songs, practices playing the harp, and learns to use a sling.

▶ When the Philistine giant Goliath challenges Saul's army, David meets the challenge and defeats the giant, using only a sling and his faith in God. He becomes a national hero.

▶ The king's jealousy causes David to flee and he becomes leader of a group of fugitives. He has two occasions to kill Saul, but out of honor and respect, he does not harm the king.

After Saul's death, David becomes king of Judah and for two years civil war wages as David tries to unite Israel and Judah. After seven years, the northern kingdom accepts David as their king. David was king for over 40 years.

Did You Know?

David, A Man After God's Heart

▶ **Read about David on pp. 276-367.**

In 1 Samuel 13:14, Samuel tells Saul that God wants a person after His own heart to be the next king. God wants a person of good character who will do what God asks him to do. He finds the qualities He is looking for in David.

As Warrior
- Is resourceful and courageous
- Demonstrates faith in God
- Shows respect for Saul by not killing him when he has the chance.

As King
- Unites the kingdom
- Makes Jerusalem—the City of David—the capital.

As Shepherd
- Responsible keeper of his father's sheep
- Shows courage by killing a lion and a bear

As Musician/Writer:
- Writes at least 73 Psalms
- Plays harp skillfully
- Organizes priestly singers for worship of God (1 Chr. 6:31)

As Religious Leader
- Moves the ark of the covenant to Jerusalem
- Organizes the worship of God
- Plans to build a temple

When David sins, he:
- Repents
- Asks God for forgiveness
- Follows God's leadership

David and Jesus were related. See Matthew 1 and Luke 3.

WHEN JOAB LEARNS OF ASAHEL'S DEATH, HE IS TORN WITH GRIEF — AND ANGER.

I'LL GET REVENGE!

THE WAR CONTINUES BETWEEN THE TWO KINGDOMS. BUT WITH EACH BATTLE DAVID GROWS STRONGER, AND IN ISH-BOSHETH'S PALACE FEAR AND TENSION MOUNT UNTIL ONE DAY ABNER TURNS ON THE KING...

HOW DARE YOU QUEST[ION] ME? FOR THAT, I WIL[L] TRANSFER MY ALLEGIANC[E] TO DAVID — AND YOUR KINGDOM WITH IT.

ABNER CARRIES OUT HIS THREAT AND OFFERS TO HELP DAVID ADD THE REST OF ISRAEL TO HIS KINGDOM. DAVID REPLIES WITH AN INVITATION TO A FEAST.

THANK YOU FOR YOUR KINDNESS. I'LL JOIN FORCES WITH YOU...YOU, MY LORD, WILL SOON REIGN OVER ALL ISRAEL!

317

Plot against the King!

FROM 2 SAMUEL 3:26—4:5

JOAB IS ANGRY BECAUSE KING DAVID HAS HONORED ABNER, THE GENERAL OF AN ENEMY KING. SECRETLY, JOAB INVITES ABNER TO SEE HIM...

HERE COMES ABNER—THE MAN WHO KILLED MY BROTHER! HE MUST BE WILLING TO BETRAY HIS OWN KING TO WIN FAVOR AND POWER WITH DAVID—MORE POWER THAN I WOULD HAVE!

WHEN ABNER ENTERS THE CITY...

WELCOME, ABNER. I HAVE AN IMPORTANT MATTER TO TAKE UP WITH YOU—WILL YOU STEP OVER HERE WHERE WE CAN TAKE IT UP QUIETLY?

GREETINGS, JOAB. OF COURSE.

JOAB LEADS ABNER TO A QUIET CORNER OF THE BUSY GATE. AND THERE, BEFORE ABNER CAN SUSPECT WHAT IS GOING ON— JOAB STABS HIM.

DAVID IS ANGRY WHEN HE LEARNS OF ABNER'S MURDER. HE CALLS THE PEOPLE TOGETHER AND ACCUSES JOAB.

THE PUNISHMENT OF JOAB IS IN THE HANDS OF GOD!

TO FURTHER SHOW HIS DISAPPROVAL FOR WHAT JOAB HAS DONE, DAVID LEADS THE MOURNERS IN ABNER'S FUNERAL PROCESSION. BUT EVEN AS KING, DAVID IS NOT SECURE ENOUGH IN HIS NEW KINGDOM TO PUNISH JOAB, FOR JOAB IS THE LEADER OF DAVID'S ARMY.

319

DAVID MOURNS THE DEATH OF ABNER, BUT ABNER'S MASTER, KING ISH-BOSHETH, IS SHAKEN WITH FRIGHT.

WHAT BAD NEWS! WITHOUT ABNER, I'M LOST.

KING ISH-BOSHETH'S FEARS ARE WELL GROUNDE FOR EVEN AS HE RECEIVES THE NEWS OF ABNER DEATH, TWO OF HIS OWN ARMY OFFICERS ARE PLOTTING...

WITHOUT ABNER, KING ISH-BOSHETH IS A WEAKLING. IF DAVID ATTACKS US, WE'LL BE WIPED OUT.

I HAVE AN ID THAT COUL GIVE US POW —AND A REWA LISTEN—JUST THE TWO OF US

WONDERFUL! LET'S DO IT NOW WHILE IT'S DARK.

NO—IT WILL BE EASIER IF WE JUST WALK INTO THE PALACE IN BROAD DAYLIGHT— AS IF WE WERE GETTING GRAIN. THEN NO ONE WOULD SUSPECT.

AT NOON THE NEXT DAY, WHILE THE KING IS TAKING HIS NAP...

THE REWARD WILL SOON BE OURS!

320

Hail to the King!

FROM 2 SAMUEL 4:6—5:4

THE WAR AGAINST KING DAVID LEAVES KING ISH-BOSHETH WITH FEW LOYAL FOLLOWERS. IN BROAD DAYLIGHT TWO OF HIS OWN OFFICERS ENTER THE KING'S PALACE...

THE KING'S ROOM IS DOWN THIS HALL.

HE IS ASLEEP.

GOOD—BUT WE MUST ACT SWIFTLY!

BOLDLY THE MEN ENTER THE KING'S BEDROOM AND—WHILE THE PALACE IS RESTING DURING THE HEAT OF THE DAY—THEY KILL HIM. THEN...

QUIETLY, SO THAT NO ONE WILL SUSPECT THEIR ERRAND...THEY WALK OUT OF THE PALACE AND INTO THE STREET. NIGHT FINDS THEM TRAVELING DOWN THE PLAIN TOWARD DAVID'S CAPITAL IN HEBRON.

BEFORE DAVID THEY PROUDLY TELL THEIR STORY.

WE BRING GOOD NEWS, O KING. **WE** HAVE KILLED YOUR ENEMY, KING ISH-BOSHETH!

WE THOUGHT SOME REWARD...

REWARD! DO YOU THINK I WILL REWARD YOU FOR KILLIN' AN INNOCENT MAN? THERE'S ROOM IN MY KINGDOM FOR TRAITORS WHO BETRAY THEIR KING! GUARDS! TAKE THEM AWAY—EXECUTE THEM.

Underground Attack

FROM 2 SAMUEL 5:5–9; 1 CHRONICLES 11:6

As king of all Israel, David begins his military conquest by attacking the stronghold of Jerusalem...

You couldn't take this city if only the blind and lame were left to defend it.

THE FIRST MAN TO STRIKE A BLOW INSIDE THAT WALL WILL BE MADE GENERAL OF MY WHOLE ARMY.

THAT'S WORTH TRYING FOR, DAVID. BE READY TO CHARGE WHEN THE GATE OPENS.

HAT NIGHT JOAB AND SOME OF HIS MEN GO TO A POOL INSIDE A CAVE NEAR THE JERUSALEM WALLS.

LOOK! HERE'S THE TUNNEL THAT TAKES WATER FROM THE SPRING INTO THE CITY! COME ON.

CAREFUL, JOAB. THEY'LL HAVE GUARDS POSTED INSIDE.

WE'LL HAVE TO RISK IT. IT'S THE ONLY WAY TO GET INSIDE THE WALLS—AND JERUSALEM MUST BE TAKEN FROM WITHIN.

God's Promise to David

FROM 2 SAMUEL 6—8; 9:5;
1 CHRONICLES 13, 15, 16

JERUSALEM, THE CAPITAL OF ISRAEL, IS NOW A WELL-FORTIFIED CITY. BUT KING DAVID KNOWS THAT HIS NATION LACKS ONE THING TO MAKE IT SPIRITUALLY STRONG—A WAY FOR ISRAEL TO WORSHIP THE LORD. HE CALLS ON THE PEOPLE TO GO WITH HIM TO BRING GOD'S HOLY ARK TO JERUSALEM.

FATHER, WHAT'S IN THE GOLDEN CHEST?

TWO STONE TABLETS ON WHICH GOD'S TEN COMMANDMENTS ARE WRITTEN.

WHERE HAS IT BEEN?

THE PHILISTINES CAPTURED IT—BUT WHEN TROUBLE CAME TO THEM, THEY WERE AFRAID AND SENT IT BACK. IT HAS BEEN STORED AWAY FOR MANY YEARS.

BUT ONE DAY DAVID LOOKS AT THE TENT AND CALLS NATHAN, THE PROPHET OF GOD, TO HIM.

IT ISN'T RIGHT FOR GOD'S HOUSE TO BE A TENT WHILE I LIVE IN A PALACE. I'D LIKE TO BUILD A TEMPLE TO GOD.

I'M SURE GOD WOULD BE PLEASED.

THAT NIGHT GOD SPEAKS TO NATHAN — AND THE NEXT DAY NATHAN TELLS DAVID THAT GOD DOES NOT WANT HIM TO BUILD THE TEMPLE. DAVID IS A MAN OF WAR, AND THE TEMPLE IS TO BE BUILT BY A MAN OF PEACE. GOD PROMISES TO GIVE DAVID A SON WHO WILL BUILD A HOUSE FOR GOD.

THEN DAVID REMEMBERS A PROMISE HE HIMSELF MADE YEARS BEFORE TO HIS BEST FRIEND, JONATHAN. EACH HAD VOWED TO BE KIND TO THE OTHER'S CHILDREN. DAVID INQUIRES ABOUT JONATHAN'S FAMILY.

YES, PRINCE JONATHAN HAD A SON, MEPHIBOSHETH.

SEND FOR HIM.

REMEMBER, HE IS ALSO KING SAUL'S GRANDSON. BUT FOR YOU HE MIGHT BE SITTING ON THE THRONE OF ISRAEL. HE MAY HATE YOU...

A King Is Tempted

FROM 2 SAMUEL 9:6—11:14

DAVID ORDERS JONATHAN'S SON BROUGHT TO HIM. BUT HE IS SHOCKED WHEN MEPHIBOSHETH APPEARS -- A CRIPPLE.

HAVE MERCY ON YOUR SERVANT AND HIS CHILD, O KING.

MERCY? WHY DO YO ASK FOR MERCY?

I AM THE GRANDSON OF YOUR ENEMY, KING SAUL. DID YOU NOT SEND FOR ME TO PUT ME TO DEATH?

NO, MEPHIBOSHETH -- NO! I SENT FOR YOU BECAUSE I LOVED YOUR FATHER, JONATHAN. I DID NOT KNOW YOU WERE LAME.

DAVID SENDS A MESSENGER TO BRING BATH-SHEBA TO HIS COURT.

YOU SENT FOR ME, O KING?

SHE IS EVEN MORE BEAUTIFUL THAN I THOUGHT!

IF ONLY I COULD MARR[...] HER! THE PROBLEM IS [...] URIAH IS HER HUSBAN[...]

BUT SOLDIERS SOMETIMES DIE IN BATTLE. THAT'S IT!

THINKING ONLY OF HIS LOVE FOR BATH-SH[...] DAVID SENDS FOR URIAH ON THE EXCUSE [...] ASKING ABOUT THE WAR.

THE ENEMY IS STRONG. BUT JOAB THINKS WE CAN FORCE THEIR SURRENDER SOON.

I AM SURE OF IT. PREPARE TO RETU[...] TO THE FRONT-- AN[...] TAKE THIS MESSAG[...] TO JOAB.

King David's Sin

URIAH, THE HUSBAND OF BATH-SHEBA, RETURNS TO THE BATTLEFRONT WITH A MESSAGE FROM KING DAVID TO JOAB, GENERAL OF THE ISRAELITE FORCES.

AND SENDS WORD TO DAVID.

E FOUGHT BRAVELY-- T THE ARCHERS ON E CITY WALLS HAD E ADVANTAGE. URIAH, E LEADER OF THE TACK, WAS KILLED.

TELL JOAB NOT TO FEEL BADLY -- WAR ALWAYS TAKES SOME OF OUR BEST MEN. STEP UP THE ATTACK AND TAKE THE CITY.

ACROSS THE CITY, BATH-SHEBA MOURNS FOR HER HUSBAND-- BUT IN HER HEART SHE KNOWS THAT NOW SHE IS FREE TO MARRY THE KING.

HEN BATH-SHEBA'S TIME OF MOURNING OVER, DAVID CALLS HER TO THE ALACE, AND THEY ARE MARRIED.

LONG LIVE THE KING! LONG LIVE THE QUEEN!

LATER, WHEN A SON IS BORN TO BATH-SHEBA, THE KING AND ALL ISRAEL REJOICE... BUT GOD IS NOT PLEASED! EVEN WHILE THE PEOPLE SHOUT THEIR PRAISES, A MAN OF GOD IS ON HIS WAY TO THE PALACE...

The King's Punishment

FROM 2 SAMUEL 12:1–14

DAVID HAS MARRIED THE BEAUTIFUL BATH-SHEBA. WHEN THEIR SON IS BORN, DAVID IS PROUD AND HAPPY UNTIL ONE DAY... NATHAN, THE PROPHET OF GOD, COMES TO SEE HIM.

WELCOME, NATHAN. WHAT CAN I DO FOR YOU?

I HAVE COME TO TELL YOU ABOUT A GREAT INJUSTICE THAT HAS BEEN DONE IN YOUR KINGDOM.

338

Flight of the Brothers

FROM 2 SAMUEL 12:15—13:29

BOLDLY THE PROPHET NATHAN CHARGES KING DAVID WITH SINNING AGAINST THE LORD, AND FORETELLS THE DEATH OF DAVID'S YOUNGEST SON. WHEN NATHAN LEAVES, DAVID IS ALONE IN HIS SHAME. HE IS TRULY SORRY FOR THE CRIME HE HAS COMMITTED, AND TURNS TO GOD IN PRAYER...

CREATE IN ME A CLEAN HEART, O GOD; AND RENEW A RIGHT SPIRIT WITHIN ME.

THE SAME DAY WORD COMES THAT THE KING'S INFANT SON IS ILL... AND DAVID RUSHES TO THE SICKROOM.

HOW IS HE?

THERE IS LITTLE HOPE.

DAVID IS SICK WITH SORROW. HE FASTS AND PRAYS... BUT ON THE SEVENTH DAY HIS CHILD DIES.

339

MEANWHILE JOAB, DAVID'S GENERAL, CONTINUES THE SIEGE AGAINST THE CITY OF RABBAH. TO HONOR DAVID, HE SENDS WORD FOR THE KING TO COME AND MAKE THE FINAL ATTACK. DAVID LEADS THE CHARGE-- AND THE CITY SURRENDERS.

RETURNING VICTORIOUS INTO JERUSALEM, DAVID IS GREETED WITH SHOUTS OF PRAISE. HE IS PLEASED AND PROUD-- ISRAEL IS STRONG, AND NO NATION WOULD DARE ATTACK IT, BUT...

DAVID DOES NOT REALIZE THAT TROUBLE BUILDING UP WITHIN HIS OWN PALACE WALLS WILL ENDANGER HIS THRONE.

SOON AFTER DAVID'S TRIUMPHAL RETURN, PRINCE ABSALOM MAKES A SPECIAL VISIT TO HIS FATHER.

IT'S SHEEPSHEARING TIME, AND I'M HAVING A BIG FEAST IN THE COUNTRY. WILL YOU HONOR MY GUESTS WITH YOUR PRESENCE?

THANK YOU, ABSALOM, BUT IF YOU ARE HAVING A BIG FEAST, I DON'T WANT TO ADD TO YOUR EXPENSES.

THEN MAY MY BROTHERS COME? SINCE AMNON CAN REPRESENT YOU.

AMNON? I THOUGHT ABSALOM HATED HIM.

YES, I'M PLEASED THAT YOU WANT TO HONOR YOUR BROTHERS THIS WAY.

ABSALOM DOES HATE HIS OLDER HALF-BROTHER, AMNON, WHO HAS FIRST RIGHT TO DAVID'S THRONE. WHEN AMNON ACCEPTS THE INVITATION, ABSALOM CALLS IN HIS SERVANTS.

AMNON IS COMING TO THE FEAST. WHEN I GIVE THE WORD -- KILL HIM!

AT THE HEIGHT OF THE FEAST, AMNON IS KILLED... AFRAID FOR THEIR LIVES, THE REST OF THE BROTHERS FLEE INTO THE NIGHT...

A Prince's Command
FROM 2 SAMUEL 13:30—14:30

MESSENGERS BRING WORD TO THE PALACE IN JERUSALEM THAT KING DAVID'S SON, ABSALOM, HAS KILLED ALL OF HIS BROTHERS. STUNNED BY SHOCK AND GRIEF, DAVID FALLS TO THE GROUND--WEEPING. BUT HIGH ON THE CITY WALLS THE MAN IN THE TOWER KEEPS WATCH...

LOOK! A BAND OF MEN RIDING THIS WAY!

THE MEN ARE DAVID'S SONS AND THEIR SERVANTS.

343

Treason?

FROM 2 SAMUEL 14:31—15:4

I'M A PRINCE, AND I SHOULD BE TREATED LIKE MY BROTHERS. GO TO MY FATHER AND ASK HIM IF HE WILL SEE ME.

BUT...

HE ASKED ME TO COME BACK TO JERUSALEM. IF HE WANTS TO PUNISH ME FOR WHAT I DID, LET HIM DO IT. IF NOT, THEN LET HIM TREAT ME LIKE A SON AGAIN.

JOAB CARRIES ABSALOM'S MESSAGE TO KING DAVID.

YOUR SON MISSES YOU—HE WISHES TO BE FORGIVEN AND WELCOMED BACK INTO THE FAMILY.

HE MISSES ME? NO MORE THAN I MISS HIM. TELL HIM TO COME TO ME.

ABSALOM PRETENDS TO BE HUMBLE AS HE BOWS BEFORE HIS FATHER--ASKING FORGIVENESS. BUT IN HIS HEART HE HAS AN EVIL PLAN.

RISE UP, ABSALOM. YOU ARE FORGIVEN. FROM NOW ON YOU WILL BE WELCOME AT THE PALACE AS A PRINCE OF ISRAEL.

Revolt!
FROM 2 SAMUEL 15:7–13

FOR SEVERAL YEARS ABSALOM CARRIES ON A CAMPAIGN TO GAIN FOLLOWERS SO THAT HE CAN OVERTHROW HIS FATHER'S KINGDOM. AT LAST THE TIME IS RIPE FOR HIS FINAL MOVE... HE GOES TO HIS FATHER...

AFTER I KILLED MY BROTHER AND WAS LIVING IN GESHUR, I MADE A VOW THAT IF I COULD RETURN AGAIN TO JERUSALEM, I WOULD SERVE THE LORD. MAY I GO TO MY BIRTHPLACE, HEBRON, TO OFFER A SACRIFICE TO GOD?

YOU HAVE MY PERMISSION, SON, AND MY BLESSING.

HSHAI RETURNS -- IN TIME TO SEE
SALOM RIDE INTO THE CITY. IN THE
OWDS THERE ARE SHOUTS OF JOY
D PRAISE -- BUT THERE IS ALSO FEAR...

THIS MEANS WAR!

KE THE MAN IN THE CROWD, HUSHAI
OWS THAT WAR WILL SOON BE UPON
EM. HE OFFERS HIS SERVICES TO
BSALOM -- AND ALONG WITH AHITHOPHEL
CALLED TO THE FIRST COUNCIL OF
R. AHITHOPHEL SPEAKS FIRST.

WE MUST
ATTACK WHILE
DAVID IS WEAK
AND ON THE
RUN.

NO, AHITHOPHEL'S ADVICE IS NOT
GOOD. DAVID AND HIS MEN ARE
ISRAEL'S BEST FIGHTERS. AND RIGHT
NOW THEY ARE ANGRY AS BEARS
ROBBED OF THEIR YOUNG. IF YOU
ATTACK AND SUFFER ANY DEFEAT,
THE PEOPLE WILL TURN AGAINST
YOU. WAIT UNTIL YOU CAN CALL
UP THOUSANDS OF MEN...
THEN IF YOU, O KING,
LEAD THEM...

Hide-out in a Well

FROM 2 SAMUEL 17:14–23

AHITHOPHEL HAS ADVISED ABSALOM TO ATTACK KING DAVID WHILE HE IS FLEEING FOR HIS LIFE. BUT HUSHAI--SECRETLY WORKING FOR DAVID-- TELLS ABSALOM TO WAIT UNTIL HIS OWN FORCES ARE BETTER PREPARED.

NO! NO! HUSHAI'S ADVICE WILL HELP YOUR FATHER MORE THAN YOU. GIVE DAVID TIME TO GET HIS FORCES PREPARED, AND THE BATTLE IS HIS. REMEMBER -- DEFEAT MEANS DEATH TO ALL OF US!

BUT ABSALOM WILL NOT LISTEN. AHITHOPHEL IS SO SURE THE REBELLION WILL FAIL -- AND HE WILL DIE A TRAITOR'S DEATH-- THAT HE GOES HOME AND COMMITS SUICIDE.

MEANWHILE, BACK IN JERUSALEM, HUSHAI'S WELL-ORGANIZED PLAN IS BEING CARRIED OUT.

TWO OF OUR MEN ARE WAITING AT THE KIDRON FOUNTAIN. TELL THEM WHAT WE HAVE TOLD YOU. BE CAREFUL -- KING DAVID'S LIFE IS IN YOUR HANDS!

WITH A WATER JUG ON HER HEAD, THE GIRL WALKS BOLDLY OUT OF THE CITY GATE...

AND AT THE APPOINTED PLACE MEETS THE TWO MEN.

TELL KING DAVID NOT TO STOP UNTIL HE HAS REACHED THE OTHER SIDE OF THE JORDAN RIVER.

THE MEN LEAVE, BUT ON THE WAY...

DON'T LOOK NOW, BUT I THINK WE HAVE BEEN SEEN. LET'S PLAY IT SAFE AND HIDE OUT IN BAHURIM.

PIES!

THE BOY RACES BACK TO THE CITY AND REPORTS WHAT HE HAS SEEN TO PRINCE ABSALOM.

FIND THOSE SPIES AND BRING THEM TO ME!

ABSALOM'S SOLDIERS FOLLOW THE TRAIL UNTIL THEY REACH A HOUSE IN BAHURIM...

WE'RE SEARCHING FOR SPIES...HAS ANYONE BEEN HERE?

YES, TWO MEN. BUT THEY LEFT-- IN THE DIRECTION OF THE RIVER.

THE SOLDIERS SEARCH THE HOUSE BUT WHEN THEY FIND NOTHING, TH MOVE ON.

COME UP-- THE SOLDIE HAVE GONE.

EVEN ABSALOM'S MEN WOULDN'T KNOW THERE WAS A WELL HERE. I'M GLAD IT WAS A DRY ONE.

I'M PROUD TO HELP MY KING, BUT--GO-- THE SOLDIERS MIGHT RETURN.

THE MESSENGERS HURRY ON.. AND THAT NIGHT DAVID AND HIS FOLLOWERS CROSS OVER THE JORDAN.

ABSALOM'S SOLDIERS SEARCH FOR THE MESSENGERS WHO HAVE EEN SENT TO WARN DAVID. WHEN HEY CANNOT FIND THEM, THEY RETURN O JERUSALEM. MEANWHILE, DAVID ND HIS FOLLOWERS REACH THE ITY OF MAHANAIM.

HERE'S SOME FOOD AND BEDDING MY MASTER HAS SENT FOR KING DAVID AND HIS FRIENDS.

GOD BLESS YOU. TELL YOUR MASTER I WILL NOT FORGET HIS KINDNESS.

DAVID QUICKLY ORGANIZES HIS ARMY AND WAITS FOR THE MESSAGE HE EXPECTS — BUT DREADS.

PRINCE ABSALOM AND HIS FORCES HAVE CROSSED THE JORDAN RIVER!

THE ARMIES MEET HEAD-ON IN THE WOODS OF EPHRAIM. DAVID'S MEN ATTACK WITH SUCH FURY THAT ABSALOM'S ARMY IS THROWN INTO PANIC AND RETREATS.

THE BATTLE IS LOST. ABSALOM IS AFRAID THAT IF HE IS CAUGHT HE WILL SUFFER A TRAITOR'S DEATH. HE TRIES TO ESCAPE...

AND IS CAUGHT IN THE LOW-HANGING BRANCH OF AN OAK!

The King Returns

FROM 2 SAMUEL 18—24; 1 KINGS 1:1-9

PRINCE ABSALOM'S REVOLT AGAINST HIS FATHER, KING DAVID, LEADS TO A TERRIBLE BATTLE IN THE WOODS OF EPHRAIM. WHEN ABSALOM SEES THAT THE FIGHT IS GOING AGAINST HIM, HE TRIES TO ESCAPE, BUT...

GENERAL JOAB! ABSALOM IS CAUGHT-- BACK THERE-- IN A TREE!

ABSALOM? WHY DIDN'T YOU KILL HIM ON THE SPOT!

361

DAVID SEES THE TRUTH OF JOAB'S WORDS. HE MAKES PEACE WITH THE TRIBES THAT HAD SIDED WITH ABSALOM... AND GOES BACK TO JERUSALEM.

SOON AFTER THE ROYAL FAMILY IS SETTLED AGAIN IN THE PALACE, QUEEN BATH-SHEBA SPEAKS TO DAVID.

WHEN OUR SON, SOLOMON, WAS BORN, YOU PROMISED THAT HE WOULD BE KING AFTER YOU. BUT I FEAR HIS HALF-BROTHERS WILL CAUSE TROUBLE.

HAVE NO FEAR. SOLOMON WILL RULE ISRAEL.

YEARS PASS -- AND DAVID GROWS OLD. FINALLY WORD SPREADS THROUGHOUT JERUSALEM THAT THE KING'S HEALTH IS FAILING FAST. THE PEOPLE KNOW THAT DAVID HAS CHOSEN SOLOMON TO BE KING AND TO BUILD THE TEMPLE OF GOD. BUT THERE ARE RUMORS...

AND IN THE PALACE, ONE OF DAVID'S SONS, ADONIJAH, MEETS WITH THE HIGH PRIEST, ABIATHAR, AND GENERAL JOAB.

MY FATHER IS GROWING WEAKER -- AND THE TIME HAS COME FOR ME TO CARRY OUT OUR PLAN. BRING ALL THE KING'S SONS -- EXCEPT MY HALF-BROTHER, SOLOMON — AND MEET ME AT THE SERPENT'S STONE.

...e Plot that Failed

...OM 1 KINGS 1:9–49

THE BOOKS, 1 AND 2 KINGS AND 2 CHRONICLES, RECORD THE HISTORY OF THE HEBREW EMPIRE THROUGH THE YEARS OF SOLOMON'S REIGN, THE DIVISION OF THE KINGDOM INTO TWO SEPARATE NATIONS, JUDAH AND ISRAEL-- AND THE FALL OF BOTH.

...NG DAVID IS GROWING WEAKER... ...S OLDEST SON, ADONIJAH, KNOWS ...AT IF HE IS TO ACCOMPLISH ...S PURPOSE, HE MUST ACT ...IFTLY. SECRETLY HE ...VITES SOME OF HIS ...IENDS TO A FEAST ...TSIDE THE CITY... ...D PROCLAIMS ...MSELF KING.

EAT AND BE MERRY — BEFORE THIS DAY IS OVER I WILL SIT ON THE THRONE OF ISRAEL. AND YOU, MY FRIENDS, WILL BE REWARDED FOR YOUR LOYALTY.

...T WHILE ADONIJAH IS FEASTING, NATHAN, THE ...OPHET OF GOD, IS TALKING WITH QUEEN BATH-SHEBA.

HAVE YOU HEARD -- ADONIJAH HAS PROCLAIMED HIMSELF KING! IF YOU WOULD SAVE YOURSELF AND YOUR SON, SOLOMON, DO AS I SAY.

TELL ME -- AND I'LL DO IT.

FOLLOWING NATHAN'S ADVICE, SHE GOES AT ONCE TO DAVID.

MY LORD, YOU PROMISED THAT MY SON SOLOMON WOULD RULE AFTER YOU—BUT EVEN NOW HIS HALF-BROTHER, ADONIJAH, HAS DECLARED HIMSELF KING.

SEND FOR NATHAN AND ZADOK, THE PRIEST.

TAKE SOLOMON TO THE SACRED SPRING OF GIHON AND DECLARE HIM KING.

ZADOK AND NATHAN ACT AT ONCE... SOLOMON RIDES HIS FATHER'S MULE TO THE SPRING OF GIHON...

AND THERE HE IS MADE KING OF ISRAEL. THE TRUMPET SOUNDS...

GOD SAVE KING SOLOMON!

AS SOLOMON RETURNS TO THE CITY, THE PEOPLE GREET THEIR NEW KING WITH SHOUTS OF JOY.

SO GREAT IS THE NOISE OF THE CELEBRATION THAT IT REACHES ADONIJAH'S FEAST.

WHAT'S GOING ON IN THE CITY?

AT THAT MOMENT A MESSENGER ENTERS...

WHAT GOOD NEWS DO YOU HAVE FOR US?

THE NOISE YOU HEAR IS THE SHOUTING OF ALL JERUSALEM! DAVID HAS MADE SOLOMON KING.

KNOWING THAT THEY MAY BE BRANDED AS TRAITORS, ADONIJAH'S GUESTS FLEE IN TERROR.

THERE'S ONLY ONE CHANCE TO SAVE MY LIFE.

Death of a King

FROM 1 KINGS 1—5; 2 CHRONICLES 2:16

WHEN PRINCE ADONIJAH LEARNS THAT HIS FATHER, KING DAVID, HAS MADE SOLOMON KING OF ALL ISRAEL, ADONIJAH KNOWS THAT HIS OWN PLOT TO STEAL THE THRONE HAS FAILED. IN FEAR FOR HIS LIFE, HE RUNS TO THE TABERNACLE AND GRABS HOLD OF THE HORNS ON THE ALTAR OF SACRIFICE.

I WILL NOT LET GO UNTIL SOLOMON PROMISES NOT TO KILL ME.

SOLOMON AGREES TO SPARE ADONIJAH'S LIFE IF HE PROVES HIMSELF WORTHY OF THE KING'S TRUST. ADONIJAH PROMISES AND IS BROUGHT BEFORE HIS YOUNG HALF-BROTHER.

MY LORD AND KING!

SOLOMON LATER BELIEVE BOTH ADONIJAH AND GEN JOAB TO BE DISLOYAL, A THEY ARE EXECUTED.

DAY DAVID CALLS
OMON TO HIM.

MY SON, I AM DYING. THIS IS MY LAST COUNSEL TO YOU: BE STRONG AND SHOW YOURSELF A MAN. KEEP GOD'S COMMANDMENTS AND WALK IN HIS WAYS...

AND IS BURIED IN A TOMB WITHIN THE WALLS OF JERUSALEM, THE CAPITAL OF HIS KINGDOM.

THEN DAVID, WHO RULED ISRAEL FOR FORTY YEARS, DIES...

ALL ISRAEL MOURNS THE DEATH OF THE SHEPHERD BOY WHO BUILT ISRAEL INTO A MIGHTY EMPIRE AND WHOSE FAITH IN GOD IS REVEALED IN ONE OF HIS PSALMS.

Psalm 23

THE LORD IS MY SHEPHERD;
SO I SHALL LACK NOTHING.
HE MAKES ME LIE DOWN IN
GREEN PASTURES;
HE LEADS ME BESIDE
STILL WATERS.
HE RESTORES MY VERY SELF.
HE GUIDES ME IN CORRECT
PATHS FOR HIS NAME'S SAKE.
YES, THOUGH I WALK THROUGH
THE VALLEY OF THE
SHADOW OF DEATH,
I WILL NOT FEAR HARM,
FOR YOU ARE WITH ME.
YOUR ROD AND STAFF
ARE A COMFORT TO ME.

YOU LAY OUT A TABLE BEFORE
ME IN THE PRESENCE OF
MY ENEMIES.
YOU'VE ANOINTED MY HEAD
WITH OIL;
MY CUP RUNS OVER.
SURELY GOODNESS AND
FAITHFULNESS WILL FOLLOW
ME ALL THE DAYS OF
MY LIFE,
AND I WILL LIVE IN THE
HOUSE OF THE LORD
FOREVER.

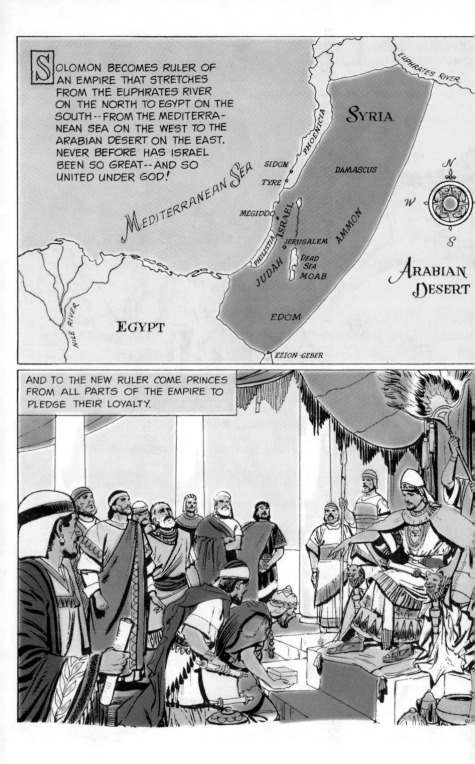

SOLOMON BECOMES RULER OF AN EMPIRE THAT STRETCHES FROM THE EUPHRATES RIVER ON THE NORTH TO EGYPT ON THE SOUTH--FROM THE MEDITERRANEAN SEA ON THE WEST TO THE ARABIAN DESERT ON THE EAST. NEVER BEFORE HAS ISRAEL BEEN SO GREAT--AND SO UNITED UNDER GOD!

EUPHRATES RIVER

SYRIA

MEDITERRANEAN SEA

SIDON

TYRE

PHOENICIA

DAMASCUS

MEGIDDO

ISRAEL

PHILISTIA

JERUSALEM

DEAD SEA

JUDAH

AMMON

MOAB

EDOM

N

W

S

ARABIAN DESERT

NILE RIVER

EGYPT

EZION-GEBER

AND TO THE NEW RULER COME PRINCES FROM ALL PARTS OF THE EMPIRE TO PLEDGE THEIR LOYALTY.

THE PEOPLE ARE HAPPY. ISRAEL IS AT PEACE. SOLOMON ESTABLISHES GOOD RELATIONS WITH MANY OF THE NEIGHBORING COUNTRIES BY MARRYING PRINCESSES OF THOSE NATIONS. RULERS OF THE COUNTRIES CONQUERED BY DAVID PAY TRIBUTE MONEY TO SOLOMON'S TREASURY. SO BEGINS THE GOLDEN AGE OF ISRAEL.

...LAUNCH HIS FIRST GREAT ...ILDING PROJECT, SOLOMON ...NDS A MESSENGER TO HIS ...THER'S OLD FRIEND, KING ...AM OF TYRE.

KING SOLOMON SENDS HIS GREETINGS--AND ASKS IF YOU WILL SEND HIM CEDAR AND CYPRESS LOGS AND SKILLED WORKERS TO HELP HIM BUILD A TEMPLE TO GOD IN JERUSALEM.

...BLESSED BE THE LORD FOR ...VING MY FRIEND DAVID SUCH ... WISE SON. TELL YOUR KING ... WILL GIVE HIM WHAT HE ASKS ... EXCHANGE FOR WHEAT AND OIL, WHICH ARE SCARCE IN OUR COUNTRY.

THE DEAL IS MADE--AND SOON MEN BY THE THOUSANDS ARE ORDERED TO WORK IN THE FORESTS OF LEBANON, CUTTING CEDAR TREES FOR SOLOMON'S TEMPLE.

ON THE SEACOAST WEST OF THE LEBANON FORESTS THE LOGS ARE TIED TOGETHER TO FORM GIANT RAFTS. THESE ARE FLOATED DOWN TO ISRAEL.

AT THE SEAPORT OF JOPPA THE LOG RAFTS ARE BROKEN UP, AND THE TIMBERS ARE DRAGGED MORE THAN THIRTY MILES ACROSS RUGGED COUNTRY TO JERUSAL...

NEAR JERUSALEM, THOUSANDS OF MEN TOIL IN THE GREAT QUARRIES.

CHISEL A BIT FROM THIS SIDE. EVERY STONE MUST BE MADE TO FIT PERFECTLY.

MEANWHILE, WOOD CARVERS AND GOLDBEATER ARE AT WORK IN JERUSALEM.

THESE DOORS WOULD BE BEAUTIFUL JUST AS THEY ARE.

COVERED WITH GOLD, THE' BE THE FINEST THE WORLD.

SLOWLY, CAREFULLY, FC SEVEN LONG YEARS T WORK GOES ON, UNT AT LAST, THE MOST BE TIFUL BUILDING IN ALL ISRAEL IS FINISHED...

The Temple of God

FROM 1 KINGS 8:1—10:1

AFTER SEVEN LONG YEARS OF HARD WORK, THE MAGNIFICENT TEMPLE OF GOD IS COMPLETED. MEN, WOMEN, AND CHILDREN FROM ALL CORNERS OF ISRAEL CROWD INTO JERUSALEM TO WATCH THE PRIESTS CARRY THE SACRED ARK INTO THE TEMPLE. INSIDE, IN THE HOLY OF HOLIES-- A DARK, WINDOWLESS, HEAVILY CURTAINED ROOM--THE ARK IS CAREFULLY PLACED BENEATH THE PROTECTING WINGS OF TWO FIFTEEN-FOOT GOLDEN CHERUBIM.

HORSES! BETWEEN FEEDING HIS FOREIGN WIVES, HIS SERVANTS, AND HIS HORSES, THERE'S LITTLE LEFT FOR THE POOR-- LIKE US!

STILL THE BUILDING PLANS GO ON...

OUR CARAVANS TRAVEL NORTH, SOUTH, EAST, AND WEST-- BUT WE HAVE MISSED ONE VITAL TRADE ROUTE.

WHERE?

THE SEA! I HAVE DECIDED TO BUILD MERCHANT SHIPS TO SAIL BEYOND THE RED SEA!

THE FLEET IS BUILT. ITS SHIPS BRING TREASURES INTO JERUSALEM AND CARRY AWAY WITH THEM STORIES OF THE CITY'S BEAUTY AND THE RULER'S WISDOM. THE STORIES REACH FAR AND WIDE — EVEN TO THE KINGDOM OF SHEBA IN THE ARABIAN PENINSULA.

SOLOMON! SOLOMON! ALL I HEAR ARE TALES OF HIS WEALTH AND WISDOM. I'M GOING TO JERUSALEM AND FIND OUT FOR MYSELF WHETHER THEY ARE TRUE!

A Queen's Visit

FROM 1 KINGS 10:2—11:8

THE FAME OF SOLOMON'S WEALTH AND WISDOM SPREADS FAR AND WIDE. IN THE ARABIAN PENINSULA, THE QUEEN OF SHEBA IS SO CURIOUS THAT SHE SETS OUT ON A TRIP TO JERUSALEM TO SEE FOR HERSELF WHETHER THE STORIES ARE TRUE.

WHAT A BEAUTIFUL CITY! IT SITS ON THE HILL LIKE A GLISTENING CROWN.

375

JERUSALEM HAS OUTGROWN ITS OLD WALLS OF DEFENSE, SO WE ARE BUILDING NEW ONES.

THAT FORE[IGN] MAN SEEM[S] TO KNOW WH[AT] HE IS DOIN[G]

HOW OBSERVING YOU ARE! THAT IS JEROBOAM, MY CHIEF LABOR FOREMAN.

SOLOMON CONTINUES TO BUILD -- BU[T] NOW THE PEOPLE ARE WORRIED AN[D] SHOCKED BY WHAT THEY SEE.

ANOTHER TEMPLE TO THE IDOL OF ONE OF THE KING'S FOREIGN WIVES. AND OUR TAXES USED TO BUILD IT!

THOSE HEATHEN TEMPLES MAKE IT CLEAR THAT SOLOMON IS NO LONGER ASKING GOD FOR GUIDANCE. THERE'S TROUBLE AHEAD FOR ISRAEL...

WHEN HER CURIOSITY IS SATISFIED, THE QUEEN OF SHEBA PRESENTS SOLOMON WITH GIFTS OF GOLD, RARE SPICES, PRECIOUS STONES — AND DEPARTS FOR HER HOME.

AHIJAH TEARS THE ROBE INTO TWELVE STRIPS.

HERE, TAKE THESE TEN PIECES. THEY REPRESENT THE TEN TRIBES OF ISRAEL OVER WHICH YOU WILL RULE WHEN SOLOMON DIES. THE OTHER TWO TRIBES WILL BE GIVEN TO SOLOMON'S SON.

SOLOMON FLIES INTO A RAGE WH HE LEARNS OF AHIJAH'S PROPHE

I MADE JEROBOAM A LEADER NOW HE IS USING HIS POSITION TURN PEOPLE AGAINST ME! FI HIM AND KILL HIM!

BUT FRIENDS WARN JEROBOAM-- AND HE ESCAPES INTO EGYPT.

I'LL STAY HERE UNTIL SOLOMON DIES. THEN WE'LL SEE IF AHIJAH SPOKE THE TRUTH ABOUT MY RULING THE NORTHERN TRIBES OF ISRAEL.

REPORTS OF YOUR PEOPLE'S COMPLAINTS HAVE BEEN REACHING US FOR SOME TIME.

BUT SOLOMON CONTINUES TO LIVE IN LUXURY -- AND SO FAR REMOVED FROM HIS PEOPLE THAT THEIR COMPLAINTS DO NO REACH HIM. HE EVEN IGNORES AHIJAH'S PROPHECY AND GOD'S WARNING THAT THE KINGDOM WILL BE DIVIDED BECAUSE HE WORSHIPS FALSE GODS.

378

AT LAST HE EVEN JOINS HIS FOREIGN WIVES IN THEIR WORSHIP OF HEATHEN IDOLS.

JUST TO PLEASE ME, PRAY TO MY GOD, SOLOMON.

IT CAN DO NO HARM--I STILL PRAY EVERY DAY TO THE GOD OF ISRAEL.

FIRST THE KING--AND NOW THE PEOPLE WORSHIP HEATHEN IDOLS. NO COUNTRY THAT TURNS AWAY FROM GOD CAN REMAIN STRONG AND FREE. ISRAEL IS DOOMED.

THEN SOLOMON DIES! WITH GOD'S HELP HE HAD BUILT ISRAEL INTO A STRONG NATION. BUT IN HIS GREED FOR MORE WEALTH AND POWER HE HAD TURNED AWAY FROM GOD--AND HIS MIGHTY KINGDOM BEGINS TO CRUMBLE...

WHILE ISRAEL MOURNS THE DEATH OF ITS KING, A MESSENGER CARRIES THE NEWS OF HIS DEATH TO EGYPT.

JEROBOAM, I BRING NEWS! KING SOLOMON IS DEAD. HIS SON, REHOBOAM, HAS TAKEN HIS PLACE. THE PEOPLE WANT YOU TO COME HOME AND PRESENT THEIR CASE TO THE NEW KING.

I'LL GO AT ONCE!

The Kingdom Is Divided

FROM 1 KINGS 12:4–27

SOLOMON IS DEAD! HIS SON, REHOBOAM, HAS GONE TO SHECHEM TO BE CROWNED KING OF ALL ISRAEL. WHEN JEROBOAM RETURNS FROM EXILE IN EGYPT, HE PLEADS FOR HIS PEOPLE.

YOUR FATHER FORCED US TO PAY HEAVY TAXES AND TO WORK HARD ON HIS BUILDING PROJECTS. WE **CANNOT** CONTINUE TO CARRY SUCH BURDENS. LIGHTEN OUR LOAD, AND WE WILL SERVE YOU, BUT...

COME BACK IN THREE DAYS, AND I WILL GIVE YOU MY ANSWER.

REHOBOAM CONSULTS HIS ADVISERS. THE OLDER MEN TELL HIM TO HEED THE CRIES OF HIS PEOPLE, BUT HIS YOUNG FRIENDS...

NOW IS THE TIME TO LET THEM KNOW THAT YOU RULE WITH AN EVEN STRONGER HAND THAN YOUR FATHER.

THREE DAYS LATER THE PEOPLE RETURN FOR THE KING'S ANSWER.

MY FATHER MADE YOUR YOKE HEAVY. I'LL MAKE IT HEAVIER. MY FATHER BEAT YOU WITH LEATHER WHIPS. I'LL STING YOU WITH LEADED LASHES.

WHY SHOULD **YOU** RULE US? KING DAVID WAS YOUR GRANDFATHER, BUT WE OWE YOU NOTHING.

JST AS THE PROPHET AHIJAH HAD SAID, TEN BES OF ISRAEL BREAK M THE KINGDOM AND KE JEROBOAM THEIR G. IN FEAR FOR HIS E, REHOBOAM RACES CK TO JERUSALEM AND E TRIBE OF JUDAH T REMAINS LOYAL HIM.

JERUSALEM, REHOBOAM CALLS UP HIS ARMY TO FIGHT E NORTHERN TRIBES THAT HAVE REVOLTED.

THE MEN ARE READY FOR YOUR ORDERS, SIR.

GOOD, I'LL SPEAK TO THEM AT ONCE.

WAIT!

Two Kingdoms

When Saul is anointed Israel's first king, all twelve tribes are considered one nation. After Solomon's reign, the kingdom is divided and each kingdom has its own kings.

Saul
↓
David
↓
Solomon

↙   ↘

Israel
Northern Kingdom
10 tribes
Has 19 kings
No godly kings

Judah
Southern Kingdom
2 tribes (Judah and Benjamin)
20 kings
Has 8 kings that please God:

Asa
Jehoshaphat
Joash (p. 440)
Amaziah
Azariah (Uzziah)
Jotham
Hezekiah (p. 449)
Josiah (p. 458)

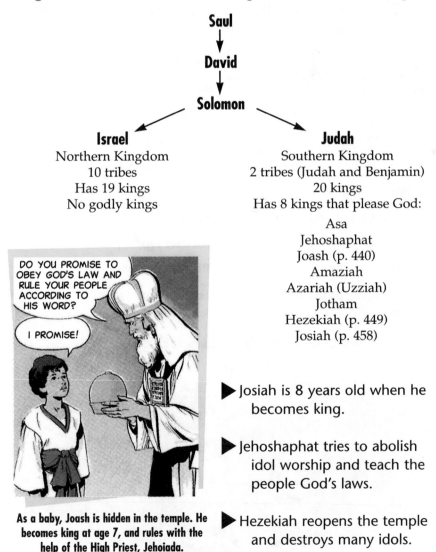

DO YOU PROMISE TO OBEY GOD'S LAW AND RULE YOUR PEOPLE ACCORDING TO HIS WORD?

I PROMISE!

As a baby, Joash is hidden in the temple. He becomes king at age 7, and rules with the help of the High Priest, Jehoiada.

▶ Josiah is 8 years old when he becomes king.

▶ Jehoshaphat tries to abolish idol worship and teach the people God's laws.

▶ Hezekiah reopens the temple and destroys many idols.

Did You Know?

Two Prophets—The Same but Different

In 1 and 2 Kings, we read about two men who are called by God to be prophets in Northern Israel. Their names are Elijah and Elisha. Sometimes it's easy to mix them up, but even though they basically have the same job, God uses them in different ways.

Elijah (See p. 389-412)	**Elisha** (See p. 402-435)
Means "The Lord is my God"	Means "God is Salvation"
Lives 800 years before Jesus	Comes after Elijah
Wears hairy clothes (2 King 1:8)	Wears Elijah's mantle (p. 402)
A loner and an outsider	Welcomed by everyone
Performs many miracles	Performs many miracles
Lives in caves (1 Kings 17:3; 19:9)	Lives in a house (2 King 6:32)
Confronts kings	Advises kings
Brings judgement	Brings compassion
Carried away in whirlwind (2 Kings 2:1-11)	Dies a natural death

Elisha's bones bring a dead man back to life (2 Kings 13:21)

ONLY GOD CAN GRANT YOUR WISH. YOU'LL HAVE TO WAIT AND SEE WHAT HAPPENS...

385

AHIJAH, THE PROPHET! HE TOLD ME I WOULD BE KING. HE KNOWS WHAT WILL HAPPEN. DISGUISE YOURSELF SO THAT HE WILL NOT KNOW YOU AND GO TO HIM.

IMMEDIATELY THE QUEEN DISGUISES HERSELF AND SETS OUT FOR AHIJAH'S HOUSE. BUT AS SHE STEPS THROUGH THE DOOR...

I AM BLIND-- BUT I KNOW WHO YOU ARE AND WHY YOU HA COME! TELL YOUR HUSBAND, JEROBOAM, THAT HE HAS DONE EVIL--AND EVIL WILL COME TO HI. HIS CHILD WILL DIE -- AND ONE DAY THE PEOPLE OF ISRAEL WILL BE SCATTERED IN OTHER LANDS BECAUSE THEY HAV WORSHIPED IDC

THE FIRST PART OF AHIJAH'S PROPHECY COMES TRUE AT ONCE-- WHEN THE QUEEN RETURNS HOME SHE FINDS HER SON DEAD! BUT JEROBOAM IS NOT WISE ENOUGH TO HEED THIS WARNING. HE CONTINUES TO LEAD HIS PEOPLE IN IDOL WORSHIP, AND EVERY KING OF ISRAEL AFTER HIM FOLLOWS HIS EVIL PRACTICE. AT LAST KING AHAB COMES TO THE THRONE, AND...

ONE DAY A CARAVAN ENTERS SAMARIA, THE CAPITAL OF NORTHERN ISRAEL, WHERE KING AHAB HAS HIS PALACE.

THAT'S A RICH CARAVAN WONDER WHERE IT'S FROM AND WHO CAN AFFORD TO TRAVEL IN SUCH STYLE?

IT'S AHAB NEW WIFE JEZEBEL -- TH DAUGHTER OF T HEATHEN KIN OF TYRE.

386

SOON A STRANGE TEMPLE IS BUILT IN SAMARIA.

IT'S FINISHED, JEZEBEL, THE TEMPLE TO YOUR GOD, BAAL.

MY GOD? YOUR GOD, AHAB, AND EVERYBODY'S GOD. ONLY BAAL SHALL BE WORSHIPED WHERE I AM QUEEN.

THAT WON'T BE EASY --THERE ARE STILL PEOPLE IN ISRAEL WHO WORSHIP ISRAEL'S GOD.

THEY'LL WORSH ISRAEL'S GOD NO LONGER-- I HAVE ORDERED THEM PUT TO DEATH

390

MONTHS GO BY AND STILL THERE IS NO RAIN
ISRAEL. AT LAST KING AHAB HIMSELF IS
RCED TO SEARCH THE COUNTRY TO FIND
STURES FOR HIS ANIMALS.
EANTIME GOD SENDS THE
ROPHET, ELIJAH, TO SEE THE
NG. THE TWO MEET.

ELIJAH! IS
IT YOU -- THE ONE
WHO HAS CAUSED US
SO MUCH TROUBLE?

IT IS NOT **I**
WHO BROUGHT DROUGHT
TO ISRAEL, BUT YOU, O KING.
IT IS **YOU** WHO HAVE BROKEN
GOD'S COMMANDMENTS
AND WORSHIPED BAAL.

ND FOR THE PROPHETS
BAAL --ALL 450 OF
EM-- AND THE LEADERS
ISRAEL. THEN MEET
ON MOUNT CARMEL.

AHAB IS SO AWED
BY THE AUTHORITY
WITH WHICH ELIJAH
SPEAKS THAT HE
DOES AS THE
PROPHET COM-
MANDS. SOON A
GREAT CROWD
GATHERS ON
TOP OF THE
MOUNTAIN BY
THE SEA.

THE PROPHETS OF BAAL ARE FORCED TO ACCEPT THE CHALLENGE. WITH GREAT CEREMONY THEY PREPARE THE SACRIFICE... AND BEGIN TO CHANT AND CALL UPON THEIR GOD.

AS THE HOURS PASS THEY SING LOUDER AND LOUDER.

CALL A LITTLE LOUDER-- PERHAPS BAAL IS TALKING --OR OFF ON A JOURNEY-- OR ASLEEP.

BY MIDAFTERNOON THE PROPHETS ARE STILL CALLING UPON BAAL TO SEND DOWN FIRE-- BUT THERE IS NO ANSWER. AT LAST THEY GIVE UP.

THEN ELIJAH BUILDS AN ALTAR TO GOD.

WHEN IT IS FINISHED, AND THE SACRIFICE PREPARED, ELIJAH ORDERS MEN TO POUR WATER OVER IT.

POUR ON MOR WATER. FILL TH TRENCH WITH I

THEN--BEFORE THE WATER-SOAKED ALTAR--ELIJAH PRAYS.

HEAR ME, O LORD, HEAR ME, THAT THE PEOPLE OF ISRAEL MAY KNOW THAT YOU ARE THE LORD GOD.

Answer by Fire!

FROM 1 KINGS 18:38—19:2

FOR HOURS THE PROPHETS OF BAAL CALL UPON THEIR GOD TO PROVE HIMSELF BY SENDING FIRE -- BUT THERE IS NO ANSWER. THEN ELIJAH CALLS UPON GOD-- INSTANTLY FIRE SWEEPS DOWN AND BURNS UP NOT ONLY THE SACRIFICE, BUT THE ALTAR MADE OF STONES.

THE LORD... HE IS GOD!

IN THE HOMES OF ISRAEL, THERE IS JOY-- THANKSGIVING -- AND REPENTANCE.

RAIN AT LAST! THE LORD BE PRAISED!

YES, IT WAS THE LORD WHO ANSWERED WITH FIRE! WE SHOULD NEVER HAVE WORSHIPED BAAL.

BUT IN THE PALACE QUEEN JEZEBEL IS FURIOUS...

WHEN THE PEOPLE SAW THE FIRE FROM GOD, THEY TURNED ON THE PROPHETS OF BAAL AND KILLED THEM. ELIJAH---

ELIJAH! ELIJAH! THAT'S ALL I HEAR! WELL, I'LL HEAR HIS NAME NO MORE!

SHE CALLS FOR A MESSENGER.

GO TO ELIJAH AND TELL HIM THAT BY THIS TIME TOMORROW HE WILL BE AS THOSE PROPHETS HE HAD PUT TO DEATH ON MOUNT CARMEL...

N A FIT OF RAGE
UEEN JEZEBEL
ENDS WORD TO
LIJAH THAT HE
LL BE PUT TO
EATH THE NEXT
AY. THAT NIGHT
LIJAH AND HIS
ERVANT MAKE
HEIR ESCAPE.

WHERE CAN WE GO TO BE SAFE?

THE DESERT-- EVEN JEZEBEL WON'T LOOK FOR US THERE.

HEIR JOURNEY TAKES
HEM SOUTH THROUGH
RAEL AND JUDAH.
HE SERVANT STAYS
THE CITY OF BEER-
HEBA, WHILE ELIJAH
ONTINUES ALONE INTO
HE WILDERNESS. BUT
FTER A DAY'S TRAVEL.

O LORD, TAKE MY LIFE. I HAVE DONE MY BEST TO BRING ISRAEL BACK TO THEE, BUT IT'S NO USE. THE PEOPLE WON'T LISTEN!

THEN, HUNGRY AND TIRED, ELIJAH FALLS ASLEEP. WHILE HE IS SLEEPING AN ANGEL APPEARS WITH BREAD AND WATER.

WAKE UP, ELIJAH, AND EAT.

ELIJAH IS ENCOURAGED BY THE FACT THAT GOD IS TAKING CARE OF HIM. AFTER HE EATS AND RESTS, HE CONTINUES HIS JOURNEY...

AND FORTY DAYS LATER HE REACHES MOUNT SINAI WHERE GOD TALKED TO MOSES.

I PRAY THAT I, TOO, MAY RECEIVE A MESSAGE FROM GOD ON THE MOUNTAIN.

SUDDENLY A GREAT STORM STRIKES. THE WIND HURLS ROCKS DOWN THE MOUNTAIN -- AN EARTHQUAKE SHAKES THE GROUND ON WHICH ELIJAH STANDS -- AND LIGHTNING SPLITS THE SKY! THE POWER OF GOD IS REVEALED IN THE STORM -- BUT THERE IS NO MESSAGE.

THEN, IN THE QUIETNESS AFTER THE STORM, ELIJAH HEARS THE STILL, SMALL VOICE OF GOD.

ELIJAH, WHAT ARE YOU DOING HERE?

O LORD, THE PEOPLE OF ISRAEL DO NOT SERVE THEE. THEY WORSHIP IDOLS. THEY HAVE KILLED ALL OF YOUR OTHER PROPHETS--AND NOW THEY WANT TO KILL ME.

WHEN GOD TELLS ELIJAH THERE IS WORK FOR HIM TO DO IN ISRAEL. --HIS COURAGE RENEWED-- ELIJAH STARTS BACK.

O GOD, I AM READY NOW TO FACE ANY DANGER.

Forged Letters

FROM 1 KINGS 19:19–21; 21:1–8

ELIJAH RETURNS TO ISRAEL TO SERVE AS GOD'S PROPHET. PASSING BY A FIELD HE STOPS AND THROWS HIS CLOAK OVER A YOUNG FARMER'S SHOULDERS.

ELIJAH! YOUR CLOAK! DOES THIS MEAN THAT YOU ARE CALLING **ME** TO BE A PROPHET?

YES, ELISHA, YOU HAVE BEEN APPOINTED BY GOD TO BE HIS SPOKESMAN IN ISRAEL.

WAIT--LET ME GO HOME AND SAY GOOD-BYE TO MY MOTHER AND FATHER; THEN I'LL GO WITH YOU.

OF COURSE--BUT JOIN ME SOON, FOR THERE IS WORK TO BE DONE FOR GOD.

SO NABOTH IS INVITED TO A PUBLIC MEETING. AND THERE-- BEFORE ALL THE PEOPLE--TWO HIRED WITNESSES BRING FALSE CHARGES AGAINST HIM.

NABOTH CURSED GOD AND THE KING.

THAT'S THE TRUTH--I HEARD HIM.

SO THE VERDICT IS GIVEN...

NABOTH IS GUILTY. TAKE HIM OUTSIDE THE CITY AND STONE HIM TO DEATH.

NO! NO! BEFORE GOD! I AM INNOCENT!

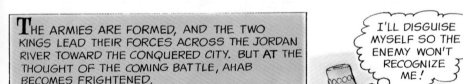

AHAB IS SO FRIGHTENED BY ELIJAH'S PROPHECY THAT FOR A TIME HE SEEKS GOD'S FAVOR. BUT WHEN THE KING OF JUDAH COMES TO VISIT HIM, HE PREPARES FOR WAR IN SPITE OF GOD'S WARNING.

THE SYRIANS TOOK ONE OF MY CITIES. WILL YOU HELP ME DRIVE THEM OUT?

YOUR WA... IS MY WAR AHAB.

THE ARMIES ARE FORMED, AND THE TWO KINGS LEAD THEIR FORCES ACROSS THE JORDAN RIVER TOWARD THE CONQUERED CITY. BUT AT THE THOUGHT OF THE COMING BATTLE, AHAB BECOMES FRIGHTENED.

I'LL DISGUISE MYSELF SO THE ENEMY WON'T RECOGNIZE ME!

The Last Journey

FROM 1 KINGS 22:30—2 KINGS 2:10

AS KING AHAB OF ISRAEL PREPARES FOR BATTLE AGAINST THE SYRIAN INVADERS, HE BECOMES SO FRIGHTENED THAT HE DISGUISES HIMSELF.

THE ENEMY WILL NEVER RECOGNIZE ME IN THIS ARMOR.

AHAB IS RIGHT—THE ENEMY DOESN'T RECOGNIZE HIM. BUT IN THE HEAT OF BATTLE A STRAY ARROW STRIKES AHAB. ALTHOUGH BADLY WOUNDED, HE STAYS WITH HIS ARMY UNTIL EVENING.

Chariot of Fire!

FROM 2 KINGS 2:11–18; 4:1

ELISHA ASKS FOR THE SPIRITUAL POWER TO CARRY ON ELIJAH'S WORK. AND ELIJAH PROMISES: "IF YOU SEE ME WHEN I AM TAKEN FROM YOU, IT WILL BE A SIGN THAT GOD HAS GRANTED YOUR WISH." SUDDENLY A CHARIOT OF FIRE SWEEPS DOWN AND SEPARATES ELIJAH FROM ELISHA, AND ELIJAH IS TAKEN UP IN A WHIRLWIND...

ELIJAH! ELIJAH! I SEE NOW--THE POWER THAT PROTECTED AND GUIDED YOU IS GREATER THAN ALL THE ARMIES OF EARTH!

FOR A LONG TIME ELISHA STANDS LOOKING UP INTO THE SKY. THEN, PICKING UP THE PROPHET'S CLOAK, HE TURNS BACK. AT THE JORDAN HE STRIKES THE WATER WITH HIS CLOAK--AND THE WATERS PART.

O GOD, I THANK THEE FOR THE GIFT OF THY POWER.

THE OTHER SIDE OF THE RIVER SHA IS MET BY A GROUP OF YOUNG OPHETS WHO HAD BEEN TRAINED ELIJAH.

WE KNOW GOD HAS TAKEN ELIJAH'S SPIRIT, BUT LET US SEARCH FOR HIS BODY THAT WE MAY BURY IT.

NO, ELIJAH WAS TAKEN UP INTO HEAVEN BY A WHIRLWIND.

BUT THE PROPHETS CANNOT BELIEVE WHAT ELISHA TELLS THEM. THEY PLEAD UNTIL ELISHA TELLS THEM TO CARRY OUT THEIR SEARCH. FOR THREE DAYS THE MEN LOOK-- THEN THEY RETURN, CONVINCED THAT THE BODY OF ELIJAH IS NOT TO BE FOUND.

NEWS THAT ELIJAH IS GONE SPREADS QUICKLY. IN THE PALACE OF SAMARIA, QUEEN JEZEBEL GLADLY PASSES THE NEWS ON TO HER SON.

WITH ELIJAH OUT OF THE WAY, WE CAN RULE ISRAEL AS WE PLEASE.

413

A Miracle of Oil

FROM 2 KINGS 4:2-7

ELISHA PROMISES A SURPRISE FOR THE MONEYLENDER WHO DEMANDS THAT A WIDOW GIVE HER SONS IN PAYMENT FOR A DEBT SHE CANNOT PAY.

TELL ME WHAT YOU HAVE IN YOUR HOUSE.

ONLY A JAR OF OIL.

BORROW ALL THE EMPTY JARS YOU CAN FROM THE NEIGHBORS. POUR THE OIL INTO THE JARS, AND TRUST GOD TO HELP YOU.

THE WOMAN QUICKLY BEGINS TO COLLECT ALL THE JARS SHE CAN.

MORE JARS, MOTHER. BUT SURELY YOUR JAR IS EMPTY NOW.

NO. I HAVE FILLED THESE JARS, BUT THERE IS STILL MORE OIL. ELISHA SAID TO FILL ALL THE JARS WE COULD FIND.

416

A Prophet's Prescription

FROM 2 KINGS 5:1–14A

AN ISRAELITE GIRL, KIDNAPPED BY SYRIAN RAIDERS, BECOMES A SERVANT TO THE WIFE OF SYRIA'S GENERAL, NAAMAN.

THANK YOU, DEAR, I'M NOT HUNGRY.

ARE YOU ILL?

NO, BUT MY HUSBAND IS. HE HAS LEPROSY AND NO ONE CAN CURE HIM.

I KNOW A PROPHET OF GOD IN ISRAEL WHO CAN.

419

420

THEN NAAMAN RETURNS TO HIS HOME IN SYRIA.

I THANK GOD EVERY DAY FOR HEALING ME, AND I OWE IT ALL TO ELISHA...

AND TO THE LITTLE GIRL WHO ALSO BELIEVES IN ELISHA'S GOD.

BUT THE HEALING OF NAAMAN DOES NOT KEEP THE KING OF SYRIA FROM PLOTTING AGAINST ISRAEL.

MY SPIES TELL ME THAT THE KING OF ISRAEL WILL SOON BE RETURNING T SAMARIA. SET UP AN AMBUSH AND CAPTURI HIM.

A FEW DAYS LATER ON THE ROAD TO SAMARIA...

STOP! ELISHA SENDS WORD FOR YOU TO TAKE ANOTHER ROAD. THE SYRIANS ARE WAITING ON THIS ROAD TO CAPTURE YOU.

R DAYS THE SYRIAN SOLDIERS WAIT FOR THE RAELITE KING -- BUT HE DOESN'T COME. AGAIN E SYRIAN KING SETS A TRAP AND AGAIN ELISHA RNS HIS KING TO ESCAPE. FINALLY THE SYRIAN KING COMES SO ANGRY THAT HE ACCUSES HIS OWN EN OF TREASON.

E'RE NOT GUILTY, KING. IT'S ELISHA, E PROPHET IN ISRAEL, HO IS TELLING YOUR PLANS.

ELISHA, IS IT? HAVE OUR SPIES FIND OUT WHERE HE IS AND I'LL SEND AN ARMY TO GET HIM.

A FEW DAYS LATER...

I HAVE GOOD NEWS FOR YOU -- ELISHA IS AT DOTHAN.

SEND AN ARMY AT ONCE TO SURROUND THE CITY.

E SYRIANS MARCH -- AND SET UP THEIR CAMP BY NIGHT. THE NEXT ORNING -- ELISHA'S SERVANT RISES EARLY AND SEES THE SYRIAN ARMY.

ELISHA! WE'RE URROUNDED -- BY HE WHOLE SYRIAN ARMY!

FEAR NOT -- THERE'S MORE POWER ON OUR SIDE THAN ON THEIRS.

One against an Army

FROM 2 KINGS 6:17–24

ELISHA'S SERVANT IS FRIGHTENED WHEN HE SEES THE SYRIAN ARMY. BUT AS ELISHA PRAYS, THE SERVANT LOOKS UP TO SEE CHARIOTS OF FIRE SURROUNDING THE PROPHET.

THE ARMY OF HEAVEN IS WITH ELISHA!

TO SAVE THE CITY FROM ATTACK, ELISHA AND HIS SERVANT GO OUT TO MEET THE ENEMY. AT ONCE THE SYRIAN SOLDIERS CLOSE IN ON THEM. BUT ELISHA PRAYS, AND SUDDENLY...

I CAN'T SEE--WHAT'S HAPPENED?

I'M BLIND-- I--

COME WITH ME. I KNOW THE ONE YOU SEEK, AND I'LL TAKE YOU TO HIM.

ELISHA LEADS THE ENEMY SOLDIERS TEN MILES SOUTH AND INTO THE CAPITAL CITY OF ISRAEL.

O LORD, OPEN THEIR EYES, THAT THEY MAY SEE.

INSTANTLY, SIGHT RETURNS TO THE SYRIANS.

WE'RE IN SAMARIA--

WE'RE TRAPPED-- THEY'LL KILL US!

SHALL WE KILL THEM, ELISHA?

NO. FEED THEM AND SEND THEM HOME.

TO THE AMAZEMENT OF THE SYRIANS, THEY ARE GIVEN FOOD AND TOLD TO RETURN HOME.

I CAN'T BELIEVE IT! WE TRIED TO KILL BOTH THE KING AND ELISHA-- AND NOW THEY TREAT US LIKE FRIENDS!

BACK HOME, THE SYRIANS TELL ABOUT THE KINDNESS OF THE ISRAELITES, AND FOR A TIME THERE IS PEACE BETWEEN THE TWO NATIONS. BUT AFTER A WHILE...

WE'LL CUT OFF ALL FOOD SUPPLIES TO SAMARIA, SURROUND IT, AND STARVE THE PEOPLE INTO SURRENDER.

EXCELLENT! AND THE LONGER THEY HOLD OUT, THE EASIER THEY WILL BE TO TAKE.

SO THE SYRIAN ARMY PITCHES ITS TENTS AROUND THE WALLS OF SAMARIA AND WAITS...

I WONDER HOW LONG THEY CAN HOLD OUT.

Starving City

FROM 2 KINGS 6:25—7:5

SAMARIA, THE CAPITAL OF ISRAEL, IS SURROUNDED BY THE SYRIAN ARMY. THE CITY MAKES A BRAVE STAND TO HOLD OUT, BUT AS MONTHS PASS, AND NO FOOD IS ALLOWED INTO THE GATES, THE PEOPLE PLEAD FOR ACTION FROM THE KING.

OUR CHILDREN ARE DYING. WE MUST HAVE FOOD.

I'D RATHER TAKE MY CHANCES FIGHTING THE ENEMY THAN STARVING TO DEATH!

WHO HAS STRENGTH ENOUGH TO FIGHT NOW?

428

THE ANXIOUS KING IS WILLING TO WAIT UNTIL THE NEXT DAY, BUT OUTSIDE THE CITY FOUR LEPERS HAVE NOT HEARD ELISHA'S PROPHECY...

I'M STARVING. I'M GOING TO TRY TO BREAK INTO THE CITY AND GET SOME FOOD.

WHY DO THAT? THERE'S NO FOOD IN THERE.

THEN LET'S GO OVER TO THE SYRIAN CAMP. MAYBE THEY'LL GIVE US SOMETHING TO EAT. MAYBE THEY'LL KILL US. EITHER WAY, THERE'S NOTHING TO LOSE-- WE'LL STARVE IF WE STAY HERE.

IN DESPERATION THE FOUR HUNGRY LEPERS APPROACH THE SYRIAN CAMP.

SOMETHING STRANGE IS GOING ON. THERE'S NOT A GUARD IN SIGHT. MAYBE IT'S A TRAP--

MAYBE IT IS— BUT I'D RATHER DIE QUICKLY THAN STARVE TO DEATH. COME ON--

THERE'S NOBODY HERE!

The Missing Enemy

From 2 Kings 7:8–16

THEIR HUNGER SATISFIED, THE LEPERS QUICKLY SEARCH THE SYRIAN TENTS.

LOOK! WON'T PEOPLE BE SURPRISED TO SEE ME IN THIS?

MORE GOLD-- WE'RE RICH!

SURPRISED? THEY'LL SAY YOU STOLE IT. THEN YOU'LL REALLY BE IN TROUBLE.

HE'S RIGHT-- LET'S HIDE EVERYTHING.

ISN'T RIGHT FOR [U]S TO KEEP ALL OF [TH]IS FOOD FROM THE [ST]ARVING PEOPLE [I]N THE CITY.

IF WE DON'T TELL THE GOOD NEWS, SOME PUNISHMENT MAY COME UPON US.

THE MEN GO BACK TO THE CITY AND POUND ON THE GATES UNTIL A GUARD ANSWERS.

THE SYRIANS ARE GONE!

GONE? WHERE? HOW DO YOU KNOW?

431

The Sound of Marching Men

FROM 2 KINGS 7:5–7, 14—9:12

THE ISRAELITE SCOUTS FOLLOW THE FLEEING SYRIAN ARMY TO THE JORDAN RIVER. ALONG THE WAY THEY OVERTAKE SOME OF THE ENEMY SOLDIERS.

PULL UP--HERE'S ONE WHO DROPPED BEHIND. MAYBE HE CAN TELL US WHAT HAPPENED.

WHY DID YOU SYRIANS DESERT CAMP IN THE MIDDLE OF THE NIGHT?

WE WERE GOING TO BE ATTACKED! WE THOUGHT THE HITTITES WERE COMING FROM THE NORTH -- AND THE EGYPTIANS FROM THE SOUTH -- TO TRAP US.

WE RODE AROUND YOUR CAMP. THERE WAS NO SIGN OF EVEN A SCOUTING PARTY-- LET ALONE **TWO** ARMIES. DID YOU REALLY **SEE** THEM?

NO-- BUT WE HEARD THEM! THOUSANDS OF SOLDIERS, HORSES AND CHARIOTS -- WE WOULDN'T HAVE HAD A CHANCE AGAINST SUCH MIGHT.

THE **SOUND** OF ARMIES-- REAL ENOUGH TO FRIGHTEN THE WHOLE SYRIAN CAMP. WHAT DO YOU MAKE OF IT?

IT WAS A MIRACLE-- USED BY ELISHA'S GOD TO FRIGHTEN THE SYRIANS AWAY.

ELISHA'S GOD-- YES. THAT FITS IN WITH THE PROMISE THAT BY TODAY THERE WOULD BE FOOD FOR EVERYONE!

BACK IN SAMARIA THE STARVING ISRAELITES RUS OUT TO THE SYRIAN CAMP, EAT THEIR FILL, AND HAUL THE REST OF THE FOOD BACK TO THE CITY.

YOU SAID THERE WOULD BE FOOD, ELISHA, BUT I DIDN'T BELIEVE YOU.

IT WAS THE LORD WHO PROMISED THE FOOD-- AN YOU CAN ALWAYS COUNT ON THE PROMISES OF GOD!

434

In spite of the fact that God has saved Israel, King Jehoram and his mother keep on worshipping Baal. When one of his border cities is attacked by the King of Syria, Jehoram goes to its defense. Wounded in the battle, he leaves Captain Jehu in charge and returns home.

...LE THE KING IS AWAY FROM THE ARMY, ...SHA CALLS FOR A YOUNG PROPHET TO ...KE A QUICK JOURNEY FOR HIM.

...KE THIS OIL--GO OUT TO ...ERE OUR ARMY IS CAMPED, ...D DO WHAT I TELL YOU.

AT THE CAMP THE YOUNG PROPHET SEARCHES UNTIL HE FINDS A GROUP OF OFFICERS.

CAPTAIN JEHU! PLEASE COME WITH ME--I MUST SPEAK TO YOU ALONE.

THUS SAYS THE LORD; "I HAVE ANOINTED YOU TO BE KING OVER ISRAEL, TO FIGHT FOR THOSE WHO WORSHIP ME, AND AGAINST THOSE WHO WORSHIP BAAL."

WHAT DID THAT FELLOW WANT?

HE WAS A MESSENGER FROM GOD--AND HE ANOINTED ME KING-- KING OF ISRAEL!

WHAT'S GOING TO HAPPEN WHEN KING JEHORAM LEARNS OF THIS?

WHEN THE NEWS REACHES KING JEHORAM, HE BELIEVES JEHU IS BRINGING NEWS OF THE WAR. SO, WITH HIS VISITOR, KING AHAZIAH OF JUDAH, HE RIDES OUT TO MEET JEHU.

DO YOU BRING NEWS OF PEACE?

HOW CAN THERE BE PEACE IN ISRAEL WHILE YOUR MOTHER, JEZEBEL, WORSHIPS BAAL?

TOO LATE, JEHORAM SEES THAT JEHU HAS COME TO OVERTHROW THE KINGDOM. HE TRIES TO ESCAPE, BUT JEHU'S ARROW STRIKES HIM DOWN.

THAT'S THE FIRST BLOW STRUCK FOR ISRAEL.

BUT NOT THE LAST! NOW JEZEBEL MUST PAY FOR HER SINS!

438

A Queen's Plot

FROM 2 KINGS 9:32—11:3

WHEN THE PALACE SERVANTS DISCOVER THAT JEHU IS NOW KING OF ISRAEL, THEY SHOW THEIR ALLEGIANCE TO HIM BY PUSHING QUEEN JEZEBEL FROM THE WINDOW TO HER DEATH IN THE STREET BELOW. SO JEZEBEL PAYS WITH HER LIFE FOR THE EVIL SHE HAS DONE -- AND ELIJAH'S PROPHECY IS FULFILLED. JEHU WIPES OUT THE WORSHIP OF BAAL IN ISRAEL.

DESTROY THE IDOL OF BAAL!

BREAK DOWN THE HEATHEN TEMPLE! FROM THIS DAY ON IT SHALL BE A PLACE TO DUMP REFUSE.

The Temple Secret

FROM 2 KINGS 11:1–12

UNDER COVER OF DARKNESS THE TWO WOMEN HURRY TO THE TEMPLE OF GOD. THE HIGH PRIEST, JEHOIADA, ANSWERS THEIR FRANTIC KNOCK.

COME IN-- HURRY!

WE HAVE BABY JOASH. HELP US SAVE HIM FROM THE QUEEN.

ONLY THE PRIESTS USE THIS ROOM. JOASH WILL BE SAFE HERE AS LONG AS IT IS NECESSARY TO HIDE HIM.

A FEW HOURS LATER THE QUEEN'S OFFICER GIVES HIS REPORT.

THE KING'S RELATIVES HAVE BEEN PUT TO DEATH AS YOU COMMANDED.

GOOD! NOW THERE IS NO ONE TO SAY I CAN-NOT RULE JUDAH.

FOR SIX YEARS ATHALIAH RULES JUDAH WITH A CRUEL HAND UNTIL AT LAST THE PEOPLE BEGIN TO COMPLAIN. UNKNOWN TO THEM -- IN A SECRET ROOM OF THE TEMPLE -- YOUNG PRINCE JOASH IS BEING TRAINED BY THE HIGH PRIEST.

WHAT'S THIS?

THE IDOL BAAL -- THE CAUSE OF ALL THE TROUBLE IN JUDAH. YOUR GRANDMOTHER WORSHIPS IT. WHEN YOU ARE KING, YOU MUST DESTROY IT AND LEAD YOUR PEOPLE BACK TO GOD.

NOW, TELL ME THE WORD OF GOD YOU HAVE LEARNED TODAY.

YOU MUST LOVE THE LORD YOUR GOD WITH ALL YOUR HEART, AND WITH ALL YOUR SOUL, AND WITH ALL YOUR MIGHT!

ONE DAY A PRIEST OF THE TEMPLE COMES TO JEHOIADA.

I PRAY THAT GOD WILL DELIVER JUDAH FROM THIS IDOL WORSHIP.

AND GOD HAS ANSWERED YOUR PRAYER. I HAVE SENT FOR ALL THE CAPTAINS OF THE GUARD TO MEET SECRETLY IN THE TEMPLE. COME--

IN THE TEMPLE...

MEN-- THIS IS PRINCE JOASH, YOUR RIGHTFUL RULER. I AM GOING TO CROWN HIM KING OF JUDAH ON THIS COMING SABBATH. BE THERE WITH ALL YOUR MEN TO PROTECT HIM.

THE NEXT SABBATH IN THE PALACE...

THE SOUND OF CHEERING --IT COMES FROM THE TEMPLE. I WONDER WHAT IT MEANS!

444

445

446

UNDER THE GUIDANCE OF JEHOIADA, THE HIGH PRIEST, JOASH DESTROYS THE TEMPLE OF BAAL AND LEADS HIS PEOPLE BACK TO THE WORSHIP OF GOD. THE HOUSE OF GOD IS REPAIRED, AND FOR YEARS JUDAH PROSPERS. BUT WHEN JEHOIADA DIES, JOASH IS TOO WEAK TO STAND UP UNDER THE PRESSURE OF THOSE WHO WOULD TURN HIM AWAY FROM GOD. FINALLY, JEHOIADA'S SON, ZECHARIAH, GOES TO THE KING...

KING JOASH, I SPEAK TO YOU AS MY FATHER WOULD SPEAK. YOUR PEOPLE ARE RETURNING TO BAAL AND FORSAKING GOD. JUDAH WILL BE DESTROYED UNLESS YOU STOP THEM!

AS SOON AS ZECHARIAH LEAVES, THE WORSHIPERS OF BAAL GIVE **THEIR** ADVICE.

ZECHARIAH IS A TROUBLE-MAKER.

HE SHOULD BE PUT TO DEATH BEFORE HE TURNS ALL JUDAH AGAINST YOU.

YOU'RE RIGHT. STIR UP THE PEOPLE SO THAT THEY WILL GET RID OF HIM.

AND SO JOASH, WHO WAS ONCE A GOOD KING, LISTENS TO EVIL ADVICE. ZECHARIAH IS STONED TO DEATH BY A MOB--AND SOON HIS PROPHECY OF DISASTER COMES TRUE...

447

Dagger in the Night

FROM 2 KINGS 12—18:10; 2 CHRONICLES 24:20–27

WHEN KING JOASH TURNED AWAY FROM GOD, ZECHARIAH PREDICTED DISASTER. IT COMES SOON-- IN AN ATTACK BY THE KING OF SYRIA WHO IS ON A CAMPAIGN OF CONQUEST. DURING THE ATTACK THE MEN WHO HAD ADVISED JOASH AGAINST ZECHARIAH ARE KILLED. IN AN ATTEMPT TO SAVE JERUSALEM, JOASH TRIES TO BUY OFF THE ENEMY.

GIFTS FROM MY LORD, KING JOASH OF JUDAH. HE ASKS THAT YOU ACCEPT THEM AND LEAVE JERUSALEM IN PEACE.

TELL YOUR KING I ACCEPT HIS OFFER.

HAVING ACQUIRED AN EASY FORTUNE, THE KING OF SYRIA CALLS BACK HIS ARMY AND MARCHES ON. JERUSALEM IS SAVED, BUT JOASH FALLS GRAVELY ILL.

HOW IS THE KING TODAY?

NO BETTER-- NO WORSE. TOO BAD THE SYRIANS DIDN'T KILL THE KING ALONG WITH THE MEN WHO ADVISED HIM TO MURDER ZECHARIAH. WITH THEM GONE WE COULD SAVE JUDAH --IF IT WEREN'T FOR...

IF YOU'RE THINKING WHAT I AM--

SH! THIS ISN'T THE TIME.

THAT NIGHT-- WHEN ALL THE PALACE IS ASLEEP...

REMEMBER-- WE'RE DOING THIS TO SAVE OUR COUNTRY.

SO KING JOASH IS MURDERED-- BY HIS OWN MEN. FOR ALMOST A HUNDRED YEARS JUDAH IS RULED BY KINGS WHO WAVER BETWEEN WORSHIPING GOD AND HEATHEN IDOLS. THEN HEZEKIAH COMES TO THE THRONE...

449

452

WHEN NEWS OF THE PEOPLE'S FEAR REACHES KING EZEKIAH, HE SEEKS ADVICE FROM ISAIAH, GOD'S PROPHET IN JUDAH.

HAVE FAITH! GOD WILL NOT FORSAKE US.

SUDDENLY THE ASSYRIAN FORCES DISAPPEAR!

THE ASSYRIANS ARE GONE!

IT MAY BE A TRICK TO GET US OUT OF THE CITY. SEND SOME MEN TO SEE WHAT IS GOING ON.

STEALTHILY HEZEKIAH'S MEN APPROACH THE MAIN CAMP OF THE ENEMY...

HOW QUIET IT IS...

AND NOT A GUARD IN SIGHT!

A Foolish King

FROM 2 CHRONICLES 32:21—33:12

WHEN THE ASSYRIANS SUDDENLY STOP THREATENING THE PEOPLE OF JERUSALEM, KING HEZEKIAH SENDS MEN TO SCOUT THE ENEMY CAMP. THEY FIND IT STRANGELY QUIET.

WHY-- THEY'RE ASLEEP, OR--

A PLAGUE MUST HAVE STRUCK DOWN THE MAIN FORCE OF THE ENEMY.

AT THE NEWS, ALL JERUSALEM GOES WILD WITH JOY...

HEZEKIAH SAID GOD WAS ON OUR SIDE.

AND GOD DOESN'T FORSAKE THOSE WHO BELIEVE AND TRUST HIM...

NO SOONER IS MANASSEH ON THE THRONE THAN THE FOLLOWERS OF BAAL BEGIN THEIR CAMPAIGN TO LEAD HIM AWAY FROM GOD.

TO BECOME RICH AND POWERFUL AS THE ASSYRIANS, WE SHOULD WORSHIP IDOLS, AS THEY DO.

...EVER AGAIN ...ILE HEZEKIAH ...ES DO THE ...SYRIANS TRY ...TAKE JERUSALEM. ...ZEKIAH CON- ...UES TO LEAD ...G PEOPLE IN ...EIR WORSHIP ...: GOD, AND ...EY ARE HAPPY. ...HIS DEATH, ...S YOUNG SON, ...ANASSEH, IS ...OWNED KING.

...NASSEH LISTENS TO THEIR ADVICE, ...D RESTORES IDOL WORSHIP IN ISRAEL. ...EVEN DARES TO PLACE AN IDOL IN ...E TEMPLE OF GOD.

BUT WORSHIPING THE IDOLS OF THE SURROUNDING NATIONS DOES NOT SAVE MANASSEH. THE ASSYRIAN KING SUSPECTS MANASSEH IS PLOTTING AGAINST HIM AND SENDS TROOPS TO JERUSALEM. IN A SURPRISE MOVE THE ASSYRIANS OVERCOME MANASSEH'S FORCES AND TAKE THE KING PRISONER.

BOUND BY CHAINS, MANASSEH IS PARADED THROUGH THE STREETS OF JERUSALEM...

WHERE ARE HIS ADVISORS NOW?

AND IN BABYLON, WHICH IS CONTROLLED BY ASSYRIA, HE IS CAST INTO PRISON

ALONE--AND IN THE DARKNESS OF HIS CELL-- MANASSEH REVIEWS THE PAST. HE REMEMBERS THAT WHEN HIS FATHER RULED JUDAH, THE ASSYRIANS TRIED TO TAKE JERUSALEM, AND GOD HAD DESTROYED THEM WITH A PLAGUE. ASSYRIA HAD NOT DARED TO STRIKE AGAIN WHILE HIS FATHER LIVED. BUT HIS FATHER HAD OBEYED GOD--AND HE, MANASSEH...

O GOD, I HAVE SINNED AGAINST THEE. I REPENT AND PRAY THAT YOU WILL FORGIVE ME.

456

NO ONE KNOWS WHAT PROMPTED THE ASSYRIAN KING TO FREE MANASSEH--BUT WHEN HE RETURNS TO JERUSALEM HIS PEOPLE WELCOME HIM...

THE KING HAS RETURNED!

LONG LIVE THE KING OF JUDAH!

BUT THE PEOPLE ARE AMAZED HIS FIRST SPEECH...

I WAS WRO TO TURN AW FROM GOD DESTROY TI IDOLS, AND JOIN ME IN WORSHIPIN GC

MANASSEH TRIES TO SAVE HIS NATION, BUT IT IS TOO LATE. MOST OF THE PEOPLE CONTINUE TO WORSHIP IDOLS. MANASSEH DIES, AND AFTER TWO YEARS, HIS EIGHT-YEAR-OLD GRANDSON, JOSIAH, COMES TO THE THRONE.

AS THE KING GROWS UP, THE IDOL WORSHIPER TRY TO INFLUENCE JOSIAH, BUT THE YOUNG KING REMAINS TRUE TO GOD. HE RULES JUDA WITH A FIRM BUT JUST HAND. ONE DAY HE CALLS FOR THREE OF HIS OFFICIALS.

THE WAL OF THE TEMPI ARE CRUMBLING I WANT THEM REPAIR IMMEDIATEL

A Prophetess Speaks

FROM 2 KINGS 22:11—24:20; 2 CHRONICLES 34:19—36:16

THE SCRIBE READS TO KING JOSIAH FROM THE LOST BOOK THAT HAS BEEN FOUND IN THE TEMPLE WALLS.

GOD'S LAWS ARE CLEARLY STATED -- AND SO IS THE PUNISHMENT FOR ANYONE WHO DISOBEYS THEM.

THEN JUDAH IS DOOMED! FOR IT HAS BROKEN GOD'S LAW MANY TIMES.

JOSIAH IS SO UPSET THAT HE QUICKLY SENDS SEVERAL HIGH-RANKING OFFICIALS TO THE PROPHETESS HULDAH.

THE KING HAS SENT US TO ASK FOR A MESSAGE FROM GOD ABOUT THE BOOK WE HAVE JUST READ.

460

THUS SAITH THE LORD: BECAUSE JUDAH HAS DISOBEYED ME, JUDAH SHALL BE DESTROYED... BUT THE DESTRUCTION WILL NOT COME IN THE DAYS OF JOSIAH.

...PING HE MAY YET WIN GOD'S FOR-...ENESS FOR HIS NATION, JOSIAH ...LLS A MEETING OF THE PEOPLE.

AT JOSIAH'S COMMAND PAGAN WORSHIP IS WIPED OUT IN ALL THE LAND. OBJECTS USED IN IDOL WORSHIP ARE REMOVED FROM GOD'S TEMPLE IN JERUSALEM, TAKEN OUTSIDE THE CITY, AND BURNED.

I HAVE READ GOD'S LAWS TO YOU. LET US NOW PROMISE TO OBEY THEM FROM THIS DAY ON. AND MAY GOD HAVE MERCY ON US.

461

THEN JOSIAH CALLS THE PEOPLE TO KEEP THE FEAST OF THE PASSOVER.

THIS REMINDS US OF HOW GOD DELIVERED OUR FORE-FATHERS FROM SLAVERY IN EGYPT CENTURIES AGO.

WHILE JOSIAH LIVES, JUDAH OBEYS THE LAWS OF GOD. BUT AFTER HIS DEATH, ONE KING AFTER ANOTHER TURNS BACK TO THE WORSHIP OF IDOLS. LACKING GOD'S HELP, JUDAH COMES UNDER THE CONTROL OF A NEW WORLD POWER, BABYLONIA.

JUDAH IS ALLOWED TO REMAIN UNDER ITS OWN RULERS, BUT AFTER KING ZEDEKIAH COMES TO THE THRONE HE FOOLISHLY TRIES TO REGAIN HIS COUNTRY'S INDEPENDENCE. IN REPLY THE GREAT BABYLONIAN ARMY SETS OUT...

The Fall of Jerusalem

FROM 2 CHRONICLES 36:17–20; 2 KINGS 25:1–11

FOR 2 YEARS AND A HALF, FORCES FROM THE GREAT BABYLONIAN ARMY BESIEGE THE CITY OF JERUSALEM. AT LAST THEY BREAK THROUGH THE WALL...

THAT NIGHT KING ZEDEKIAH AND HIS ARMY TRY TO ESCAPE.

IF WE CAN MAKE IT TO THE HILL REGION EAST OF THE JORDAN, THEY'LL NEVER FIND US.

IT'S OUR ONLY CHANCE -- IF THEY CAPTURE US...

BUT THE BABYLONIANS PURSUE THEM, AND ZEDEKIAH IS CAPTURED BEFORE HE CAN REACH THE RIVER. HE IS BLINDED AND TAKEN TO BABYLON.

HUNGRY, WEARY, AND AFRAID, THE PEOPLE OF JERUSALEM ARE FORCED TO BEGIN THE LONG MARCH OF 900 MILES FROM JERUSALEM TO BABYLON -- AS CAPTIVES.

GOD HAS FORSAKEN US.

NO. GOD WARNED US, BUT WE WOULD NOT LISTEN. IT IS WE WHO HAVE FORSAKEN GOD!

VER, GOLD, AND ALL OBJECTS OF VALUE
E STRIPPED FROM THE TEMPLE AND
ACE BUILDINGS.

SET FIRE TO EVERY CORNER OF THE CITY-- LET NOTHING REMAIN THAT WILL GIVE ANYONE IDEAS ABOUT REBUILDING IT.

R DAYS THE FIRES RAGE -- UNTIL
THAT IS LEFT OF THE BEAUTIFUL
Y OF JERUSALEM IS A HEAP OF
HES AND BLACKENED STONES...

BUT ON THE WAY TO BABYLON A FEW BRAVE CAPTIVES DREAM OF A DAY WHEN THEY MAY RETURN...

Return of the Captives

FROM EZRA 1—2; DANIEL 5; ISAIAH 45:1-2,13

FROM THE MOMENT THEY ARE CARRIED AWAY AS CAPTIVES TO BABYLON, THE JEWS DREAM OF RETURNING TO THEIR HOMELAND, JUDAH. THE BOOK OF **EZRA** TELLS WHAT HAPPENS TO THAT DREAM.

FOR MANY YEARS THE J... LIVE AS CAPTIVES OF GREAT BABYLONIAN EMPI... THEY WATCH ANXIOUSLY A PERSIA, A STRONG COUN... TO THE EAST, RISES UP ... CHALLENGE BABYLON.

WHEN THE PERSIAN ARMY APPEARS OUTSIDE THE CITY WALLS, KING BELSHAZZAR IS SO SURE OF BABYLON'S STRENGTH THAT HE SPENDS THE NIGHT IN A DRUNKEN FEAST WITH HIS COURT. PERSIAN TROOPS STEAL INTO THE CITY-- INVADE THE PALACE--AND SLAY BELSHAZZAR. WITHIN HOURS THE BABYLONIAN EMPIRE FALLS TO PERSIA.

[TW]O WEEKS LATER KING CYRUS OF PERSIA [RI]DES TRIUMPHANTLY INTO THE CITY.

[S]O THAT'S OUR [NE]W RULER. I [WO]NDER--DOES [THI]S MEAN GOOD [O]R EVIL FOR [US] JEWS?

I'VE HEARD THAT CYRUS IS A JUST MAN. WE'LL HAVE TO WAIT AND SEE.

[SOO]N AFTER CYRUS TAKES OVER [THE] BABYLONIAN EMPIRE, AN [OFFI]CIAL ANNOUNCEMENT IS [MA]D.

THESE ARE THE WORDS OF KING CYRUS: THE GOD OF ISRAEL COM-MANDS THAT A HOUSE BE [B]UILT FOR HIM IN JERU-[S]ALEM. ANY OF HIS PEOPLE [W]HO WANT TO DO SO MAY [R]ETURN. THOSE WHO DO NOT GO BACK SHOULD GIVE OF THEIR POSSESSIONS TO HELP THOSE WHO RETURN TO JUDAH.

GIFTS OF MONEY, HORSES, MULES, CAMELS, GOLD AND SILVER, FOOD AND CLOTHING POUR IN. AT LAST THE DAY COMES WHEN THE GREAT CARAVAN IS READY TO LEAVE.

THANK GOD, I'LL SEE MY HOMELAND AGAIN.

467

ON THE LONG ROAD HOME, THEY FOLLOW MUCH THE SAME ROUTE THAT ABRAHAM, THE FATHER OF THE JEWISH NATION, TRAVELED 1,500 YEARS BEFORE WHEN HE OBEYED GOD'S COMMAND TO LEAVE UR AND MAKE A NEW NATION IN PALESTINE.

WHEN WE LEFT JERUSALEM IT WAS IN FLAMES -- I WONDER WHAT IT LOOKS LIKE NOW.

BUT NO MATTER HOW MUCH THEY PREPARE THEMSELVES FOR THE RUINED CITY, THEY A BROKENHEARTED WHEN THEY WALK THROUG THE RUBBLE OF JERUSALEM.

SOLOMON'S BEAUTIFUL TEMPLE STOOD OVER THERE.

OUR HOME-- LET'S TRY T FIND IT.

HOW PROUD WE WERE WHEN WE BUILT IT-- WITH OUR OWN HANDS, TOO. NOW LOOK AT IT-- A HOME FOR WILD DOGS.

MAYBE WE SHOULD NOT HAVE COME BACK. MAYBE...

OUR FOREFATHERS BUILT MUCH OF THIS CITY. WE'LL REBUILD IT -- JERUSALEM WILL RISE AGAIN. YOU'LL SEE...

Jerusalem Rises Again

From Ezra 3—10

ALTHOUGH THE CITY OF JERUSALEM IS IN RUINS, THE JEWS WHO HAVE RETURNED FROM CAPTIVITY IN BABYLON SET TO WORK TO REBUILD IT. WHEN THE FOUNDATION OF THE TEMPLE IS IN PLACE, THE HIGH PRIEST LEADS THE PEOPLE IN A SERVICE OF WORSHIP AND REJOICING.

O GIVE THANKS UNTO THE LORD, FOR HE IS GOOD. HIS MERCY ENDURETH FOR EVER.

BUT THE SOUND OF REJOICING BRINGS TROUBLE. THE SAMARITANS WHO LIVE NEAR JERUSALEM COME WITH A REQUEST TO HELP BUILD THE TEMPLE.

WE'RE SORRY-- BUT YOU DO NOT WORSHIP AS WE DO, SO WE CANNOT LET YOU HELP US BUILD OUR TEMPLE TO GOD.

SO THEY "CAN'T" LET US HE THEM BUILD THE TEMPLE! WE WE'LL MAKE THEM SORRY TH EVER CAME BACK TO JERUSALEM TO BUILD ANYTHING.

WHAT DO YOU MEAN?

THE JEWS SOON LEARN WHAT THE SAMARITAN MEANT. ONE DAY WHILE THEY ARE AT WORK AN OFFICER OF KING CYRUS RIDES UP.

BY ORDER OF THE KING, THIS WORK IS TO STOP!

STOP? WHY? IT WAS KING CYRUS HIM- SELF WHO TOLD US WE SHOULD RETURN TO JERUSALEM TO REBUILD THE TEMPLE!

UNHAPPILY, THE WORKMEN LAY DOWN THEIR TOOLS AND GO HOME

FATHER, WHAT COULD HAVE HAPPENED? KING CYRUS SAID...

YES, BUT THE SAMAR TANS WROTE HIM THA WE WERE TRYING TO DESTROY HIS POWER HERE. THE KING IS INVESTIGATING THE CHARGES AND HAS ORDERED WORK ON THE TEMPLE STOPPED.

470

ORCED TO OBEY, THE WS TURN TO WORK THEIR HOMES AND RDENS. SEVERAL ARS PASS -- CYRUS ES AND NEW KINGS OME TO THE THRONE PERSIA, BUT STILL HE TEMPLE IN ERUSALEM IS NOT OMPLETED. THEN, NE DAY, THE JEWS RE APPROACHED BY WO PROPHETS OF GOD.

HAGGAI, ZECHARIAH! WHAT BRINGS YOU HERE?

WE HAVE NEWS.

A NEW KING, DARIUS, HAS COME TO THE THRONE. LET'S START WORK AGAIN ON THE TEMPLE -- MAYBE HE WON'T STOP US.

KING DARIUS NOT ONLY LETS THE JEWS COMPLETE THE TEMPLE -- HE EVEN ORDERS HIS OFFICERS TO GIVE THEM THE MATERIAL THEY NEED.

D -- AT LAST -- E NEW TEMPLE GOD IS FINISHED. H THANKFUL ARTS THE PEO- E OFFER THEIR CRIFICES AND AYERS TO GOD.

SOME YEARS LATER, EZRA, A PRIEST, GAINS PERMISSION FROM THE PERSIAN KING TO GO TO JERUSALEM TO TEACH THE PEOPLE THE LAWS OF GOD. HE TAKES A GROUP OF JEWS WITH HIM. UNDER EZRA JERUSALEM GROWS IN SIZE AND SPIRITUAL STRENGTH, BUT IS STILL WITHOUT WALLS AND SUR- ROUNDED BY HOS- TILE NEIGHBORS.

E NIGHT, WHILE THE CITY SLEEPS, STRANGER AND HIS GUARDS E TOWARD JERUSALEM ...

Two Lines of Defense

FROM NEHEMIAH

THE BOOK OF **NEHEMIAH** CONTINUES THE STORY OF THE JEWS' STRUGGLE TO REBUILD JERUSALEM.

AT NIGHT, SO THAT NO ONE WILL SEE HIM, A STRANGER TO JERUSALEM RIDES AROUND THE CITY AND EXAMINES THE WALLS.

THIS CITY COULD BE WIPED OUT IN ONE QUICK ATTACK.

YOU'RE RIGHT, NEHEMIAH. BUT IT MUST HAVE BEEN A GREAT FORTRESS AT ONE TIME. THESE WALLS ARE AS THICK AS ANY WE HAVE IN PERSIA.

BUT WHILE THE ENEMIES OF JERUSALEM PLAN TO TAKE THE CITY, NEHEMIAH PREPARES TO DEFEND IT.

PASS THESE OUT TO EVERY WORKER. LET NO MAN WORK WITHOUT A WEAPON IN HIS HAND -- READY TO FIGHT!

THE ENEMY APPROACHES -- BUT TO THEIR SURPRISE ARMED WORKERS RISE UP -- THEIR SPEARS RAISED AND THEIR BOWS PULLED.

THEY'RE ARMED!

RETREAT!

THE WORKERS GO BACK TO THEIR JOBS, AND SOON STRONG WALLS AND HEAVY GATES AGAIN PROTECT THE CITY OF JERUSALEM. BUT INSIDE THERE IS AN EVEN STRONGER LINE OF DEFENSE -- A NATION LED BY EZRA AND NEHEMIAH TO LOVE AND OBEY GOD!

HE BOOK OF
STHER IS THE
ORY OF A
UNG JEWISH
OMAN WHO
ISKS HER
IFE TO SAVE
HER PEOPLE.

WHEN THE BABYLONIANS CAPTURE JERUSALEM, THEY TAKE THOUSANDS OF JEWS BACK HOME AS CAPTIVES. LATER, WHEN THE PERSIAN KING CONQUERS BABYLON, HE FREES THE JEWS. MANY RETURN TO JERUSALEM, BUT OTHERS REMAIN IN BABYLON AND PERSIA.

AT THIS TIME THE PERSIAN EMPIRE IS THE MOST POWERFUL IN ALL THE WORLD-- REACHING FROM INDIA TO ETHIOPIA. ON THE THRONE AT SHUSHAN SITS KING AHASUERUS.

FOR MONTHS THE KING HAS BEEN ENTERTAINING HIGH-RANKING OFFICIALS OF HIS REALM. HOW MUCH LONGER WILL THIS FEASTING GO ON?

UNTIL HE HAS IMPRESSED ALL OF HIS SUBJECTS WITH HIS WEALTH AND POWER.

A Plot against the King

FROM ESTHER 2:11—3:6

OR MONTHS, ESTHER, ALONG WITH HUNDREDS OF BEAUTIFUL WOMEN OF PERSIA, LIVES IN THE PALACE, WAITING FOR THE KING TO CHOOSE ONE OF THEM TO BE HIS WIFE. AT LAST THE KING MAKES HIS CHOICE--

ESTHER, YOU ARE NOW MY WIFE, QUEEN OF ALL PERSIA!

I AM HONORED, MY LORD.

BUT ESTHER'S COUSIN, MORDECAI, IS NOT INVITED TO THE WEDDING. HE SITS, AS HE DOES EVERY DAY, AT THE PALACE GATE, WAITING FOR A CHANCE WORD ABOUT ESTHER.

THE QUEEN OF PERSIA IS A JEWESS. BUT ONLY ESTHER AND I KNOW THAT!

A New Law

FROM ESTHER 3:8—4:16

ANGERED BECAUSE MORDECAI WILL NOT BOW BEFORE HIM, HAMAN PREPARES HIS REVENGE...

THERE'S A RACE OF PEOPLE IN YOUR KINGDOM, SIR, WHO DO NOT OBEY YOU. FOR YOUR SAFETY, THEY SHOULD BE DESTROYED. GIVE ME PERMISSION TO MAKE A LAW THAT WILL RID PERSIA OF THEM.

YOU ARE A LOYAL MAN, HAMAN. HERE IS MY RING. USE ITS SEAL TO SHOW THAT YOUR LAW IS MY LAW.

HAMAN ACTS AT ONCE...

WRITE THIS DOWN AND SEE THAT EACH GOVERNOR IN THE KINGDOM RECEIVES A COPY OF IT: "EVERY JEW IN PERSIA IS TO BE DESTROYED ON THE 13TH DAY OF THE 12TH MONTH. THOSE WHO KILL THE JEWS MAY KEEP AS REWARDS ALL THE MONEY AND GOODS OF THE JEWS THEY KILL."

480

THE FRIGHTENED SERVANT CARRIES THE MESSAGE TO ESTHER.

GO TO SEE THE KING? MORDECAI KNOWS THAT ANYONE WHO APPEARS BEFORE THE KING WITHOUT BEING INVITED IS SUBJECT TO DEATH. AND I HAVE NOT BEEN CALLED TO SEE THE KING FOR THIRTY DAYS.

NOW, MORE FRIGHTENED THAN EVER, THE SERVANT REPORTS BACK TO MORDECAI.

TELL THE QUEEN I UNDERSTAND HER FEAR. BUT TELL HER, TOO, THAT PERHAPS GOD RAISED HER UP TO THE PALACE FOR SUCH A TIME AS THIS.

AFTER RECEIVING MORDECAI'S LAST MESSAGE, ESTHER PREPARES TO GO TO THE KING.

BRING THE ROYAL ROBES — I WILL GO LOOKING AS A QUEEN SHOULD.

NO! NO! THIS COULD MEAN YOUR DEATH!

A Queen Risks Her Life

FROM ESTHER 5:1—6:10

QUEEN ESTHER BREAKS A LAW BY APPEARING UNINVITED BEFORE THE KING--AN ACT PUNISHABLE BY DEATH. BUT THE LIVES OF HER PEOPLE, THE JEWS, ARE IN DANGER, AND SHE IS THE ONLY ONE WHO MAY BE ABLE TO SAVE THEM.

ESTHER WHAT DOES WANT THAT S WOULD RISK LIFE TO GE

...RPRISED AS HE IS BY HER SUDDEN ...PEARANCE, THE KING IS PLEASED AT THE ...GHT OF HIS BEAUTIFUL QUEEN. HE HOLDS ...T HIS SCEPTOR TO SHOW THAT SHE IS ...RGIVEN, AND ASKS WHAT SHE WANTS.

I ASK THAT YOU AND HAMAN COME TO A DINNER THAT I SHALL PREPARE FOR YOU.

...E KING ACCEPTS. SO DOES HAMAN ...WHO IS OVERJOYED UNTIL HE ...AVES THE PALACE.

THAT STUBBORN JEW -- HE STILL WON'T BOW BEFORE ME! WELL, HE'LL SOON BE DEAD WITH ALL THE OTHER JEWS.

AT HOME HAMAN COMPLAINS THAT MORDECAI HAS INSULTED HIM.

DON'T STAND FOR IT, HAMAN. BUILD A GALLOWS AND TELL THE KING YOU WANT MORDECAI HANGED. THEN YOU CAN ENJOY YOUR DINNER WITH THE QUEEN.

I'LL DO IT! I'LL HAVE THE GAL- LOWS MADE AND GO TO SEE THE KING EARLY IN THE MORNING.

BUT THAT NIGHT THE KING CANNOT SLEEP. HE CALLS FOR A SCRIBE TO READ TO HIM FROM THE RECORDS OF THE KINGDOM. WHEN THE READING REACHES THE STORY OF MORDECAI, THE KING INTERRUPTS.

STOP! WHAT REWARD DID HE RECEIVE FOR SAVING MY LIFE?

NONE, MY LORD.

AT THAT MOMENT HAMAN ENTE THE COURT AND IS BROUGH BEFORE THE KING.

HAMAN, YOU'RE JUST THE MAN I WANTED TO SEE. WHAT SHALL I DO TO HONOR A MAN WHO HAS PLEASED ME?

I KNEW THE KING WOULD RECOGNIZE MY SERVICES.

LET HIM WEAR ONE OF YOUR ROBES -- AND RIDE YOUR HORSE. THEN HAVE ONE OF YOUR NOBLES LEAD HIM THROUGH THE CITY TELLING EVERYONE THAT THIS IS THE WAY THE KING HONORS THOSE WHO PLEASE HIM.

GOOD! GET THE ROBE AND THE HORSE AND DO EXACTLY AS YOU HAVE SUGGESTED -- FOR MORDECAI.

MORDECAI! BUT I -- YES -- SIR!

The Unchangeable Law

FROM ESTHER 6:11—10

NGRY AND HUMILIATED, HAMAN IS FORCED TO PERFORM FOR HIS ENEMY, MORDECAI, THE CEREMONY THAT HE HAD PLANNED FOR HIMSELF...

THE CEREMONY OVER, HAMAN COVERS HIS HEAD IN SHAME AND HURRIES HOME TO TELL HIS FAMILY.

THIS LOOKS BAD FOR YOU, HAMAN.

ALL IS NOT LOST! THE KING HAS SIGNED AN ORDER TO KILL THE JEWS, AND NOT EVEN HE CAN CHANGE IT! NOW I MUST DRESS TO GO TO QUEEN ESTHER'S DINNER. AT LEAST SHE RECOGNIZES ME!

LATER AT THE PALACE.

QUEEN ESTHER, WHEN YOU DARED TO COME TO THE THRONE ROOM I THINK YOU WANTED A GREATER FAVOR THAN TO ASK ME TO DINNER. DIDN'T YOU?

YES, MY LORD, I DID.

485

WHAT IS IT? I'LL GRANT WHATEVER YOU ASK.

I ASK FOR THE LIFE OF MYSELF AND MY PEOPLE. BY THE CRUEL PLAN OF A CERTAIN MAN WE ARE TO BE PUT TO DEATH.

PUT **YOU** TO DEATH? WHO WOULD DARE DO SUCH A THING?

HAMAN!

N OW, FOR THE FIRST TIME THE KING KNOWS THAT HIS WIFE IS JEWISH, AND THAT HAMAN TRICKED HIM INTO SIGNING HER DEATH WARRANT. IN ANGER THE KING LEAVES THE ROOM.

QUEEN ESTHER! I'LL DO ANYTHING YOU SAY-- ONLY SPARE ME! SPARE ME!

THE KING'S SERVANT KNOWS THAT HAMA IS DOOMED TO DIE AND HE COVERS TH MAN'S HEAD WITH A CLOTH.

487

Women Who Change Their World . . .

Deborah is a judge and a prophetess who becomes a military advisor. See pp. 214-217 (Judges 4–5).

Delilah is bribed by the enemy to get information from her boyfriend. She betrays him and he is taken prisoner. See pp. 240–243 (Judges 16).

Esther is an orphan who wins a beauty contest and later risks her life to save her people. See pp. 476–488 (the Book of Esther).

Eve is created, not born as a baby, but becomes known as the mother of all human beings. She disobeys God in a big way when she and her husband eat fruit that God tells them not to eat. See pp. 19–26 (Genesis 2–4).

Hannah is falsely accused by a priest of being drunk when she prays earnestly for a child. God grants her request and a son is born. When he is young, she takes her son to be raised in God's house. See pp. 253–254 (1 Samuel 1–2).

Did You Know?

Women Who Change Their World . . .

Jezebel is a wicked queen who worships idols. She tries to kill all the prophets of God, and in the end is thrown over a wall and run over by horses. See pp. 386-439 (1 Kings 16,18–21; 2 Kings 9).

Mary is a young woman who becomes mother to the Son of God. See pp. 550-566 (Matthew 1–2 and Luke 1–2).

Miriam helps her mother save her little brother by putting him in a basket riverboat. See pp. 125–128 (Exodus 2).

Rahab hides two spies in her house and later she and her whole family are saved because she hangs a red cord out of her window. See pp. 193–202 (Joshua 2 and 6).

Rebekah agrees to move away from home and marry a man she has never met. Later she becomes the mother of twin boys. See pp. 68-81 (Genesis 24–28).

Ruth is from an enemy country, but she risks her future to help her mother-in-law. It pays off and she becomes King David's grandmother. See pp. 247–252 (the Book of Ruth).

Man with a Message

FROM ISAIAH

AT THIS POINT IN OUR BIBLE STORY, WE NOW RETURN TO PICK UP MATERIAL NOT COVERED AT OTHER PLACES IN THE BIBLE.

THINGS SEEMED TO BE GOING WELL IN THE LAND OF JUDAH, BUT TROUBLE WAS ON THE WAY. IN THEIR HEARTS THE PEOPLE WERE TURNING AWAY FROM GOD. THE RICH WERE CHEATING THE POOR. AND ALTHOUGH THE WALLS OF JERUSALEM WERE STRONG, THERE WAS ALWAYS THE DANGER OF INVASION BY AN ENEMY. IN THIS TIME OF NEED, GOD SENT A YOUNG MAN WITH A MESSAGE. HE WAS ISAIAH, ONE OF THE GREATEST OF THE HEBREW PROPHETS.

HOLY, HOLY, HOLY, IS THE LORD GOD OF HOSTS.

THE CALL TO BECOME A PROPHET OF GOD COMES TO ISAIAH WHEN HE IS WORSHIPING IN THE TEMPLE. AS HE PRAYS, HE SEES A GLORIOUS VISION.

O GOD, I AM NOT WORTHY TO BE IN THY PRESENCE. I AM A SINFUL MAN IN A SINFUL NATION.

AN ANGEL TOUCHES ISAIAH'S LIPS WITH A COAL OF FIRE AND SAYS, "YOUR SIN IS TAKEN AWAY." THEN ISAIAH HEARS GOD ASK: "WHOM SHALL I SEND TO SPEAK TO THIS SINFUL NATION?"

HERE I AM; SEND ME.

FOR MORE THAN FIFTY YEARS ISAIAH PLEADS WITH HIS PEOPLE TO DESTROY THEIR IDOLS AND WORSHIP GOD. BUT ONLY A FEW LISTEN. HE WARNS THE KINGS OF WHAT WILL HAPPEN IF THEY DISOBEY GOD, BUT THE KINGS IGNORE THE WARNINGS. AT LAST ISAIAH PROPHESIES DESTRUCTION...

BECAUSE JUDAH HAS TURNED AWAY FROM GOD, IT WILL BE DESTROYED AND ITS PEOPLE CARRIED AWAY AS CAPTIVES.

IS THERE NO HOPE FOR GOD'S PEOPLE?

YES, GOD WILL SEND A DELIVERER TO SAVE ALL WHO BELIEVE IN HIM. AND HIS NAME SHALL BE CALLED WONDERFUL, COUNSELLOR, THE MIGHTY GOD... THE PRINCE OF PEACE.

BUT GOD PROMISES THAT HE WILL GIVE JEREMIAH THE WORDS TO SPEAK AND THE COURAGE TO SAY THEM. THAT EVENING...

A WONDERFUL THING HAPPENED TO ME TODAY --GOD CALLED ME TO BE A PROPHET.

A PROPHET! KING JOSIAH WORSHIPS GOD--BUT MANY OF THE COURT LEADERS SECRETLY WORSHIP IDOLS. THEY WILL MAKE IT HARD FOR YOU--AND YOU'RE SO SHY...

THE PEOPLE C JUDAH ARE DOOMED UNLES THEY TURN BAC TO GOD. GOD HA CALLED ME TO WARN THEM.

THE MESSAGE JEREMIAH IS TO GIVE HIS PEOPLE COMES TO HIM WHILE HE IS WATCHING A BOILING KETTLE.

INVADERS COMING DOWN FROM THE NORTH TO DESTROY JUDAH! BUT WILL ANYONE BELIEVE ME?

...SOON FINDS OUT-- WHEN HE TELLS THE PRIESTS [H]IS OWN TOWN THAT JUDAH WILL BE DESTROYED [BEC]AUSE THE PEOPLE HAVE TURNED FROM GOD [TO] WORSHIP IDOLS.

WHO IS THIS YOUNG UPSTART TO TELL US HOW TO LIVE?

LET'S GET RID OF HIM BEFORE HE STARTS TROUBLE.

SO, TO SAVE HIS LIFE, JEREMIAH IS FORCED TO LEAVE HIS HOME TOWN AND GO TO JERUSALEM.

KING JOSIAH LOVES AND WORSHIPS GOD; HE WILL HELP ME TRY TO SAVE JUDAH.

[FOR] SEVERAL YEARS JEREMIAH AND THE KING [WO]RK TOGETHER TO DESTROY IDOL WORSHIP. THEN, [ON]E DAY, JEREMIAH HEARS SOME FRIGHTENING NEWS.

[TH]E ASSYRIAN EMPIRE [IS C]RACKING UP. EGYPT [IS] MARCHING NORTH TO [GR]AB WHAT'S LEFT. KING [JO]SIAH DECLARES HE [WIL]L STOP THE EGYPTIAN [AR]MY FROM MARCHING [TH]ROUGH JUDAH.

STOP EGYPT? WHY, IT'S ONE OF THE STRONG-EST COUNTRIES IN THE WORLD! THE KING IS MAKING A BIG MISTAKE.

MEDITERRANEAN

EGYPT

JUDAH

ASSYRIAN EMPIRE

BUT KING JOSIAH LEADS HIS SOLDIERS OUT OF THE GATES OF JERUSALEM — AND INTO THE PATH OF THE ONCOMING EGYPTIAN ARMY.

The Broken Vase

FROM JEREMIAH 18—20:2;
2 KINGS 23:29–37

KING JOSIAH IS KILLED AS HE ATTEMPT
TO DEFEAT THE EGYPTIANS. NOW HIS
SON, JEHOIAKIM, SITS ON THE THRONE O
JUDAH AS A PUPPET RULER FOR EGYPT. A
ONCE THE IDOL WORSHIPERS BEGIN THEIR
CAMPAIGN AGAINST GOD AND HIS PROPHET
JEREMIAH.

O KING, YOUR FATHER ORDERED US NOT TO WORSHIP ANY GOD BUT JEHOVAH. AND WHAT HAPPENED? JUDAH IS NO LONGER A FREE COUNTRY. JOIN US IN WORSHIPING OUR GODS SO THAT JUDAH WILL BECOME STRONG-- LIKE OUR NEIGHBORS.

JEHOIAKIM AGREES--AND IN SPITE OF JEREMIAH'S WARNINGS, MANY OF THE PEOPLE FOLLOW THE KING'S LEAD.

GO AWAY, JEREMIAH. NOBODY WANTS TO LISTEN TO YOUR FAR-FETCHED STORIES ABOUT JUDAH BEING DESTROYED!

JUDAH DOESN'T HAVE LONG TO WAIT FOR ITS ANSWER. BABYLON ATTACKS JERUSALEM, AND KING JEHOIAKIM IS FORCED TO SURRENDER.

YOU MAY REMAIN ON THE THRONE, JEHOIAKIM, BUT NOW YOU MUST PAY TRIBUTE MONEY TO ME. AND TO SEE THAT YOU DO, I'LL TAKE YOUR BEST PRINCES AS HOSTAGES.

WITHIN DAYS ALL JER SALEM SADLY WATCHE ITS FINEST YOUNG M BEING MARCHED AWA

KNOWING THAT THE DOWNFALL OF JUDAH IS NOT FAR OFF, JEREMIAH DICTATES ALL OF THE MESSAGES HE HAS RECEIVED FROM GOD.

THE PEOPLE MUST BE TOLD THAT GOD IS ALLOWING JUDAH TO BE PUNISHED FOR ITS SINS.

THEN--BECAUSE HE IS NOT ALLOWED IN THE TEMPLE--JEREMIAH ASKS BARUCH TO READ GOD'S WORD TO THE PEOPLE.

WE MUST S THAT THE KI LEARNS ABC THIS.

THE SCROLL IS READ TO THE KING, HE BE-
COMES SO ANGRY THAT HE CUTS IT UP PIECE BY
PIECE AND THROWS IT INTO THE FIRE.

ARREST JEREMIAH AND BARUCH. THROW THEM INTO PRISON. THAT WILL KEEP THEM QUIET.

BUT JEREMIAH AND BARUCH ARE PREPARED FOR THE KING'S ANGER-- ALREADY THEY ARE IN HIDING.

THE KING BURNED THE SCROLL-- BUT WE WILL WRITE ANOTHER.

WHILE JEREMIAH AND BARUCH ARE BUSY RE-
PLACING THE BURNED SCROLL, TROUBLE IS
BREWING IN THE PALACE.

WHY SHOULD WE PAY TRIBUTE TO BABYLON? I SAY LET'S STOP IT AND USE THE MONEY TO BUILD UP OUR OWN ARMY. THEN WE'LL BE READY IF BABYLON ATTACKS US AGAIN.

YOU'RE RIGHT-- THOSE HOSTAGES IN BABYLON ARE NOT AS IMPORTANT AS ALL OF US HERE IN JUDAH.

IN TIME, WORD LEAKS OUT THAT KING JEHOIAKIM IS BREAKING HIS AGREEMENT WITH BABYLON. JEREMIAH IS ALARMED.

THE KING'S DECISION IS AGAINST THE WILL OF GOD. AND NO MAN CAN DEFY GOD!

Babylon Strikes!

FROM 2 KINGS 24—25:4
JEREMIAH 27; 28:1–12
37:1–10

WITH FULL FORCE THE ARMY OF BABYLON STORMS THE WALLS JERUSALEM.

YOUNG KING JEHOIACHIN, WHO HAS RULED THREE MONTHS, IS FORCED TO SURRENDER TO KING NEBUCHADNEZZAR.

THIS TIME I WILL TAKE YOUR TREASURES, YOUR NOBLES, YOUR SKILLED WORKERS **AND** YOUR KING. LET THIS BE A LESSON TO YOU WHO ARE LEFT!

SO JEREMIAH'S PROPHECY COMES TRUE! THE TEMPLE TREASURES ARE LOOTED, THE KING AND 10,000 OF JUDAH'S ABLEST MEN ARE LED AWAY. PRINCE ZEDEKIAH IS MADE KING-- **AFTER** HE PROMISES LOYALTY TO BABYLON.

FOR A FEW YEARS KING ZEDEKIAH PAYS TRIBUTE TO BABYLON. THEN, IN SPITE OF JEREMIAH'S WARNINGS, HE BEGINS TO LISTEN TO SOME HOT-HEADED YOUNG ADVISERS IN HIS COURT.

WHAT DO **WE** GET FROM THE MONEY PAID TO BABYLON?

WELL-- WE GET PEACE.

PEACE--BUT NOT FREEDOM! MAYBE THE EGYPTIANS WILL HELP US-- THEY HATE BABYLON, TOO.

LET ME THINK ABOUT IT.

WHEN JEREMIAH LEARNS THAT THERE IS TALK OF ANOTHER REVOLT, HE PUTS AN OX YOKE ON HIS SHOULDERS AND WALKS THROUGH THE STREETS.

WHAT'S THE MEANING OF THIS?

BABYLON HAS STRUCK TWICE, AND IT WI STRIKE AGAIN. THE NEXT TIME IT WILL DESTROY JERUSALEM. JUDAH'S ONLY HOPE OF SURVIVAL IS TO WE THE YOKE OF BABYLON AS I AM WEARING THIS ONE.

I'LL SHOW YOU WHAT TO DO WITH THE YOKE OF BABYLON. BREAK IT!

DURING ALL OF THIS TIME, EGYPT KEEPS AN ANXIOUS EYE ON THE GROWING TENSIONS IN JUDAH. AT THE RIGHT MOMENT IT SENDS AN AMBASSADOR TO KING ZEDEKIAH

BABYLON IS YOUR ENEMY AS WELL AS OURS. ALONE, NEITHER ONE OF US CAN DEFEAT THEM, BUT--

TOGETHER WE CAN! AN WE WILL!

Accused

FROM JEREMIAH 37—38:6

Backed by Egypt's promise to help, King Zedekiah of Judah revolts against the control of Babylon. Jeremiah argues against the decision.

BABYLON HAS SPARED JERUSALEM TWICE BEFORE. BUT IF YOU GO THROUGH WITH THIS REVOLT, BABYLON WILL NOT SPARE THE CITY AGAIN.

BUT THIS TIME WE'LL WIN. JUDAH WILL BE FREE!

S JEREMIAH PROPHESIED, BABYLON ANSWERS THE REVOLT WITH A SWIFT ATTACK. FOR WEEKS THE SOLDIERS OF JUDAH FIGHT TO DEFEND JERUSALEM'S WALLS.

THE EGYPTIANS! WHY DON'T THEY COME AS THEY PROMISED?

SPITE OF HIS [IN]OCENCE, JEREMIAH [is] THROWN INTO [PRI]SON. WITHIN A [FE]W WEEKS THE [BA]BYLONIANS, AFTER [DE]FEATING THE [E][G]YPTIANS, RETURN [TO] THE GATES OF [JE]RUSALEM. JEREMIAH'S [EN]EMIES BRING HIM [BE]FORE THE KING [AN]D ACCUSE HIM OF [BEI]NG A TRAITOR.

I REPEAT THE WARNING GOD HAS GIVEN ME. INVADERS FROM THE NORTH WILL CONQUER JUDAH. GOD HAS CHOSEN THE BABYLONIANS TO DESTROY OUR NATION BECAUSE OF THE SINS OF ITS PEOPLE.

IT'S THIS KIND OF TALK THAT MAKES OUR SOLDIERS LOSE COURAGE. PUT THIS TRAITOR TO DEATH-- OR THE CITY **WILL** FALL.

HE IS IN YOUR [H]ANDS-- DO WHAT YOU WANT WITH HIM.

QUICKLY-- BEFORE THE KING CAN CHANGE HIS MIND-- JEREMIAH IS PUT INTO AN OLD CISTERN BENEATH THE PRISON FLOOR.

LET HIM STARVE TO DEATH!

505

A Prophecy Comes True

FROM JEREMIAH 38:7—43:7

DURING THE SIEGE OF JERUSALEM, SOME NOBLES ACCUSE JEREMIAH OF BEING A TRAITOR AND HAVE HIM THROWN INTO AN OLD CISTERN. BUT EBED-MELE SERVANT IN THE PALACE, PERMISSION FROM THE TO PUT JEREMIAH IN TH PRISON YARD.

THANK GOD FOR YOUR HELP. I WOULD HAVE DIED IN THAT AWFUL HOLE.

AS THE SIEGE CONTINUES, PEOPLE IN JERUSALEM ARE STARVING AND BEG FOR FOOD. AT LAST THE FRIGHTENED KING CALLS FOR JEREMIAH.

WHAT WILL HAPPEN TO US?

IF YOU SURRENDER, JERUSALEM WILL BE SAVED. IF YOU DO NOT, IT WILL BE BURNED.

SURRENDER? I D DARE. MY OWN P WOULD TURN AGAINST ME!

...REMIAH IS TAKEN BACK TO PRISON... ...E SIEGE GOES ON, BUT AT THE END ...F 30 MONTHS...

...E BABYLONIANS ...VE BROKEN ...ROUGH THE ...WALL!

JERUSALEM WILL BE DESTROYED! BUT IT WILL RISE AGAIN... AND SOMEDAY GOD'S COMMANDMENTS WILL BE WRITTEN IN THE HEARTS OF MEN WHO CHOOSE TO OBEY GOD. THEY WILL LIVE TOGETHER IN PEACE.

KING ZEDEKIAH TRIES TO ESCAPE, BUT IS CAPTURED AND BLINDED. THE KING, JEREMIAH, AND MOST OF THE ABLE-BODIED PEOPLE ARE CAPTURED TO BE TAKEN TO BABYLON.

...T IN THE CAPTIVE CAMP AT RAMAH...

...HE KING OF BABYLON ...AS LEARNED THAT ...OU TRIED TO KEEP ...UR COUNTRY FROM ...EBELLING AGAINST ...IM, SO HE HAS ...ENT ORDERS TO ...ET YOU FREE.

THANK GOD! NOW I CAN HELP THE PEOPLE WHO HAVE BEEN LEFT IN ISRAEL WITHOUT A LEADER.

ABOUT A MONTH AFTER JERUSALEM IS TAKEN, A BABYLONIAN OFFICER RETURNS, TAKES MORE CAPTIVES, AND THEN SETS FIRE TO THE CITY.

THE FIRE RAGES FOR DAYS -- UNTIL THE ONCE-PROUD CAPITAL OF JUDAH BECOMES A HEAP OF SMOULDERING RUINS.

THE BABYLONIANS SET UP HEADQUARTERS AT MIZPAH AND APPOINT AN ISRAELITE TO ACT AS GOVERNOR. JEREMIAH JOINS HIM -- AND BECOMES HIS ADVISER.

TOGETHER WE'LL ENCOURAGE THE PEOPLE TO BUILD UP THEIR HOMES AND REPLANT THEIR VINEYARDS AND FIELDS.

SOMEDAY THE CAPTIVES WILL RETURN-- AND JUDAH WILL BECOME A NATION AGAIN.

BUT BEFORE THE GOVERNOR'S DREAM CAN COME TRUE HE IS MURDERED BY SOME ISRAELITES WHO ARE JEALOUS OF HIS POWE IN THE COUNTRY. FEARFUL THAT BABYLON WILL BLAME ALL ISRAE FOR THE MURDER, A GROUP OF PEOPLE GO TO JEREMIAH...

WE WANT TO GO TO EGYPT-- WHERE THERE IS PEACE AND PLENTY TO EAT.

YOU WILL FIN[NEITHER PEAC NOR PLENTY IN EGYPT. STA HERE -- THE BABYLONIANS W NOT HURT YOU

BUT THE PEOPLE DO NOT BELIEVE JEREMIAH. THEY FLEE TO EGYPT, FORCING HIM TO GO WITH THEM. AND THERE, UNTIL HE DIES, JEREMIAH TRIES TO LEAD HIS PEOPLE BACK TO GOD.

HE GRIEF OF THE JEWS OVER THE DESTRUCTION OF JERUSALEM IS EXPRESSED IN A GROUP OF POEMS FOUND IN THE

BOOK OF LAMENTATIONS

IN THE MONTHS THAT FOLLOW, EZEKIEL WORKS HARD TO MAKE A LIVING IN THE NEW LAND.

IT IS NOT AS BAD AS I FEARED. WE ARE WELL TREATED--AND WE ARE TOGETHER.

YES. WE MAY HAVE TO STAY HERE THE REST OF OUR LIVES, BUT GOD IS WITH US WHEREVER WE ARE.

BUT NOT ALL OF THE CAPTIVI FEEL THE SAME WAY.

WHAT DO YOU THINK OF EZEKIEL PLANTING TREES AND PLANNING TO BUILD A HOUSE? LOOKS AS IF HE INTENDS TO STAY IN BABYLONIA.

HE'S WASTIN HIS TIM WE'LL B ON OUR W. HOME IN A COUPLE OF YEARS

WHEN THIS NEWS REACHES GOD'S PROPHET, JEREMIAH, IN JUDAH, HE WRITES A LETTER TO THE CAPTIVES.

JEREMIAH SAYS IT IS GOD'S WILL THAT WE STAY HERE. WE SHOULD BUILD HOMES AND WORK FOR THE GOOD OF OUR NEW COUNTRY. WE WILL BE HERE FOR SEVENTY YEARS.

DID YOU HEAR THAT, EZEKIEL? SEVENTY YEARS --I DON'T BELIEVE IT!

JEREMIAH SPEAKS THE WILL OF GOD.

EZEKIEL SHOWS HIS FAITH BY BUILDING A HOUSE.

WE'LL MAKE A LARGE COURTYARD--BIG ENOUGH INVITE PEOPLE HERE TO WORSH GOD. I USED TO THINK THA WE COULD WORSHIP GOD ONLY IN THE TEMPLE I JERUSALEM, BUT NO I KNOW WE CAN WORSHIP HIM ANYWHERE.

THE NEXT DAY...

YOU HAVE ALL PASSED -- NOW YOU'LL BE GIVEN THREE YEARS TO STUDY UNDER OUR WISE MEN. AFTER THAT THE KING HIMSELF WILL CHOOSE THOSE BEST QUALIFIED TO BE HIS ADVISERS.

O GOD, THANK YOU. HELP US TO PASS THESE NEW TESTS SO THAT WE MAY ADVISE THE KING IN A WAY THAT WILL PLEASE YOU.

THE YOUNG MEN ARE TAKEN AT ONCE TO THE PALACE TO BEGIN THEIR STUDIES. THEY ARE GIVE THE BEST OF EVERYTHING -- EVEN FOOD FROM THE KING'S TABLE.

THANK YOU, BUT W CANNOT EAT THIS MEAT AND DRINK THIS WINE. OUR HEBREW L FORBID IT. GIVE US PLAIN FOOD AND WATER, PLEASE.

BUT IT'S THE KING'S ORDER -- WE DARE NOT DISOBEY. I LIKE YOU, DANIEL, BUT I DON'T WANT TO GET INTO TROUBLE.

GIVE US A TEN-DA TRIAL. LET US EAT OUR FOOD AND THEN SEE IF WE ARE NOT STRONGER THAN THE OTHERS.

THE TEST IS MADE, AND AT THE END OF TEN DAYS, THERE'S NO DOUBT--DANIEL AND HIS FRIENDS NOT ONLY **LOOK** STRONGER, THEY **ARE** STRONGER.

AT THE END OF THREE YEARS, THE YOUNG MEN ARE BROU BEFORE THE KING. HE TALKS WITH EACH ONE, THEN MAI HIS DECISION.

I HAVE CHOSEN THESE FOUR--DANIEL, SHADRACH, MESHACH, AND ABEDNEGO -- TO SERVE AS MY ADVISERS.

THERE IS NONE EQUAL TH S

NIEL AND HIS FRIENDS BECOME
PULAR MEMBERS OF THE KING'S
URT. BUT ONE DAY THE KING HAS
UNUSUALLY DIFFICULT
OBLEM AND HE CALLS
R ONLY HIS OLDER,
RE EXPERIENCED
VISERS.

I HAD A STRANGE DREAM, BUT I HAVE FORGOTTEN IT. TELL ME WHAT IT WAS AND WHAT IT MEANS.

WE CAN TELL YOU WHAT A DREAM MEANS, SIR, BUT NO MAN CAN TELL YOU WHAT YOU DREAMED.

WHAT GOOD ARE ADVISERS F THEY CAN'T TELL ME HAT I WANT TO KNOW? UT THESE MEN TO DEATH -- AND EVERY WISE MAN IN KINGDOM!

THE CAPTAIN OF THE KING'S GUARD IS FORCED TO CARRY OUT HIS UGLY TASK.

DANIEL, YOU AND YOUR FRIENDS ARE UNDER ARREST --THE KING HAS ORDERED ALL OF HIS WISE MEN PUT TO DEATH.

TO DEATH? WHY? WHAT HAVE WE DONE?

THE FOUR YOUNG HEBREWS PRAY,
VISION COMES TO DANIEL.
O GOD, HANK YOU R MAKING E DREAM KNOWN TO ME.
THE NEXT DAY--
HAVE YOU COME TO ASK FOR MORE TIME--OR CAN YOU TELL ME MY DREAM?
GOD IN HEAVEN HAS REVEALED YOUR DREAM TO ME.
OU SAW A MIGHTY STATUE TS HEAD WAS MADE OF LD AND ITS FEET OF AY. THEN YOU SAW LARGE STONE STRIKE T THE FEET OF THE TATUE AND BREAK INTO MANY PIECES.
YES! YES! THAT'S RIGHT. BUT WHAT DOES IT MEAN?
THE HEAD OF GOLD STANDS FOR YOU AND YOUR GREAT KINGDOM, O KING. OTHER LESSER KINGDOMS WILL FOLLOW. BUT AFTER THEY FALL, GOD WILL SET UP A KINGDOM WHICH SHALL NEVER BE DESTROYED.
YOUR GOD IS A GOD ABOVE ALL GODS. AND YOU SHALL BE RULER OF THE PROVINCE OF BABYLON--OVER ALL THE WISE MEN WHOSE LIVES YOU SAVED THIS DAY.

DANIEL RELAYS THE GOOD NEWS TO HIS HEBREW FRIENDS.

THE KING HAS MADE ME RULER OVER BABYLON AND EACH OF YOU HAS AN IMPORTANT OFFICE IN THE KINGDOM.

THAT'S WONDERFUL!

BUT THE NEWS DOES NOT PLEASE THE KING'S OTHER ADVISERS.

SO THE KING HAS PUT THIS YOUNG HEBREW OVER **US!** WE MUST GET RID OF HIM.

NOT NOW HE'S TOO POWERFUL BUT IF WE CAN TURN THE KING AGAINST DANIEL'S FRIENDS WE MIGHT BE ABLE TO CAUSE DANIEL TROUBLE.

THEIR OPPORTUNITY COMES WHEN THE KING BUILDS A STATUE AND ORDERS HIS OFFICIALS TO WORSHIP IT--OR BE THROWN INTO A FIERY FURNACE.

THE KING IS PLAYING RIGHT INTO OUR HANDS --HE DOESN'T KNOW THAT HEBREWS WILL WORSHIP ONLY THEIR GOD.

DANIEL HOLDS TOO HIGH A POSITION FOR ANY ONE OF US TO REPORT ON HIM-- BUT NOT HIS FRIENDS...

RIGHT--AND TOMORROW WHEN THE TRUMPET SOUNDS FOR ALL MEN TO BOW BEFORE THE STATUE, WE'LL KEEP OUR EYES ON SHADRACH, MESHACH AND ABEDNEGO.

Trial by Fire

FROM DANIEL 3:1–25

AT KING NEBUCHADNEZZAR'S COMMAND, A GIANT STATUE--90 FEET HIGH--IS BUILT ON THE PLAINS OF DURA. ALL OF THE OFFICIALS OF BABYLON ARE ORDERED TO WORSHIP IT. THE HOUR OF WORSHIP COMES-- THE MOMENT FOR WHICH THE KING'S JEALOUS ADVISERS HAVE BEEN WAITING...

THE MUSICIANS HAVE TAKEN THEIR PLACES. THE SIGNAL WILL SOON BE GIVEN-- THE ONE THAT MEANS DEATH TO DANIEL'S FRIENDS -- SHADRACH, MESHACH, AND ABEDNEGO!

MUSIC FILLS THE AIR-- SOLEMNLY THE OFFICIALS OF BABYLON BOW DOWN AND WORSHIP THE GOLDEN STATUE--ALL BUT SHADRACH, MESHACH, AND ABEDNEGO.

SEE? THEY REFUSE TO BOW DOWN!

EAGERLY, THE JEALOUS ADVISERS REPORT TO THE KING.

O KING, THREE OF YOUR HEBREW OFFICIALS HAVE DEFIED YOU. THEY REFUSE TO WORSHIP YOUR STATUE.

WHAT? HAVE THEM BROUGHT TO ME AT ONCE!

WORSHIP THE STATUE -- OR BE THROWN INTO THE FIERY FURNACE. AND TELL ME -- WHAT GOD CAN SAVE YOU FROM THAT?

IF WE ARE CAST INTO THE FIRE, THE GOD WHOM WE SERVE WILL BE ABLE DELIVER US! BUT EVEN IF WE MUST DIE, WE WILL NOT WORSHIP AN IDOL.

HEAT THE FURNACE -- SEVEN TIMES HOTTER THAN EVER BEFORE -- AND THROW THEM IN IT!

THE THREE HEBREWS ARE QUICKLY BOUND AND THROWN INTO THE RAGING FIRE.

THE KING IS UPSET BY WHAT DANIEL SAYS, BUT IN TIME HE FORGETS... ONE DAY AS HE WALKS IN HIS PALACE ROOF GARDEN...

LOOK AT THE GREAT CITY **I** HAVE BUILT! LONG AFTER I AM GONE IT WILL BE A TRIBUTE TO **MY** POWER AND MIGHT!

HE TREE YOU DREAMED BOUT IS YOU, O KING-- LL, STRONG, AND PROUD. U SAW THE TREE CUT OWN. THIS MEANS THAT UR POWER AS KING LL BE TAKEN FROM YOU F YOU DO NOT HONOR OD ABOVE YOURSELF.

THE BOASTFUL WORDS ARE SPOKEN, DANIEL'S RNING COMES TRUE. THE KING LOSES HIS MIND-- D FOR SEVEN YEARS HE LIVES LIKE A BEAST OF E FIELD. THEN ONE DAY THE KING REALIZES HE IS NG PUNISHED FOR FAILING TO HONOR GOD.

O GOD OF DANIEL AND THE HEBREWS, I HONOR AND PRAISE THEE, WHOSE KINGDOM IS GREAT AND EVERLASTING-- WHOSE WORK IS TRUTH AND JUSTICE.

INSTANTLY KING NEBUCHADNEZZAR'S MIND IS RESTORED. HE RETURNS TO THE THRONE AND RULES WISELY WITH DANIEL AS HIS ADVISER.

BUT AFTER HIS DEATH THE RULERS WHO FOLLOW HIM TURN AWAY FROM DANIEL. ONE OF THEM, BELSHAZZAR, IS SO SURE OF HIS OWN WISDOM THAT...

HE LAUGHS AT TWO GREAT THREATS TO HIS KINGDOM: ANGRY PRIESTS WHO ARE TURNING AGAINST HIM, AND THE APPROACH OF THE MIGHTY PERSIAN ARMY. INSTEAD, HE PREPARES A GREAT FEAST TO WHICH HE INVITES A THOUSAND GUESTS...

THE PARTY IS AT ITS MERRIEST WHEN SUDDENLY BELSHAZZAR STARES AT A PLACE HIGH ON THE BANQUET WALL. HE TURNS PALE-- HIS HANDS TREMBLE...

LOOK! ON THE WALL! WHAT IS IT? WHAT DOES IT MEAN?

It is midnight! Outside the walls of Babylon the Persian army waits for traitors within to open the city gates. But inside-- in the banquet hall of the palace-- King Belshazzar eats and drinks merrily with his guests. Suddenly he sees a hand write four words on the wall.

MENE MENE TEKEL UPHARSIN

TERRIFIED, BELSHAZZAR CALLS FOR HIS ADVISERS TO EXPLAIN THE WORDS, BUT THEY CANNOT. WHEN THE KING'S MOTHER HEARS THE EXCITEMENT IN THE BANQUET HALL SHE RUSHES TO HER SON.

MY SON, THERE'S A MAN IN YOUR KINGDOM NAMED DANIEL WHO CAN INTERPRET DREAMS. CALL HIM.

DANIEL! YES! YES! BRING HIM HERE AT ONCE!

NOT A SOUND IS HEARD IN THE GREA BANQUET HALL UNTIL DANIEL APPEA BEFORE THE KING.

TELL ME WHAT THOSE WORDS MEAN AND YOU SHALL BE SECOND ONLY TO ME IN ALL BABYLON.

O KING, THE ARE A WARN FROM GOD HAVE BE MEASURED FOUND LACK IN THE QUALI OF A RULER. YO KINGDOM WILL GIVEN TO PERSI

I DON'T BELIEVE YOUR MESSAGE, BUT I'LL KEEP MY PROMISE. HERE, THIS CHAIN MAKES YOU NEXT TO ME IN ALL THE KINGDOM. NOW, ON WITH THE FEAST!

AS BELSHAZZAR SPEAKS, PERSIAN SOLDIE SUDDENLY FILL THE HALL--AND TAKE HI PRISONER.

SOLDIERS WHERE DID T COME FROM? GUARDS! WHE ARE MY GUAR

BEFORE MORNING THE CITY IS IN THE HANDS OF THE ENEMY. BELSHAZZAR IS KILLED. DANIEL IS BROUGHT BEFORE DARIUS, THE COMMANDER, WHO RECOGNIZES DANIEL'S ABILITY AS A LEADER.

YOU WILL RULE OVER MY NOBLES AS LONG AS YOU OBEY ME.

DARIUS FINDS DANIEL VERY WISE AND OFTEN TURNS TO HIM FOR ADVICE.

DARIUS HAS APPOINTED DANIEL RULER OVER ALL OF US.

WE MUST GET RID OF HIM-- AND I KNOW JUST HOW TO DO IT!

O KING, YOUR NOBLES, WHO HONOR YOU ABOVE ALL, BEG YOU TO SIGN THIS LAW SO THAT **EVERYONE** WILL HONOR YOU. IT FORBIDS ANYONE TO BOW DOWN TO ANY GOD OR MAN BUT YOU, FOR THIRTY DAYS.

IF YOU WANT SUCH A LAW, I'LL SIGN IT.

529

e Lions' Den

M DANIEL 6:16–28

LOOK! DANIEL OESN'T SEEM O BE AFRAID.

HE WILL BE WHEN HE GETS TO THE LIONS' DEN. OUR PLAN TO GET RID OF HIM IS WORKING PERFECTLY.

KING DARIUS HAS BEEN TRICKED BY JEALOUS NOBLES INTO SIGNING A LAW THAT CONDEMNS DANIEL TO DEATH.

EW MINUTES LATER DANIEL, WHO BROKE THE KING'S LAW PRAYING TO GOD, IS CAST INTO THE LIONS' DEN.

MAY THE GOD HOM YOU SERVE ROTECT YOU.

SEAL THE DEN WITH A STONE SO THAT EVERYONE WILL KNOW I AM ENFORCING THE LAW.

IF ONLY I COULD CHANGE THIS ONE LAW TO SAVE MY FRIEND.

THAT NIGHT THE KING CAN NEITHER EAT NOR SLEEP. HE PACES UP AND DOWN HIS ROOM -- THINKING OF DANIEL.

AT DAYBREAK HE RUSHES TO THE LIONS' DEN.

ROLL AWAY THAT STONE!

DANIEL! DANIEL! DID YOUR GOD PROTECT YOU?

MY GOD HAS SHUT THE LIONS' MOUTHS!

THE KING IS OVERJOYED, AND ORDERS A ROPE THROWN DOWN, AND DANIEL IS PULLED OUT OF THE DEN. THEN HE SENDS FOR THE NOBLES WHO PLOTTED DANIEL'S DEATH.

YOU SENT DANIEL TO THE LIONS -- NOW WE'LL SEE HOW **YOU** LIKE IT!

GUARDS! THROW THEM INTO THE DEN!

EN DARIUS ISSUES A DECREE...

I, DARIUS, COMMAND ALL PEOPLE IN THIS KINGDOM TO HONOR THE GOD THAT DANIEL WORSHIPS AND SERVES.

AND FOR THE REST OF HIS LIFE, DANIEL HELPS TO RULE BABYLON, THE COUNTRY HE ENTERED AS A CAPTIVE. AGAINST ALL ODDS, HE BOLDLY STANDS FOR GOD-- AND GOD REWARDS HIM.

Twelve Men of God

FROM THE MINOR PROPHETS

THE LAST TWELVE BOOKS OF THE OLD TESTAMENT ARE CALLED THE MINOR PROPHETS. EACH IS NAMED FOR A MA WHOM GOD CALLED TO SPEAK FOR HIM AT A CH TIME IN THE HISTORY OF ISRAEL AND JUD

HOSEA -- the Prophet of Lov

HOSEA LOVES HIS WIFE, GOMER, MUCH. BUT ONE DAY SHE RUNS A HOSEA IS BROKENHEARTED. THEN DENLY HE SEES THAT THE PEOPL ISRAEL HAVE TREATED GOD THE GOMER HAS TREATED HIM. GO HIS PEOPLE, BUT THEY HAVE RU AWAY TO WORSHIP IDOLS.

CAN GOD FORGIVE THEM? "YES HOSEA SAYS, "FOR I CAN FORGI GOMER, AND GOD'S LOVE IS GREA THAN MINE."

"GOD LOVES YOU. HE WILL FORC YOUR SINS IF YOU CONFESS THEM WORSHIP HIM." THIS IS HOSEA'S ME TO THE PEOPLE OF ISRAEL.

AMOS -- and the Crooked Wal

JOEL -- and the Plague of Locusts

LIKE A MIGHTY ARMY DESTROYING EVERY-THING IN ITS PATH, MILLIONS OF LOCUSTS SWARM OVER THE LAND OF JUDAH. THEY DEVOUR THE CROPS--LEAVING ONLY BARREN FIELDS BEHIND.

"WHAT WILL WE DO?" THE PEOPLE CRY.

THE PROPHET JOEL ANSWERS: "REPENT OF YOUR SINS. SEEK GOD'S HELP, AND HE WILL RESTORE THE LAND."

THEN HE ADDS THIS PROMISE: "ONE DAY GOD WILL SEND HIS HOLY SPIRIT INTO THE HEARTS OF HIS PEOPLE."

AMOS, A SHEPHERD OF JUDAH, IS W ING HIS SHEEP WHEN GOD CALLS HIM DANGEROUS JOB. "GO," GOD SAYS, "-NEIGHBORING COUNTRY OF ISRAEL A TELL THE PEOPLE THAT THEY ARE GC TO BE PUNISHED FOR THEIR SINS."

WITHOUT PROTESTING, AMOS ACCEF THE JOB AND GOES TO THE CITY OF IN ISRAEL.

"PREPARE TO MEET THY GOD," HE TE THE PEOPLE OF ISRAEL, "FOR YOU ARE CROOKED WALL THAT MUST BE DESTROY FORE A NEW ONE CAN BE BUILT."

OBADIAH --
the Angry Prophet

JONAH --
the Man Who Ran Away

BADIAH IS ANGRY AT JUDAH'S NEIGHBOR, NATION OF EDOM. "YOU CHEERED," HE S TO EDOM, "WHEN BABYLON DESTROYED JSALEM. YOU HELPED TO ROB THE CITY TS TREASURES. YOU CAPTURED THE PLE AS THEY TRIED TO ESCAPE AND TURNED M OVER TO THE ENEMY."

EN HE PREDICTS EDOM'S PUNISHMENT: AUSE YOUR CAPITAL CITY IS PROTECTED ROCKY CLIFFS, YOU THINK IT CANNOT DESTROYED. BUT IT CAN! AND IT L -- AS WILL EVERY NATION THAT OBEYS GOD."

NINEVEH IS ONE OF THE MOST WICKED CITIES IN THE WORLD. SO, WHEN GOD TELLS JONAH TO GO TO NINEVEH WITH A MESSAGE TO SAVE THE CITY FROM ITS ENEMIES, JONAH RUNS THE OTHER WAY.

BUT AFTER A LESSON FROM GOD, JONAH OBEYS. HE TELLS NINEVEH TO REPENT OF ITS SINS -- AND HE PREACHES HIS MESSAGE SO SUCCESSFULLY THAT THE CITY DOES REPENT AND IS SAVED FROM DESTRUCTION.

THE MESSAGE OF THE BOOK OF JONAH IS THIS: GOD LOVES ALL PEOPLE. THOSE WHO KNOW GOD MUST TELL OTHERS ABOUT HIM.

MICAH --
Champion of the Poor

NAHUM
Condemns a City

ICAH, A SMALL-TOWN PROPHET, IS A MPION OF THE POOR. HE DARES TO CON- IN THE WEALTHY LEADERS OF JUDAH ISRAEL.

OU HATE JUSTICE," HE SHOUTS, "AND YOU RESS THE POOR. BECAUSE YOU DO, AH AND ISRAEL HAVE BECOME SO WEAK CORRUPT THAT THEY WILL BE DESTROYED." HEN THE PEOPLE ASK WHAT GOD EXPECTS M TO DO, MICAH ANSWERS: "DO JUSTLY, E MERCY, AND WALK HUMBLY WITH GOD."

ND TO THOSE WHO WILL LISTEN HE MAKES ONDERFUL PROMISE: "IN THE LITTLE TOWN BETHLEHEM A SAVIOR WILL BE BORN--A SAVIOR OSE KINGDOM OF PEACE WILL LAST FOREVER."

WHEN THE PROPHET JONAH WARNED NINEVEH OF ITS WICKEDNESS, THE CITY REPENTED -- AND WAS SPARED.

NOW, ONE HUNDRED AND FIFTY YEARS LATER, ANOTHER PROPHET, NAHUM, IS CALLED TO CONDEMN NINEVEH FOR RETURN- ING TO A LIFE OF SIN.

"THE LORD IS SLOW TO ANGER," NAHUM TELLS THE CITY, "BUT HE IS NOT BLIND. HE WILL NOT LET THE WICKED GO UNPUNISHED."

THIS TIME THE CITY IS NOT SPARED-- THE ARMIES OF BABYLON SO COMPLETELY DESTROY NINEVEH THAT IT IS NEVER REBUILT.

HABAKKUK-- The Man Who Asks Questions

HABAKKUK IS A MAN WHO ASKS QUESTIONS-- OF GOD.

HABAKKUK: THE PEOPLE OF JUDAH ARE GETTING MORE WICKED EVERY DAY. HOW LONG WILL THEY GO UNPUNISHED?

GOD: NOT FOR LONG. THE BABYLONIANS ARE COMING. I AM USING THEM TO TEACH JUDAH THAT EVIL MUST BE DESTROYED.

HABAKKUK: THE BABYLONIANS? AREN'T THEY MORE WICKED THAN JUDAH?

GOD: YES, BUT HAVE FAITH. IN TIME YOU WILL UNDERSTAND MY PLANS.

IN THE MIDST OF ALL THE EVIL AROUND HIM, HABAKKUK IS COMFORTED IN KNOWING THAT GOD IS IN CHARGE OF THE WORLD. "GOD IS IN HIS HOLY TEMPLE," HABAKKUK SAYS, "AND NO MATTER WHAT HAPPENS, I AM NOT AFRAID, FOR THE LORD IS MY STRENGTH."

ZECHARIAH and the Triumphal Entry

ZECHARIAH IS A FRIEND OF HAGGAI AND WORKS WITH HIM TO REBUILD THE TEMPLE IN JERUSALEM.

ZEPHANIAH: Repent or Die

"THE DAY OF THE LORD IS AT HAND," ZEPHANIAH WARNED JUDAH. "GOD WILL PUNISH ALL NATIONS OF THE EARTH THAT HAVE DISOBEYED HIM. NEITHER GOLD NOR SILVER WILL BE ABLE TO DELIVER THOSE WHO HAVE TURNED FROM GOD."

ZEPHANIAH PLEADS WITH HIS PEOPLE TO REPENT AND SEEK GOD'S FORGIVENESS. "THOSE WHO DO," HE PROMISES, "WILL LIVE IN PEACE UNDER THE RULE OF GOD."

HAGGAI -- A Temple Builder

WHEN THE HEBREWS FIRST RETURN TO JERUSALEM--AFTER YEARS OF CAPTIVITY IN BABYLON--THEIR FIRST THOUGHT IS TO REBUILD THE TEMPLE. THEY START-- BUT THEY SOON GET DISCOURAGED AND QUIT. FOR FIFTEEN YEARS NOTHING IS DONE.

GOD SPEAKS TO HAGGAI AND HE TAKES THE MESSAGE TO THE PEOPLE.

"BUILD GOD'S TEMPLE," HE PREACHES. AND IN FOUR YEARS IT IS BUILT!

MALACHI -- The Final Warning

THE PEOPLE OF JUDAH HAVE RETURNED T JERUSALEM FROM CAPTIVITY IN BABYLON-- THE TEMPLE HAS BEEN REBUILT. BUT STILL THEY ARE UNHAPPY. AND MALACHI TELLS THEM WHY--

"YOU DO NOT SHOW RESPECT TO GOD. YO WOULD NOT DARE BRING CHEAP GIFTS TO THE GOVERNOR. YET YOU BRING CHEAP AND FAULTY OFFERINGS TO GOD."

"GOD KNOWS THOSE WHO ARE FAITHFUL TO HIM. HE WILL REWARD THEM. BUT THE UNFAITHFUL WILL PERISH AS STUBBLE IN TH BURNING FIELDS AFTER THE HARVEST."

The Final Message FROM MALACHI

THE VOICE OF THE PROPHET MALACHI IS THE LAST TO BE HEARD IN THE STORY OF THE OLD TESTAMENT. BUT BEFORE WE HEAR HIS FINAL MESSAGE--WHICH IS FOUND IN THE BOOK THAT BEARS HIS NAME -- LET US BRIEFLY REVIEW THE HISTORY OF THE PEOPLE TO WHOM HE SPOKE.

IN OUR STORY OF THE BIBLE WE HAVE BEEN TRACING THE LIVES OF THE PEOPLE WHO DESCENDED FROM ABRAHAM. GOD CALLED HIM TO BE THE FATHER OF A NATION THAT WOULD TEACH THE WORLD ABOUT THE ONE TRUE GOD. ABRAHAM OBEYED GOD AND WENT TO CANAAN WHERE HIS FAMILY LIVED AND GREW. HIS GRANDSON, JACOB (OR ISRAEL), BECAME THE FATHER OF 12 SONS. THEIR FAMILIES WERE CALLED THE 12 TRIBES OF ISRAEL.

WHEN A FAMINE STRUCK CANAAN THE TRIBES WENT DOWN TO EGYPT WHERE THEY LIVED FOR MANY YEARS. BUT AFTER A TIME THE EGYPTIANS TURNED AGAINST THE ISRAELITES AND FORCED THEM TO WORK AS SLAVES. THE PEOPLE CRIED TO GOD FOR HELP...

GOD HEARD THE CRIES OF HIS PEOPLE AND SENT MOSES TO LEAD THEM OUT OF EGYPT -- ACROSS THE RED SEA -- AND BACK TO THE PROMISED LAND OF CANAAN. WITH GOD'S HELP THEY CONQUERED THE LAND AND MADE IT THEIR HOME. FOR MANY YEARS JUDGES RULED OVER THE TRIBES OF ISRAEL, BUT THE PEOPLE LONGED FOR A KING.

GOD HEARD THEIR PLEA AND GAVE THEM A KING, SAUL. HE WAS FOLLOWED BY DAVID, WHO BUILT ISRAEL INTO A POWERFUL NATION. BUT IN THE YEARS THAT FOLLOWED, THE PEOPLE TURNED FROM GOD TO WORSHIP IDOLS. THEY QUARRELED AMONG THEMSELVES, AND THE NATION WAS SPLIT INTO TWO KINGDOMS -- ISRAEL IN THE NORTH AND JUDAH IN THE SOUTH. WEAK AND CORRUPT, THEY WERE OPEN TO THE ATTACKS OF STRONGER NATIONS AROUND THEM.

...ME BOTH KINGDOMS WERE ...NQUERED. MANY OF THE PEOPLE ...E TAKEN AWAY TO FOREIGN LANDS. ...R TO YEARS OF CAPTIVITY, THE ...S WERE ALLOWED TO RETURN TO ...AH AND REBUILD JERUSALEM.

BUT STILL THE PEOPLE WERE UNHAPPY, AND THE PROPHET MALACHI TELLS THEM WHY...

DO YOU CALL THAT GOD'S SHARE OF YOUR GRAIN? HOW CAN YOU BE HAPPY WHEN YOU ROB GOD? BRING YOUR RIGHTFUL GIFTS AND OFFERINGS TO GOD, AND YOU WILL PROSPER.

BUT PEOPLE WHO CHEAT AND BRING NONE OF THEIR GRAIN TO THE TEMPLE PROSPER MORE THAN WE DO.

...OD KNOWS WHO ...VES AND OBEYS ...M. HE WILL REWARD ...E RIGHTEOUS AND ...NISH THE WICKED.

WHEN WILL HE DO THIS?

FIRST, GOD WILL SEND A PROPHET AS HIS MESSENGER TO GET THE PEOPLE READY. THEN THE LORD HIMSELF WILL COME AND DELIVER HIS OWN PEOPLE FROM EVIL. BUT HE WILL DESTROY THE WICKED WHO DISOBEY.

..., WITH A WARNING-- ...A PROMISE -- THE OLD ...TAMENT ENDS. BUT ...THE JEWS THE QUESTION ...AINS: WHEN WILL THE ...AT DELIVERER COME?

The Years of Waiting

BETWEEN THE OLD TESTAMENT AND THE NEW TESTAMENT

THE LAND OF JUDAH IS STILL UNDER THE RULE OF THE
PERSIANS WHEN ALEXANDER, THE YOUNG KING OF MACEDONIA,
SETS OUT TO CONQUER THE WORLD.
RIDING HIS FAMOUS HORSE, BUCEPHALUS,
HE LEADS HIS ARMY AGAINST THE COUNTRIES
OF THE MIGHTY PERSIAN EMPIRE. ONE
AFTER ANOTHER THEY FALL, AND IN 332 B.C....

ON TO JERUSALEM!

HE CITY WAITS IN TERROR! BUT WHEN
EXANDER'S ARMY COMES IN SIGHT, THE
GH PRIEST OPENS THE GATES AND LEADS
PROCESSION OUT TO GREET THE
NQUEROR. ALEXANDER RECOGNIZES
E PRIEST AS A MAN OF GOD AND BOWS
EFORE HIM. THEN HE ENTERS THE CITY
D WORSHIPS IN THE TEMPLE.
DER THE RULE OF THIS DARING
UNG WARRIOR THE JEWS ARE
LOWED TO KEEP THEIR OWN
LIGIOUS CUSTOMS -- AND
EY ARE HAPPY.

JT -- SUDDENLY -- ALEXANDER DIES...
D THE GIANT EMPIRE IS DIVIDED
ONG HIS GENERALS. WHEN THE
LER OVER JUDAH COMMANDS THE
OPLE TO WORSHIP AN IDOL, A PRIEST
AYS THE KING'S MESSENGER. THIS
LD ACT STIRS ALL JUDAH TO REVOLT...

UNDER THE LEADERSHIP OF THE PRIEST'S
BRAVE FAMILY (KNOWN AS THE MACCABEES),
THE JEWS DRIVE THE ENEMY FROM THEIR
LAND. ONE OF THE FIRST THINGS THEY DO
IS TO REDEDICATE THE TEMPLE, WHICH THE
ENEMY HAD USED TO WORSHIP IDOLS. FOR A
HUNDRED GLORIOUS YEARS JUDAH IS FREE!

BUT ONCE AGAIN A CONQUEROR COMES FROM ACROSS THE MEDITERRANEAN SEA. ROMAN SHIPS AND ROMAN SOLDIERS CONQUER EVERYTHING IN THEIR PATH. AND IN 63 B.C. THE MIGHTY ROMAN ARMY TAKES JERUSALEM. AGAIN JUDAH IS DOWN-- AND THIS TIME IT IS TOO WEAK TO RISE.

AFTER A TIME THE ROMANS APPOINT A MAN NAMED HEROD TO RULE THE JEWS. A CRAFTY, CRUEL MAN, HE TRIES TO WIN THEIR FAVOR BY BUILDING THEM A NEW AND MORE BEAUTIFUL TEMPLE, BUT THEY DESPISE HIM. BITTERLY THE JEWS CRY OUT: "WHEN WILL GOD SEND THE DELIVERER PROMISED TO US BY THE PROPHETS OF OLD?"

Next week: THE WORLD INTO WHICH JESUS CAME

STORIES FROM THE

New Testament

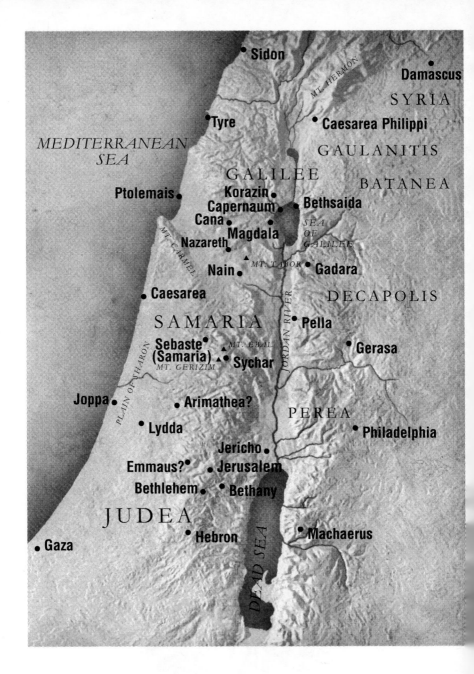

New Testament
Palestine

e Life of Jesus

м MATTHEW, MARK, LUKE, AND JOHN

THE FIRST FOUR BOOKS OF THE NEW TESTAMENT ARE CALLED THE GOSPELS, WHICH MEANS "GOOD NEWS"--ABOUT JESUS: HIS LIFE, TEACHINGS, DEATH, AND URRECTION. BECAUSE THE BOOKS ARE ALIKE AANY WAYS, THE FACTS HAVE BEEN COMBINED E TO TELL ONE STORY.

TO EVERYONE, JESUS SAYS-- I AM THE WAY... NO ONE CAN COME TO GOD BUT BY ME.

A Secret from God

FROM LUKE 1:23–55

SO THE BABY IS NAMED ACCORDING TO THE INSTRUCTIONS OF THE ANGEL-- AND AT THAT MOMENT ZACHARIAS IS ABLE TO SPEAK.

BLESSED BE THE LORD GOD OF ISRAEL; FOR HE HAS VISITED AND REDEEMED HIS PEOPLE... AND YOU, CHILD, SHALL BE CALLED THE PROPHET OF THE HIGHEST: FOR YOU WILL GO BEFORE THE FACE OF THE LORD TO PREPARE HIS WAYS.

ON THEIR WAY HOME THE PEOPLE TALK ABOUT THE STRANGE EVENTS CONNECTED WITH THE BIRTH OF ZACHARIAS' SON.

THE NAME JOHN --WHAT DOES IT MEAN?

IT MEANS, "GOD HAS BEEN GRACIOUS." GOD MUST HAVE A SPECIAL PURPOSE FOR THAT CHILD.

HOME AGAIN IN NAZARETH, MARY THINKS ABOUT THE PURPOSE GOD HAS FOR HER CHILD. BUT JOSEPH, THE CARPENTER TO WHOM SHE IS ENGAGED, DOES NOT UNDERSTAND WHAT THE ANGEL HAS TOLD MARY ABOUT THE SON THAT IS TO BE BORN. ONE NIGHT AN ANGEL COMES TO HIM.

GOD HAS CHOSEN MARY TO BE THE MOTHER OF HIS SON. YOU MUST CALL THE CHILD JESUS, FOR HE WILL SAVE HIS PEOPLE FROM THEIR SINS.

EARLY THE NEXT MORNING, JOSEPH HURRIES TO SEE MARY.

O MARY, IN A DREAM LAST NIGHT AN ANGEL TOLD ME THAT YOU ARE TO BE THE MOTHER OF THE LORD. I SEE NOW THAT GOD HAS CHOSEN ME TO TAKE CARE OF YOU AND YOUR SON.

SO MARY AND JOSEPH ARE MARRIED, AND MOVE INTO JOSEPH'S HOUSE BESIDE THE CARPENTER SHOP. IN THE EVENINGS WHEN THE DAY'S WORK IS DONE, THEY REST ON THE ROOF TOP--WATCHING THE STARS AND TALKING ABOUT GOD'S PROMISE TO MARY.

BUT ONE DAY JOSEPH COMES HOME FROM THE MARKET PLACE WITH BAD NEWS: CAESAR AUGUSTUS HAS ORDERED EVERYONE TO REGISTER HIS NAME AND PROPERTY. SINCE JOSEPH AND MARY ARE DESCENDANTS OF KING DAVID, JOSEPH MUST GO TO BETHLEHEM, THE CITY OF DAVID.

BUT I CAN'T GO NOW-- AND LEAVE YOU...

YOU MUST GO, JOSEPH, AND I'LL GO WITH YOU. DON'T WORRY-- GOD WILL BE WITH US.

EAGER TO HAVE THE REGISTRATION OVER, THEY SET OUT. SOON OTHERS JOIN THEM ON THE WAY. BUT THE JOURNEY TAKES SEVERAL DAYS, AND AFTER A WHILE JOSEPH AND MARY FALL BEHIND-- UNTIL THEY ARE AMONG THE LAST TO REACH BETHLEHEM.

WE HAVE TRAVELED A LONG WAY AND MY WIFE IS VERY TIRED. I NEED A ROOM.

I'M SORRY, BUT BETHLEHEM IS CROWDED THESE DAYS. THERE'S NO ROOM HERE.

THAT SAME NIGHT SOME SHEPHERDS ARE WATCHING THEIR SHEEP ON THE HILLS OUTSIDE THE CITY. THEY TALK OF THE CROWDS THAT HAVE COME TO BETHLEHEM.

I'VE HEARD THAT CAESAR AUGUSTUS ORDERED THIS REGISTRATION SO THAT HE CAN COLLECT MORE TAXES. WILL WE NEVER BE FREE FROM THESE FOREIGN TYRANTS?

GOD HAS PROMISED US A DELIVERER. AND ALL MY LIFE I HAVE PRAYED THAT I WOULD LIVE TO SEE HIM.

SUDDENLY-- A GREAT LIGHT SHINES AROUND THE SHEPHERDS.

WHAT IS IT?

O GOD, PROTECT US.

FEAR NOT; FOR I BRING YOU GOOD NEWS OF GREAT JOY FOR ALL THE PEOPLE. FOR TO YOU IS BORN IN THE CITY OF DAVID A SAVIOR, WHO IS CHRIST THE LORD. YOU WILL FIND THE BABY LYING IN A MANGER.

THEN THE SKY IS FILLED WITH A GREAT CHOIR OF ANGELS -- SINGING THEIR PRAISE TO GOD.

Glory to God in the highest, and on earth peace, good will toward men.

THE ANGELS LEAVE -- THE BEAUTIFUL LIGHT DISAPPEARS. ONCE AGAIN IT IS DARK AND STILL ON THE BETHLEHEM HILLS.

I CAN SCARCELY BELIEVE WHAT I HAVE SEEN AND HEARD. GOD HAS SENT OUR DELIVERER, OUR SAVIOR--**TONIGHT**!

AND TO THINK HE SENT HIS ANGEL TO TELL POOR SHEPHERDS LIKE US!

THE ANGEL SAID WE WOULD FIND THE SAVIOR IN A MANGER. LET'S GO TO BETHLEHEM AND SEE HIM.

EAGERLY--AND WITH AWE AND WONDER--THE SHEPHERDS HURRY TO BETHLEHEM. INSIDE THE GATE THEY TURN TOWARD THE INN...

LOOK-- THERE'S A LIGHT IN THE STABLE!

OUR SAVIOR IS HERE! AND I'M GOING TO SEE HIM!

A King Is Born

FROM LUKE 2:7, 16–20;
MATTHEW 2:1–8

IT IS A STRANGE AND HOLY NIGHT. WHILE THE CROWDED CITY OF BETHLEHEM SLEEPS, THE SON OF GOD IS BORN. LOVINGLY, MARY WRAPS HER BABY IN SWADDLING CLOTHES AND LAYS HIM IN A MANGER... AND THERE THE SHEPHERDS FIND HIM.

AN ANGEL TOLD US THAT THE SAVIOR HAS BEEN BORN. MAY WE SEE HIM?

MARY NODS, AND JOSEPH TURNS THE LAMP A LITTLE SO THAT ITS LIGHT FALLS ON THE MANGER. REVERENTLY THE SHEPHERDS LOOK AT THE BABY JESUS.

O GOD, WE THANK YOU FOR SENDING OUR SAVIOR, AND FOR LETTING US SEE HIM.

QUIETLY, THE SHEPHERDS TURN AWAY...

558

WHEN THE WISE MEN INQUIRE AT THE PALACE, KING HEROD-- WHO HAS COMMITTED MORE THAN ONE MURDER TO PROTECT HIS THRONE-- IS FRIGHTENED. HE CALLS FOR THE CHIEF PRIESTS AND SCRIBES.

IS THERE ANYTHING IN THE SACRED BOOKS TELLING ABOUT A BABY WHO WILL BECOME KING OF THE JEWS?

YES, THE SCRIPTURES SAY HE WILL BE BORN IN BETHLEHEM.

SECRETLY HEROD SENDS FOR THE WISE MEN AND ASKS THEM WHEN THEY SAW THE STAR AND HOW LONG IT TOOK THEM TO COME TO JERUSALEM. THEN HE SPEAKS VERY SLYLY.

LOOK FOR THE CHILD IN BETHLEHEM. WHEN YOU FIND HIM, COME BACK AND TELL ME WHERE HE IS SO THAT I MAY WORSHIP HIM, TOO.

AND WHEN I FIND THAT CHILD, I'LL KILL HIM. NO ONE IS GOING TO BE KING OF THE JEWS BUT ME!

light in the Night

om MATTHEW 2:9–14

OLLOWING HEROD'S INSTRUCTIONS, THE WISE MEN SET OUT FOR BETHLEHEM. AS THEY AVE JERUSALEM, THEY AGAIN SEE THE STAR EY HAD SEEN IN THE EAST. IT LEADS THEM O BETHLEHEM, AND THERE...

LOOK! THE STAR HAS STOPPED ABOVE THAT HOUSE!

OUR JOURNEY IS FINISHED! SOON WE'LL SEE THE CHILD WHO IS TO BE KING OF THE JEWS!

EOPLE IN BETHLEHEM ARE SURPRISED TO SEE THE IMPORTANT-OOKING STRANGERS STOP BEFORE THE HOUSE WHERE JOSEPH AND ARY NOW LIVE. WHEN THE WISE MEN TELL THEIR REASON FOR OMING, THEY ARE INVITED INSIDE. THERE THEY KNEEL BEFORE HE BABY JESUS.

WE HAVE COME A LONG WAY TO WORSHIP THE ROYAL CHILD.

AND TO BRING HIM GIFTS OF GOLD, FRANKINCENSE, AND MYRRH.

THAT NIGHT AT THE INN THE WISE MEN MAKE PLANS FOR THEIR RETURN HOME.

I'M GLAD THAT WE CAN GO BACK TO JERUSALEM AND TELL KING HEROD WHERE HE CAN FIND THE BABY.

THE NEXT MORNING...

I HAD A DREAM—

SO DID I! IN MY DREAM GOD WARNED US NOT TO RETURN TO JERUSALEM BECAUSE HEROD IS JEALOUS AND WANTS TO KILL THE CHILD.

I HAD THE SAME DREAM! HEROD WILL FIND OUT NOTHING FROM US. WE'LL GO HOME BY ANOTHER ROUTE.

563

Boy in the Temple

FROM MATTHEW 2:16–23; LUKE 2:40–52

FEARING THAT THE BABY JESUS WILL TAKE HIS THRONE, HEROD ORDERS ALL BOY BABIES IN BETHLEHEM KILLED. BUT JOSEPH AND MARY ESCAPE WITH JESUS TO EGYPT. AFTER A FEW MONTHS, AN ANGEL TELLS JOSEPH THAT HEROD IS DEAD AND THAT IT IS NOW SAFE TO TAKE JESUS HOME. IN NAZARETH...

MARY! AND JOSEPH! HOW GOOD TO HAVE YOU BACK. WHAT IS THE BABY'S NAME?

HIS NAME IS JESUS.

JESUS. THE NAME MEANS "GOD SAVES." WE NEED SOMEONE TO SAVE US FROM THE TYRANTS WHO RULE PALESTINE.

JOSEPH SETS UP HIS CARPENTER SHOP--AND AS THE YEARS PASS, JESUS LEARNS TO HELP HIM. WHEN THE DAY'S WORK IS OVER JESUS LISTENS TO THE ELDERS OF THE TOWN...

IN THE DAYS OF KING DAVID, **WE** WERE THE RULERS.

YES, BUT IN THOSE DAYS PEOPLE OBEYED GOD. TODAY, TOO MANY IGNORE HIS LAWS.

BUT JOSEPH AND MARY OBEY GOD'S COMMANDMENTS, AND TEACH JESUS TO OBEY THEM, TOO. EACH SPRING THEY ATTEND THE PASSOVER FEAST IN JERUSALEM TO THANK GOD FOR DELIVERING THEIR ANCESTORS FROM SLAVERY IN EGYPT. IN THE CARAVAN THAT MAKES THE ANNUAL JOURNEY FROM NAZARETH, THERE IS NO ONE MORE EXCITED THAN JESUS.

THIS YEAR, AS HE WORSHIPS IN THE TEMPLE, JESUS THINKS OF MANY QUESTIONS HE WOULD LIKE TO ASK THE TEACHERS OF THE JEWS.

AFTER THE FEAST IS OVER, THE PEOPLE SET OUT FOR THEIR HOMES. THAT NIGHT WHEN THEY MAKE CAMP...

JOSEPH, WHERE IS JESUS?

HE'S WITH HIS FRIENDS. I'LL FIND HIM.

BUT NO ONE HAS SEEN JESUS. FRANTICALLY, JOSEPH AND MARY TURN BACK TO JERUSALEM. THEY SEARCH THE INNS, THE CROWDED STREETS, AND FINALLY THE TEMPLE.

JESUS! WE HAVE BEEN LOOKING FOR YOU EVERYWHERE.

BUT, MOTHER, DIDN'T YOU KNOW THAT I WOULD BE IN MY FATHER'S HOUSE?

WE ARE SURPRISED AT YOUR SON'S KNOWLEDGE OF THE SCRIPTURES. HIS QUESTIONS SHOW THAT HE HAS THOUGHT A GREAT DEAL ABOUT GOD AND HIS LAWS FOR MAN.

JESUS IS NOT LIKE ANYONE ELSE. EVEN I, HIS MOTHER, DO NOT UNDERSTAND EVERYTHING ABOUT HIM.

JESUS RETURNS WITH JOSEPH AND MARY TO NAZARETH, WHERE HE LIVES UNTIL HE IS 30 YEARS OLD. HE GROWS TALL AND STRONG, AND IS WELL LIKED BY THE PEOPLE OF NAZARETH. GOD IS ALSO PLEASED WITH HIM. SEVENTY MILES AWAY, IN THE WILDERNESS NEAR THE DEAD SEA, A MAN OF THE SAME AGE PREPARES FOR AN ASSIGNMENT THAT WAS PLANNED FOR HIM -- EVEN BEFORE HE WAS BORN.

Tempted!

FROM LUKE 3:1—4:4

As soon as John, the cousin of Jesus, is old enough to understand, his father tells him: "Before you were born, God planned for you to serve him in a special way." John grows up preparing to serve God. And after the death of his parents he goes into the wilderness to pray and study. There God calls him to begin his work.

O GOD, I'M READY TO PREPARE THE WAY FOR THE COMING OF THE SAVIOR.

John puts his words into action and begins preaching along the Jordan River.

REPENT OF YOUR SINS AND BE BAPTIZED, FOR GOD'S KINGDOM IS CLOSE AT HAND.

NEWS SPREADS FAR AND WIDE ABOUT THE MAN WHO LOOKS AND SPEAKS LIKE A PROPHET OF OLD. CROWDS COME OUT FROM JERUSALEM TO HEAR THE MAN CALLED JOHN THE BAPTIST. SOME ARE ONLY CURIOUS, BUT JOHN KNOWS THEIR THOUGHTS.

DO YOU THINK THAT JUST BECAUSE YOU ARE JEWS YOU WILL BE ALLOWED IN GOD'S KINGDOM? NO, YOU MUST REPENT—

THE SCOFFERS TURN AWAY, BUT MANY PEOPLE LISTEN EAGERLY. ONE DAY A CROWD GATHERS AT THE JORDAN RIVER.

ARE YOU THE SAVIOR GOD HAS PROMISED US?

NO. I BAPTIZE WITH WATER, BUT HE WILL BAPTIZE WITH THE HOLY SPIRIT OF GOD. PREPARE YOURSELVES; THE SAVIOR IS COMING!

UNKNOWN TO JOHN, THE VERY ONE HE IS TALKING ABOUT IS IN THE CROWD. JESUS HAS COME DOWN FROM NAZARETH TO HEAR HIM. HE ASKS TO BE BAPTIZED.

WHY DO YOU COME TO **ME** FOR BAPTISM? IT IS **I** WHO NEED TO BE BAPTIZED BY YOU.

JOHN, THIS IS WHAT GOD WOULD WANT US TO DO.

SO JOHN BAPTIZES JESUS. AND WHEN JESUS COMES UP OUT OF THE WATER, THE SPIRIT OF GOD DESCENDS LIKE A DOVE UPON HIM. THEN A VOICE FROM HEAVEN SPEAKS:

THIS IS MY BELOVED SON IN WHOM I AM WELL PLEASED.

THE CROWDS DO NOT UNDERSTAND WHAT HAS HAPPENED-- THEY GO HOME, NOT REALIZING THAT THEY HAVE SEEN THEIR SAVIOR. JOHN CONTINUES PREACHING -- REPENT OF YOUR SINS, FOR THE KINGDOM OF GOD IS COMING SOON.

TO JESUS, THE WORDS OF HIS FATHER ARE A SIGN OF APPROVAL, AND THE GIFT OF THE HOLY SPIRIT IS AN ASSURANCE OF HELP FOR THE WORK GOD HAS SENT HIM TO DO. HE GOES INTO THE WILDERNESS-- ALONE -- TO THINK ABOUT HIS PLAN FOR ESTABLISHING GOD'S KINGDOM.

AT THE END OF FORTY DAYS, JESUS IS HUNGRY. AS HE THINKS OF FOOD, HE HEARS THE VOICE OF THE DEVIL TEMPTING HIM TO USE HIS DIVINE POWER FOR HIS OWN BENEFIT. "IF YOU ARE REALLY THE SON OF GOD," THE DEVIL SAYS, "TURN THIS STONE INTO BREAD. AFTER ALL, GOD WOULD NOT WANT HIS BELOVED SON TO BE HUNGRY."

SCRIPTURE SAYS, "MAN SHALL NOT LIVE BY BREAD ALONE, BUT BY THE WORD OF GOD."

THE DEVIL DOESN'T GIVE UP EASILY. HE TRIES AGAIN-- AND THIS TIME WITH A MORE POWERFUL TEMPTATION ...

Victory in the Wilderness

FROM MATTHEW 4:5–11; JOHN 1:35–46

TO PREVENT JESUS FROM CARRYING OUT GOD'S WORK, THE DEVIL TEMPTS HIM TO SEEK EARTHLY POWERS FOR HIMSELF. BUT JESUS REFUSES. THE DEVIL TRIES AGAIN -- THIS TIME HE TEMPTS JESUS TO MAKE HIMSELF POPULAR BY DOING SOMETHING SENSATIONAL.

"LET PEOPLE SEE YOUR DIVINE POWER BY THROWING YOURSELF FROM THE ROOF OF THE TEMPLE," THE DEVIL SAYS. "FOR, IF YOU ARE THE SON OF GOD, HIS ANGELS WILL TAKE CARE OF YOU."

THE SCRIPTURES SAY, "THOU SHALT NOT TEMPT GOD."

HAVING REJECTED EVERY TEMPTATION, JESUS LEAVES THE WILDERNESS AND GOES BACK TO BETHANY BEYOND THE JORDAN.

AS JESUS ENTERS BETHANY, JOHN THE BAPTIST POINTS HIM OUT TO TWO OF HIS OWN DISCIPLES — ANDREW AND JOHN.

THERE IS THE SAVIOR I HAVE BEEN TELLING YOU ABOUT.

THE TWO MEN TURN AND QUICKLY FOLLOW JESUS.

MASTER-- MAY WE TALK WITH YOU?

YES, COME WITH ME TO MY LODGING PLACE.

LISTENING TO JESUS IS SUCH A WONDERFUL EXPERIENCE THAT HOURS GO BY BEFORE ANDREW SUDDENLY REMEMBERS...

MY BROTHER! HE CAME DOWN HERE FROM CAPERNAUM WITH ME TO HEAR JOHN THE BAPTIST. I MUST FIND HIM AND BRING HIM TO SEE YOU.

ANDREW RUNS TO THE HOUSE WHERE HE AND HIS BROTHER ARE STAYING.

SIMON! I HAVE FOUND THE SAVIOR!

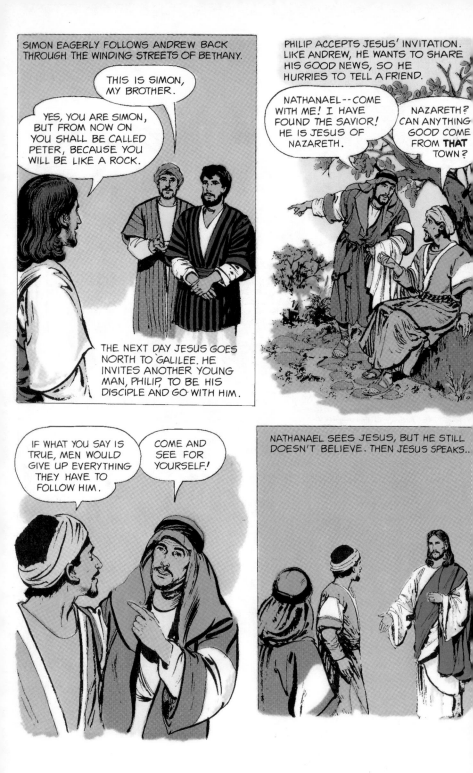

SIMON EAGERLY FOLLOWS ANDREW BACK THROUGH THE WINDING STREETS OF BETHANY.

THIS IS SIMON, MY BROTHER.

YES, YOU ARE SIMON, BUT FROM NOW ON YOU SHALL BE CALLED PETER, BECAUSE YOU WILL BE LIKE A ROCK.

THE NEXT DAY JESUS GOES NORTH TO GALILEE. HE INVITES ANOTHER YOUNG MAN, PHILIP, TO BE HIS DISCIPLE AND GO WITH HIM.

PHILIP ACCEPTS JESUS' INVITATION. LIKE ANDREW, HE WANTS TO SHARE HIS GOOD NEWS, SO HE HURRIES TO TELL A FRIEND.

NATHANAEL -- COME WITH ME! I HAVE FOUND THE SAVIOR! HE IS JESUS OF NAZARETH.

NAZARETH? CAN ANYTHING GOOD COME FROM **THAT** TOWN?

IF WHAT YOU SAY IS TRUE, MEN WOULD GIVE UP EVERYTHING THEY HAVE TO FOLLOW HIM.

COME AND SEE FOR YOURSELF!

NATHANAEL SEES JESUS, BUT HE STILL DOESN'T BELIEVE. THEN JESUS SPEAKS..

Six Jars of Water

FROM JOHN 1:47–51; 2:1–11, 23–25; 3:1–2

PHILIP IS SO EXCITED ABOUT SEEING JESUS THAT HE HURRIES TO TELL A FRIEND. "NATHANAEL, COME WITH ME. I HAVE FOUND THE SAVIOR!" NATHANAEL DOUBTS SUCH NEWS, BUT HE AGREES TO SEE FOR HIMSELF. AS THEY APPROACH JESUS...

BEHOLD, A MAN IN WHOM THERE IS NOTHING DECEITFUL.

HOW DO **YOU** KNOW ANYTHING ABOUT ME?

BEFORE PHILIP CALLED YOU, YOU WERE SITTING UNDER A FIG TREE THINKING ABOUT GOD. I SAW YOU THERE.

YOU **ARE** THE SAVIOR FOR WHOM WE HAVE WAITED SO LONG!

HAVING FOUND HIS SAVIOR, NATHANAEL FORGETS EVERYTHING ELSE AND JOINS JESUS AND HIS FRIENDS AS THEY TRAVEL NORTH TO GALILEE. AT THE CROSSROADS, PETER AND ANDREW TURN OFF TO THEIR HOME NEAR THE SEA OF GALILEE; THE OTHERS GO ON TO CANA.

THE HEADWAITER IS SO SURPRISED WHEN HE TASTES THE WINE THAT HE CALLS THE GROOM AWAY FROM THE FEAST.

SIR, THE BEST WINE IS USUALLY SERVED FIRST. BUT YOU HAVE SAVED THE BEST TO THE LAST.

I'M GLAD IF PEOPLE ARE HAPPY.

WHEN JESUS' DISCIPLES HEAR ABOUT THE MIRACLE, THEY TOO ARE EXCITED. THEY TALK ABOUT IT AS THEY GO DOWN TO JERUSALEM WITH JESUS FOR THE PASSOVER FEAST. THE CITY IS CROWDED WITH PEOPLE WHO HAVE HEARD JOHN THE BAPTIST TELL ABOUT THE COMING OF THE MESSIAH. "HOW WILL WE RECOGNIZE HIM?" THEY ASK.

AS JESUS WALKS THROUGH THE BUSY STREETS, HE HEALS THE LAME AND THE SICK.

I CAN WALK! PRAISE BE TO GOD--THIS MAN HEALED ME!

BECAUSE OF THESE MIRACLES, PEOPLE BEGIN TO ASK: "IS JESUS THE MESSIAH?" ONE NIGHT, AFTER THE STREETS ARE EMPTY, A JUDGE OF THE JEWISH SUPREME COURT STEALS THROUGH THE STREETS OF JERUSALEM ON A SECRET MISSION.

The Judge's Problem

FROM JOHN 3:3—4:6; MARK 6:14–17

NICODEMUS, A JUDGE OF THE JEWISH SUPREME COURT, HAS A PROBLEM HE CAN'T SOLVE. PEOP IN JERUSALEM ARE ASKING, "IS JESUS THE SAVIOR WHO WILL OVERTHROW THE ROMANS AND SET UP GOD'S KINGDOM IN PALESTINE?"

NICODEMUS ISN'T SURE, AND HE WONDERS: "WHAT MUST A MAN DO TO ENTER GOD'S KINGDOM?" HE HAS TO FIND OUT. SO SECRETLY-- BY NIGHT-- HE GOES TO THE PLACE WHERE JESUS IS STAYING, AND JESUS ANSWERS HIS QUESTION EVEN BEFORE HE ASKS IT...

A MAN MUST BE BORN OVER AGAIN TO ENTER GOD'S KINGDOM.

BORN AGAIN? HOW CAN I BE BORN AGAIN WHEN I AM OLD?

YOU WERE BORN ONCE OF EARTHLY PARENTS. BUT YOU MUST BE BORN AGAIN OF GOD'S SPIRIT TO LIVE IN GOD'S KINGDOM.

I DON'T UNDERSTAND.

YOU CAN'T SEE THE WIND, BUT YOU CAN SEE WHAT IT DOES. YOU CANNOT SEE THE SPIRIT OF GOD, BUT YOU CAN TELL BY THE WAY A MAN LIVES IF HE HAS BEEN BORN AGAIN AND HAS THE SPIRIT OF GOD IN HIS HEART. GOD LOVES THE WORLD, AND HE HAS SENT ME TO GIVE THIS NEW LIFE TO ALL WHO BELIEVE IN ME.

NICODEMUS GOES AWAY -- STILL PUZZLED, BUT WANTING TO LEARN MORE ABOUT JESUS AND HIS TEACHINGS.

JESUS SEES THAT MANY OF THE PEOPLE IN JERUSALEM ARE NOT READY TO RECEIVE HIM AS THEIR SAVIOR, SO HE LEAVES THE CITY. IN JUDEA HE TELLS THE PEOPLE ABOUT GOD'S KINGDOM AND WHAT THEY MUST DO TO ENTER IT. HERE, THE PEOPLE LISTEN EAGERLY.

THIS TEACHER IS GREATER THAN ALL THE PROPHETS.

NEWS OF JESUS' SUCCESSFUL MINISTRY IN JUDEA REACHES JOHN THE BAPTIST.

I'VE HEARD THAT JESUS IS BECOMING MORE POPULAR EVERY DAY.

THANK GOD, I HAVE FULFILLED MY MISSION OF PREPARING THE WAY FOR HIM. JESUS' INFLUENCE MUST INCREASE, AND MINE DECREASE.

577

WHEN JESUS TELLS HER THAT HE IS THE SAVIOR FROM GOD, SHE BELIEVES HIM AND RUNS BACK TO THE TOWN TO TELL THE WONDERFUL NEWS.

COME! SEE A MAN WHO HAS TOLD ME THINGS ABOUT MY LIFE THAT NO STRANGER COULD KNOW. HE IS THE PROMISED MESSIAH! THE SAVIOR!

WHILE THE WOMAN IS IN THE TOWN, JESUS' DISCIPLES RETURN AND INVITE HIM TO SHARE THE FOOD THEY HAVE BOUGHT.

THANK YOU, BUT NOT NOW-- I HAVE FOOD THAT YOU DON'T KNOW ABOUT.

WHAT DO YOU MEAN?

MY FOOD IS TO DO THE WILL OF HIM WHO SENT ME. LOOK AT THE PEOPLE WHO ARE EAGER TO HEAR WHAT GOD HAS SENT ME TO TELL THEM.

ALTHOUGH THE SAMARITANS HATE JEWS, MANY OF THEM BELIEVE JESUS TO BE THEIR SAVIOR "STAY," THEY PLEAD, "AND TELL US MORE ABOUT GOD AND HIS KINGDOM." JESUS REMAINS FOR TWO DAYS -- THEN GOES ON TO THE REGION OF GALILEE.

BUT--SUDDENLY--JESUS TURNS AND LOOKS INTO THE FACES OF THE MEN AND WOMEN WHO HAVE KNOWN HIM FOR THIRTY YEARS. THEN HE WALKS--SLOWLY--THROUGH THEIR MIDST... AND, STRANGELY, NOT A PERSON DARES TO TOUCH HIM.

FROM NAZARETH JESUS GOES TO CAPERNAUM ON THE SEA OF GALILEE. THERE HE FINDS THE BROTHERS HE MET NEAR THE JORDAN RIVER.

PETER! ANDREW! COME WITH ME, AND I'LL MAKE YOU FISHERS OF MEN.

THEY LEAVE THEIR NETS AND GO AT ONCE WITH JESUS. FARTHER DOWN THE SHORE JESUS SEES TWO MORE FRIENDS --JAMES AND JOHN.

COME WITH ME AND BE MY DISCIPLES.

582

THE PEOPLE ARE AMAZED. BUT THE PHARISEES,* WHO HAVE COME OUT OF CURIOSITY TO HEAR JESUS, ARE ANGRY.

WHO IS THIS MAN WHO PRETENDS TO FORGIVE SINS?

HOW DARE HE ACT AS IF HE IS GOD!

*The Pharisees are a group of Jews who believe in obeying not only the laws God gave to Moses but the hundreds of rules they have made -- such as how far a man can walk on the Sabbath. Because Jesus is more concerned about helping people than obeying their rules, the Pharisees turn against him.

JESUS KNOWS WHAT THE PHARISEES ARE THINKING.

WHICH IS EASIER-- TO SAY TO THE SICK, "YOUR SINS ARE FORGIVEN," OR TO SAY, "ARISE, TAKE UP YOUR BED, AND WALK"?

BUT SO THAT ALL MAY KNOW THAT I HAVE DIVINE POWER TO DO BOTH, I SAY TO YOU, "ARISE, TAKE UP YOUR BED, AND GO TO YOUR HOME."

585

One Man's Answer

From Matthew 9:9–13; 12:9–14

In all Capernaum there is no one more despised than Matthew, a tax collector for Rome. One day as he and a merchant are arguing about taxes on a caravan of goods, Jesus passes by. He looks straight into the eyes of the hated tax collector...

MATTHEW, FOLLOW ME.

TO THE AMAZEMENT OF THE CROWD, MATTHEW TURNS FROM HIS WORK AND FOLLOWS JESUS.

I CAN'T BELIEVE IT! MATTHEW IS GIVING UP HIS JOB TO GO WITH A MAN OF GOD!

STRANGE -- NO GOOD JEW EVER WANTED MATTHEW FOR A FRIEND.

MATTHEW IS SO HAPPY TO START A NEW LIFE WITH JESUS THAT HE GIVES A BIG FEAST AND INVITES HIS FRIENDS TO MEET JESUS. SOME PHARISEES WHO ARE PASSING BY LOOK ON -- SURPRISED.

WHY DOES YOUR MASTER EAT WITH ALL THOSE SINNERS?

JESUS ANSWERS FOR HIS DISCIPLE.

ONLY THE SICK NEED A DOCTOR. I HAVE COME NOT TO CALL THE RIGHTEOUS BUT SINNERS TO REPENT.

THE PHARISEES HAVE NO ANSWER TO THIS -- BUT IT MAKES THEM EVEN MORE ANGRY. SO EVERYWHERE JESUS GOES THEY WATCH FOR A CHANCE TO CRITICIZE HIM. ONE SABBATH DAY IN THE SYNAGOGUE...

LOOK -- JESUS IS TALKING TO THAT MAN WITH THE WITHERED HAND. LET'S SEE IF WE CAN CATCH HIM BREAKING A SABBATH LAW. THEN WE'LL HAVE A CASE AGAINST HIM.

ermon on the Mount

FROM LUKE 6:12–16;
MATTHEW 5; 6; 7; 8:5–13; 13:45–46;
MARK 4:35–37

JESUS KNOWS THAT THE PHARISEES ARE PLOTTING TO TAKE HIS LIFE, BUT HE DOES NOT LET THIS KEEP HIM FROM CARRYING ON THE WORK GOD SENT HIM TO DO. HE GOES TO A NEARBY MOUNTAIN-- AND SPENDS THE NIGHT IN PRAYER...

...AND FATHER, I THANK THEE FOR GUIDING ME IN THE CHOICES I HAVE MADE THIS NIGHT.

IN THE MORNING HE CALLS HIS DISCIPLES TO HIM--AND FROM THE GROUP HE NAMES TWELVE TO BE HIS FULL-TIME HELPERS: SIMON PETER, ANDREW, JAMES, JOHN, PHILIP, NATHANAEL BARTHOLOMEW, MATTHEW, THOMAS, JAMES THE SON OF ALPHEUS, THADDEUS, SIMON THE ZEALOT, AND JUDAS ISCARIOT. THESE ARE KNOWN AS THE TWELVE APOSTLES.

SIMON THE ZEALOT — JAMES SON OF ALPHEUS — MATTHEW — PETER — JAMES — NATHANAEL — JOHN — THOMAS — PHILIP — JUDAS — ANDREW — THADDEUS

AS THEY COME DOWN THE MOUNTAIN, THEY FIND A LARGE CROWD WAITING FOR JESUS. SO THERE--ON--THE MOUNTAINSIDE JESUS PREACHES A SERMON IN WHICH HE EXPLAINS WHAT MEMBERS OF GOD'S KINGDOM ARE LIKE:

BLESSED ARE THE MERCIFUL: FOR THEY SHALL OBTAIN MERCY.
BLESSED ARE THE PURE IN HEART: FOR THEY SHALL SEE GOD.
BLESSED ARE THE PEACEMAKERS: FOR THEY SHALL BE CALLED THE CHILDREN OF GOD....
YOU ARE THE LIGHT OF THE WORLD.... LET YOUR LIGHT SO SHINE BEFORE OTHERS, THAT THEY MAY SEE YOUR GOOD WORKS, AND GLORIFY YOUR FATHER WHO IS IN HEAVEN....
LOVE YOUR ENEMIES, BLESS THOSE WHO CURSE YOU, DO GOOD TO THOSE WHO HATE YOU, AND PRAY FOR THOSE WHO MISUSE YOU, AND PERSECUTE YOU;
THAT YOU MAY BE THE CHILDREN OF YOUR FATHER WHO IS IN HEAVEN: FOR HE MAKES HIS SUN TO RISE ON THE EVIL AND ON THE GOOD, AND SENDS RAIN ON THE JUST AND ON THE UNJUST.... THEREFORE ALL THINGS YOU WOULD WANT PEOPLE TO DO TO YOU, DO THOSE THINGS TO OTHERS: FOR THIS IS THE SUM OF THE LAW AND THE PROPHETS.

(THE FULL SERMON IS FOUND IN MATTHEW, CHAPTERS 5, 6, 7.)

591

EVEN THOUGH THE PHARISEES ARE STILL PLOTTING AGAINST HIM, JESUS KEEPS ON TEACHING IN CAPERNAUM. ONE DAY THE CROWDS THAT COME TO HEAR HIM ARE SO GREAT THAT HE HAS TO GET INTO A BOAT AND PUSH OUT FROM SHORE IN ORDER TO TEACH THEM.

A MERCHANT ONCE SAW A RARE AND BEAUTIFUL PEARL. HE WANTED IT MORE THAN ANYTHING ELSE. SO HE SOLD EVERYTHING HE OWNED AND BOUGHT IT. THE KINGDOM OF GOD IS LIKE THAT PEARL -- IT IS WORTH EVERYTHING YOU HAVE TO POSSESS IT.

WHEN EVENING COMES JESUS SUGGESTS TO HIS DISCIPLES THAT THEY CROSS OVER TO THE OTHER SIDE OF THE LAKE.

IT'S THE KIND OF A NIGHT WHEN A SUDDEN STORM COULD HIT.

592

Mad Man by the Sea

FROM MARK 4:37–41; 5:1–24, 35

AT THE END OF A DAY OF TEACHING, JESUS ASKS HIS DISCIPLES TO TAKE HIM ACROSS THE SEA OF GALILEE. BUT SOON AFTER HE LIES DOWN TO SLEEP A SUDDEN AND VIOLENT STORM STRIKES.

LOWER THE SAIL!

SECONDS LATER GIANT WAVES ARE POURING OVER THE SHIP.

HELP! WE'RE BEING SWAMPED!

IN TERROR THE DISCIPLES RUSH TO THE STERN OF THE BOAT.

MASTER! DON'T YOU CARE IF WE DROWN?

JESUS RISES AND FACES THE STORMY SEA

PEACE, BE STILL!

INSTANTLY THE WIND DIES AND THE WAVES VANISH.

WHO IS HE, THAT EVEN THE WINDS AND THE SEA OBEY HIM?

IN THE MORNING THE BOAT REACHES SHORE; AND AS JESUS AND HIS DISCIPLES ARE WALKING UP THE BEACH, A MAN POSSESSED BY AN EVIL SPIRIT RUSHES DOWN THE BANK TO MEET JESUS.

BE CAREFUL-- HE'S BROKEN HIS CHAINS.

QUIETLY JESUS LEADS THE CHILD'S PARENTS INTO HER ROOM. THERE HE TAKES THE GIRL'S HAND AND SAYS, "ARISE." INSTANTLY SHE GETS UP-- AND LOOKS AT JESUS IN SURPRISE AND WONDER.

GIVE HER SOMETHING TO EAT-- BUT DO NOT TELL ANYONE WHAT HAS HAPPENED IN THIS ROOM.

BUT JAIRUS IS AN IMPORTANT MAN. NEWS ABOUT HIS DAUGHTER SPREADS QUICKLY. AND AS JESUS TRAVELS THROUGH GALILEE, PREACHING AND HEALING, HIS FAME INCREASES. THE PHARISEES WATCH ANGRILY. AS YET THEY HAVE NO REAL CASE AGAINST JESUS AND WITH- OUT ONE THEY DARE NOT STIR UP THE EXCITED CROWDS THAT FOLLOW HIM.

BUT JESUS IS CONCERNED ABOUT THE MANY PEOPLE WHO STILL HAVE NOT HEARD HIS MESSAGE. HE CALLS HIS DISCIPLES ASIDE.

THE PEOPLE ARE LIKE SHEEP WITHOUT A SHEPHERD. I WANT YOU TO GO OUT BY TWOS TO PREACH AND HEAL THE SICK AS I HAVE DONE. DO NOT BE WORRIED ABOUT WHAT TO SAY, FOR THE SPIRIT OF GOD WILL SPEAK THROUGH YOU.

THE DISCIPLES PREACH THROUGHOUT GALILEE. WHEN THEY RETURN JESUS PREPARES TO TAKE THEM TO A QUIET PLACE TO REST AND TALK ABOUT FUTURE PLANS. AS THEY ARE STARTING, A DISCIPLE OF JOHN THE BAPTIST BRINGS THEM TRAGIC NEWS.

JOHN HAS BEEN BEHEADED BY KING HEROD!

HEROD IS A WICKED MAN. BUT THIS IS THE WORST OF HIS SINS.

Jesus—A Miracle Worker ▶ Read more about miracles on pp. 573-634 in your Picture Bible.

Did You Know?

A miracle is an extraordinary happening—something that couldn't happen without God stepping in to do what no human being could do. It is a way for God to show His power and love for people. Jesus, God's Son, did many miracles while He was on earth. Here are a few:

Blind man gets his sight (p. 614).

▶ Dead man comes to life (p. 626).

▶ 153 large fish caught (p. 670).

▶ Jesus' resurrection is the greatest miracle of all! (p. 665)

▶ 1st miracle

Turns water into wine at a wedding reception (p. 573).

▶ Jairus' daughter healed (p. 595).

▶ Walks on water. Disciples think He is a ghost (p. 601).

Stormy sea is made calm (p. 593).

There are about 35 miracles recorded in the Gospels. Jesus did many, many more. The Bible says that if all the miracles were written down, the world would not have room for all the books (John 21:25).

Did You Know?

The Great Storyteller

▶ There are 40 parables in the New Testament.

Jesus tells many stories called parables during His ministry. A parable is a story that teaches a spiritual lesson by comparing one situation with another. For example, Jesus teaches the disciples about His kingdom by comparing it to types of soil or a treasure in a field. By telling stories, Jesus can explain important truths in a way that people can easily understand.

Check out these stories Jesus tells:

The Boy Who Ran Away from Home (p. 623)

▶ A Widow Woman Who Wouldn't Quit (Luke 18:2-8)

▶ Mystery of the Lost Coin (Luke 15:8-10)

▶ Ten Bridesmaids Wait for Groom to Show Up for Wedding (Matthew 25:1-13)

▶ Building on Sand Is Risky Business! (Matthew 7:24-27)

▶ An Expensive Pearl (p. 562)

▶ One Lamb Is Lost! (Luke 15:3-7)

▶ Hidden Treasure Found in Field (Matthew 13:44)

Man Attacked on Road to Jericho (p. 617)

WHEN THE PEOPLE HAVE FINISHED EATING, JESUS TURNS AGAIN TO HIS DISCIPLES.

GATHER UP THE FOOD THAT REMAINS.

TWELVE BASKETS OF FOOD ARE LEFT OVER! THE PEOPLE ARE NOW MORE AMAZED THAN EVER.

MAYBE JESUS IS THE KING THE PROPHETS TALKED ABOUT.

A KING LIKE DAVID--WHO WILL DESTROY OUR ENEMIES AND MAKE US RICH AND POWERFUL!

UT GOD SENT JESUS TO BE THE SAVIOR, TO BRING PEOPLE INTO THE KINGDOM OF GOD--NOT TO COMMAND ARMIES AND CONQUER THRONES. WHEN JESUS SEES THAT THE CROWD WANTS TO FORCE HIM TO BE A KING, HE QUICKLY CALLS HIS DISCIPLES.

LAUNCH THE BOAT AND CROSS OVER TO THE OTHER SIDE OF THE SEA. I WILL JOIN YOU LATER.

QUICKLY--BEFORE THE EXCITEMENT OF THE PEOPLE GROWS STRONGER--JESUS DISMISSES THEM. THEN HE GOES UP ON A MOUNTAIN TO PRAY. LATER THAT NIGHT --ON THE SEA OF GALILEE...

THE WIND IS RISING! WE'RE IN FOR A STORM!

SOON THE STORM HITS...

HOW MUCH FARTHER TO LAND?

WE'RE ONLY HALF WAY.

SUDDENLY THEY LOOK UP TO SEE A FIGURE WALKING ON THE WATER. "A SPIRIT!" THEY CRY IN TERROR. ACROSS THE WAVES A CALM VOICE CALLS OUT: "IT IS I; DON'T BE AFRAID."

COME!

LORD! IF IT IS YOU, TELL ME TO COME TO YOU.

INSTANTLY PETER JUMPS FROM THE BOAT AND STARTS WALKING TOWARD JESUS, BUT WHEN HE SEES THE POWER OF THE WIND, HE LOSES FAITH-- AND BEGINS TO SINK...

Miracle on the Sea

FROM MATTHEW 14:30–36; JOHN 6:22–71; MARK 7:1–23;
MATTHEW 16:13–26; 17:1–2

JESUS RESCUES PETER, AND AS THEY REACH THE BOAT, THE WIND DIES, AND THE SEA IS CALM.

HE REALLY IS GOD'S SON!

AT DAYBREAK THE DISCIPLES BRING THE BOAT TO SHORE. WHEN THE PEOPLE SEE JESUS, THEY HURRY TO BRING THEIR SICK AND CRIPPLED TO HIM. PATIENTLY AND LOVINGLY HE HEALS THEM ALL.

IF ONLY I CAN TOUCH HIS GARMENT I WILL BE HEALED.

LATER THAT DAY JESUS GOES TO THE SYNAGOGUE IN CAPERNAUM. THE CROWD THAT HE FED THE DAY BEFORE IS THERE ASKING TO BE FED AGAIN. WHEN JESUS PREACHES A SERMON ABOUT THEIR SPIRITUAL NEEDS, MANY OF THEM ARE DISAPPOINTED AND TURN AWAY.

SEEING THIS, THE PHARISEES RESUME THEIR PUBLIC CRITICISM OF JESUS.

WE HAVE SEEN YOUR DISCIPLES EAT WITHOUT WASHING THEIR HANDS. WHY DO YOU LET THEM BREAK OUR LAWS AND DEFILE THEMSELVES?

NOTHING THAT GOES INTO A PERSON'S MOUTH IS DEFILING, BUT THE EVIL WORDS THAT COME OUT DO DEFILE.

SHOCKED BECAUSE HE DEFENDS HIS DISCIPLES, THE PHARISEES TURN AWAY, MORE DETERMINED THAN EVER TO DESTROY JESUS.

DON'T YOU KNOW THAT YOU HAVE MADE THE PHARISEES ANGRY?

THE PHARISEES ARE BLIND TO THE WILL OF GOD—AND THEY ARE LEADING THE PEOPLE TO BE AS BLIND AS THEY ARE.

BECAUSE MOST OF THE PEOPLE WILL ACCEPT HIM ONLY AS AN EARTHLY KING, JESUS LEAVES GALILEE. HE TAKES HIS DISCIPLES TO THE COUNTRY OF PHOENICIA—AND LATER TO THE REGION OF CAESAREA PHILIPPI, WHERE HE TEACHES THEM IN PRIVACY. THERE, ONE DAY, HE ASKS THEM: "WHO DO PEOPLE SAY THAT I AM?"

JOHN THE BAPTIST... ELIJAH...

BUT WHO DO YOU SAY THAT I AM?

YOU ARE THE CHRIST, THE SON OF THE LIVING GOD.

BLESSED ARE YOU, PETER--FOR MY FATHER IN HEAVEN HAS REVEALED THIS TO YOU.

NOW THAT THE DISCIPLES TRULY UNDERSTAND THAT HE IS THE PROMISED MESSIAH, JESUS TELLS THEM WHAT WILL HAPPEN WHEN HE GOES TO JERUSALEM.

THE PHARISEES AND PRIESTS DO NOT BELIEVE THAT I AM THE MESSIAH. THEY WILL HAVE ME KILLED--BUT IN THREE DAYS I WILL RISE AGAIN.

A Boy—And His Father's Faith

FROM MATTHEW 17:3–23; MARK 3:26, 33; LUKE 9:37–45

ALONE WITH JESUS ON THE MOUNTAIN, PETER, JAMES AND JOHN SEE HIM TRANSFIGURED. HIS FACE SHINES WITH THE BRIGHTNESS OF THE SUN--HIS CLOTHES BECOME DAZZLING WHITE. THEN TWO GREAT MEN OF THE PAST, MOSES AND ELIJAH, APPEAR TO TALK WITH HIM.

BUT AS PETER SPEAKS A BRIGHT CLOUD DESCENDS ON THE MOUNTAINTOP...AND OUT OF THE CLOUD COMES THE VOICE OF GOD:

THIS IS MY BELOVED SON, IN WHOM I AM WELL PLEASED; LISTEN TO HIM.

THE DISCIPLES ARE SO FRIGHTENED THAT THEY FALL TO THE GROUND BUT JESUS BENDS DOWN AND TOUCHES THEM...

DO NOT BE AFRAID.

THE NEXT MORNING-- ON THE WAY DOWN THE MOUNTAIN --JESUS WARNS HIS DISCIPLES TO TELL NO ONE OF HIS TRANS- FIGURATION UNTIL AFTER HIS RESURRECTION. AFTER WHAT THEY HAVE JUST SEEN THE DISCIPLES CANNOT BELIEVE THAT JESUS WILL DIE -- SO THEY ARE PUZZLED WHEN JESUS TALKS ABOUT RISING FROM THE DEAD.

THEY REACH THE VAL- LEY TO FIND A GREAT CROWD GATHERED AROUND THE OTHER DISCIPLES.

AT THE SIGHT OF JESUS THE PEOPLE QUICKLY SURROUND HIM.

MY SON HAS SPELLS AND OFTEN FALLS INTO THE FIRE. I BROUGHT HIM TO YOUR DISCIPLES, BUT THEY COULD NOT HEAL HIM.

BRING YOUR SON TO ME.

THE FATHER OBEYS --BUT THE BOY HAS A SPELL AND FALLS TO THE GROUND AT JESUS' FEET.

IF YOU CAN HELP US-- PLEASE DO.

ALL THINGS ARE POSSIBLE TO ONE WHO HAS FAITH.

I BELIEVE! HELP ME, PLEASE, TO HAVE MORE FAITH.

THOU UNCLEAN SPIRIT--COME OUT OF THE BOY!

Seventy Times Seven

FROM MATTHEW 18:1–14, 21–22;
JOHN 7:11–52; 8:21–59

ON THE WAY TO CAPERNAUM THE DISCIPLES QUARREL ABOUT WHICH ONE OF THEM WILL BE THE MOST IMPORTANT PERSON IN THE KINGDOM THEY EXPECT JESUS TO ESTABLISH. WHEN THEY REACH THE CITY JESUS ASKS WHY THEY ARE QUARRELING AND THEY ARE ASHAMED TO SAY. HE CALLS A LITTLE CHILD TO HIM.

WHICHEVER ONE OF YOU WANTS TO BE GREATEST IN GOD'S KINGDOM MUST BE AS HUMBLE AND WILLING TO LEARN AS THIS LITTLE CHILD.

612

WHEN THE CHIEF PRIESTS AND PHARISEES HEAR WHAT THE PEOPLE ARE SAYING, THEY QUICKLY JOIN FORCES AGAINST JESUS.

IF WE DON'T GET RID OF HIM THE PEOPLE WILL ACCEPT HIM AS THE MESSIAH.

I'LL STOP HIM.. CALL THE TEMPLE GUARDS

ARREST JESUS. BUT DO IT AT A TIME WHEN IT WILL CAUSE THE LEAST TROUBLE.

ON THE LAST DAY OF THE FEAST THE OFFICERS RETURN TO THE PRIESTS AND PHARISEES.

WHERE IS JESUS?

WE'VE NEVER HEARD ANYONE SPEAK AS THIS MAN DOES. WE COULD NOT ARREST HIM.

JESUS RETURNS TO THE TEMPLE TO PREACH. IN THE COURSE OF HIS SERMON HE NOT ONLY POINTS OUT THE SINS OF THE PRIESTS AND PHARISEES BUT DECLARES THAT HE WAS WITH GOD EVEN BEFORE THE DAYS OF THEIR GREAT FOREFATHER, ABRAHAM.

HOW DARE HE CLAIM SUCH RELATIONSHIP WITH GOD!

STONE HIM! STONE HIM!

THE PRIESTS AND PHARISEES ARE FURIOUS -- BUT THEY ARE AFRAID TO FORCE THE ISSUE WHILE THE CITY IS FILLED WITH PEOPLE ATTENDING THE FEAST. BUT THE NEXT DAY...

A Beggar Meet Jesus

FROM JOHN 9:1—10:21; LUKE 10:25

THE PRIESTS AND PHARISEES ATTEMPT TO STONE JESUS -- BUT HE ESCAPES. LATER -- ON THE SABBATH -- HE AND HIS DISCIPLES COME UPON A BLIND MAN BEGGING AT A TEMPLE GATE. JESUS MOISTENS SOME CLAY AND PLACES IT TENDERLY OVER THE MAN'S EYES.

GO, WASH IN THE POOL OF SILOAM.

THE MAN OBEYS JESUS, AND FOR THE FIRST TIME IN HIS LIFE HE CAN SEE! HE IS SO EXCITED THAT HE HURRIES HOME, WHERE HE IS MET BY HIS NEIGHBORS.

IS THIS THE BLIND MAN WHO BEGGED OUTSIDE THE TEMPLE?

IMPOSSIBLE -- BUT HE **DOES** LOOK LIKE HIM!

I AM THE GOOD SHEPHERD; THE GOOD SHEPHERD GIVES HIS LIFE FOR HIS SHEEP. NO ONE CAN TAKE MY LIFE FROM ME, BUT I GIVE IT MYSELF. I HAVE THE POWER TO GIVE IT AND TO TAKE IT AGAIN, FOR I RECEIVED THIS POWER FROM GOD MY FATHER.

THIS MAN IS CRAZY AND IS POSSESSED BY AN EVIL SPIRIT. WHY LISTEN TO HIM?

BUT CAN AN EVIL SPIRIT OPEN THE EYES OF THE BLIND?

WHILE JESUS IS PREACHING IN ONE OF THE CITIES A LAWYER IN THE CROWD WAITS FOR A CHANCE TO TEST HIM.

THE PHARISEES AND PRIESTS CONTINUE TO ARGUE. SOME THINK THAT JESUS IS WORKING WITH THE DEVIL. OTHERS DECLARE THAT HE IS NOT, BUT THEY REFUSE TO BELIEVE THAT HE IS THE SON OF GOD. A FEW DAYS LATER JESUS AND HIS DISCIPLES LEAVE JERUSALEM FOR A TOUR THROUGH JUDEA.

I'LL FIND OUT FOR MYSELF HOW THIS YOUNG TEACHER HANDLES A HARD QUESTION.

YOU ARE RIGHT--
DO THAT AND
YOU WILL HAVE
ETERNAL LIFE.

BUT WHO
IS MY
NEIGHBOR?

JESUS REPLIES WITH A STORY WHICH FORCES THE LAWYER AGAIN TO ANSWER HIS OWN QUESTION:

A MAN IS TRAVELING FROM JERUSALEM TO JERICHO. ON THE WAY HE IS ATTACKED BY BANDITS, ROBBED, AND LEFT FOR DEAD.

BY CHANCE A PRIEST COMES BY-- HE SEES THE WOUNDED MAN BUT HE QUICKLY PASSES BY.

A LITTLE LATER A LEVITE, AN ASSISTANT TO THE PRIESTS, COMES ALONG-- BUT HE, TOO, HURRIES BY.

BUT WHEN A SAMARITAN SEES THE INJURED MAN, HE STOPS. ALTHOUGH SAMARITANS ARE BITTER ENEMIES OF THE JEWS, HE BINDS UP THE MAN'S WOUNDS, TAKES HIM TO AN INN, AND PAYS FOR HIS CARE.

WHEN HE FINISHES THE STORY OF THE GOOD SAMARITAN, JESUS ASKS: WHICH ONE OF THE THREE WAS A NEIGHBOR TO THE MAN WHO WAS ROBBED?

THE MAN WHO HELPED HIM.

GO AND DO THE SAME.

THE LAWYER GOES AWAY-- AMAZED AT THE SKILL WITH WHICH JESUS ANSWERED HIS QUESTIONS.

JESUS CONTINUES ON HIS PREACHING TOUR. IN BETHANY HE STOPS TO VISIT HIS FRIENDS: MARY, MARTHA, AND LAZARUS. MARY DROPS EVERYTHING SHE IS DOING TO LISTEN TO JESUS...

NOW I SEE-- MY NEIGHBOR IS ANYONE WHO NEEDS ME.

BUT HER SISTER MARTHA...

IT ISN'T FAIR-- AND I WON'T STAND FOR IT ANY LONGER!

The Lord's Prayer

FROM LUKE 10:40—11:2; MATTHEW 6:9–13;
JOHN 10:22–40; LUKE 15:1–19

WHEN JESUS VISITS IN THE HOME OF HIS FRIENDS, MARY, MARTHA, AND LAZARUS, MARY STOPS HER WORK TO LISTEN TO JESUS. BUT MARTHA HURRIES TO THE KITCHEN TO PREPARE FOOD. AS SHE WORKS SHE BECOMES UPSET BECAUSE MARY DOES NOT HELP HER. AT LAST SHE COMPLAINS TO JESUS.

DON'T YOU THINK IT'S WRONG FOR MARY TO LEAVE ME WITH ALL THE WORK TO DO? TELL HER TO HELP ME.

MARTHA! MARTHA! YOU ARE WORRYING ABOUT TOO MANY THINGS. ONLY ONE THING IS IMPORTANT --TO LEARN THE WILL OF GOD, AS MARY HAS CHOSEN TO DO.

DURING THE REST OF JESUS' VISIT, MARTHA SEEKS TO LEARN MORE ABOUT GOD. THEN JESUS LEAVES HIS FRIENDS IN BETHANY AND JOINS HIS DISCIPLES FOR A TEACHING TRIP IN JUDEA.

LISTENING TO JESUS MAKES ME FEEL SO CLOSE TO GOD.

DURING HIS TRAVELS JESUS STOPS OFTEN TO PRAY. HIS DISCIPLES SEE THE POWER OF PRAYER IN JESUS' LIFE, AND ONE DAY A DISCIPLE SPEAKS TO HIM ABOUT IT.

TEACH US TO PRAY.

JESUS ANSWERS: WHEN YOU PRAY, SAY,

OUR FATHER WHO IS IN HEAVEN: LET YOUR NAME BE TREATED AS HOLY. LET YOUR KINGDOM COME. LET YOUR WILL BE DONE ON EARTH AS IT IS IN HEAVEN. GIVE US OUR FOOD FOR THIS DAY. AND FORGIVE US OUR DEBTS AS WE HAVE FORGIVEN OUR DEBTORS. AND DON'T LEAD US INTO TEMPTATION, BUT DELIVER US FROM THE EVIL ONE. FOR TO YOU BELONGS THE KINGDOM AND THE POWER AND THE SPLENDOR FOREVER, AMEN.

FOR A MOMENT NO ONE SPEAKS. THEN SOFTLY THE DISCIPLES SAY "AMEN" TO THE SIMPLE PRAYER THAT BECOMES A MODEL FOR THEIR FUTURE PRAYERS TO GOD. AFTER THIS, JESUS AND HIS HELPERS CONTINUE THROUGH JUDEA, PREACHING AND HEALING. BY THE TIME JESUS RETURNS TO JERUSALEM FOR A RELIGIOUS FEAST THE CITY IS FILLED WITH PEOPLE TALKING AND WONDERING ABOUT HIM.

622

The Prodigal's Return

From Luke 15:20–32; John 11:1–8

When the pharisees complain because Jesus associates with sinners, he tells them a story about a young man who leaves home. The young man spends his money so foolishly that at last he has to take care of a farmer's pigs in order to keep alive. In his misery he decides to go home and work for his father-- not as his son, but as one of his servants. When he reaches home his father rushes out to meet him.

FATHER! I HAVE SINNED AGAINST HEAVEN AND YOU. I'M NO LONGER WORTHY TO BE CALLED YOUR SON.

WHEN JESUS FINISHES THE STORY THE PEOPLE TURN TO ONE ANOTHER IN WONDER.

DOES HE MEAN THAT GOD IS LIKE THE FATHER IN THE STORY?

YES--I SEE IT. GOD WANTS TO FORGIVE EVEN US SINNERS IF WE WILL COME BACK TO HIM.

WHEN THE PHARISEES SEE THE REACTION OF THE PEOPLE, THEY TURN AWAY IN ANGER. JESUS CONTINUES TO TEACH, BUT HE IS SOON INTERRUPTED...

JESUS! MARY AND MARTHA HAVE SENT ME TO TELL YOU THAT THEIR BROTHER, LAZARUS, IS ILL. THEY WANT YOU TO COME TO BETHANY--

BETHANY? THAT'S TOO CLOSE TO HIS ENEMIES IN JERUSALEM. THEY'LL KILL HIM!

Called from the Tomb

FROM JOHN 11:38–54; LUKE 18:15–23; 19:1–3

By the time Jesus and his disciples reach Bethany Lazarus, the brother of Mary and Martha, has been dead four days. At the tomb Jesus asks to have the stone rolled away. He prays aloud to God and then calls out in a strong voice...

LAZARUS, COME FORTH.

TO THE AMAZEMENT OF THE CROWD, LAZARUS APPEARS!

LAZARUS!

O JESUS, WE THANK YOU!

A MAN RAISED FROM THE DEAD! THE PEOPLE CAN SCARCELY BELIEVE WHAT THEY HAVE SEEN. MANY OF THEM TURN TO JESUS CRYING, "MESSIAH! SON OF GOD!" BUT OTHERS GO INTO JERUSALEM TO TELL THE PHARISEES WHAT JESUS HAS DONE.

IN ANGER AND DESPERATION THE PHARISEES AND CHIEF PRIESTS CALL A MEETING.

IF NEWS OF THIS GETS AROUND THE PEOPLE WILL TRY TO MAKE JESUS A KING.

AND IF THERE'S A REBELLION THE ROMANS WILL BLAME US. WE'LL LOSE OUR POSITIONS AND THE NATION WILL BE DESTROYED.

DON'T YOU SEE? IT IS BETTER TO KILL JESUS THAN TO GET THE WHOLE COUNTRY IN TROUBLE.

CAIAPHAS IS A SHREWD ONE. HE'S FOUND A REASON TO KILL JESUS -- AND HE'LL ALSO FIND A WAY.

WHEN JESUS LEARNS OF THIS NEW PLOT AGAINST HIM, HE GOES OFF TO A QUIET PLACE -- TO WAIT UNTIL THE TIME COMES TO FACE HIS ENEMIES.

AS THE TIME FOR THE PASSOVER FEAST APPROACHES, PEOPLE FROM ALL OVER PALESTINE SET OUT FOR JERUSALEM -- AND JESUS JOINS THEM.

ON THE WAY THE CROWDS BEG TO SEE AND HEAR JESUS.

NO -- NO -- TAKE YOUR CHILDREN AWAY. JESUS IS TOO BUSY --

BUT I WANT JESUS TO BLESS MY LITTLE SON.

LET THE LITTLE ONES COME TO ME -- FOR GOD'S KINGDOM IS MADE UP OF PEOPLE WITH LOVE AND TRUST SUCH AS THEIRS.

628

Man in the Tree

FROM LUKE 19:4–10; JOHN 12:1–8; LUKE 19:29–35

ZACCHEUS, THE WEALTHY TAX COLLECTOR,
IS SO SHORT THAT HE CAN'T LOOK
OVER THE HEADS OF THE PEOPLE. FRANTICALLY
HE RUNS AHEAD OF THE CROWD, CLIMBS A TREE
AND WAITS. WHEN JESUS
SEES HIM, HE STOPS . . .

ZACCHEUS, COME DOWN, FOR I WANT TO STAY AT YOUR HOUSE!

ZACCHEUS IS AMAZED THAT JESUS WOULD EVEN SPEAK TO HIM, BUT HE CLIMBS DOWN AT ONCE AND LEADS THE WAY TO HIS HOUSE.

WHY WOULD A TEACHER AS GREAT AS JESUS WANT TO STAY WITH THAT CROOKED LITTLE TAX COLLECTOR?

ZACCHEUS WONDERS, TOO, BUT HE SOON DISCOVERS THAT BEING IN THE PRESENCE OF JESUS MAKES HIM ASHAMED OF EVERY WRONG THING HE HAS EVER DONE. HE WANTS TO BE FORGIVEN AND START OVER...

HALF OF MY GOODS I WILL GIVE TO THE POOR. AND IF I HAVE CHEATED ANYONE I WILL PAY HIM BACK FOUR TIMES AS MUCH.

SALVATION HAS COME TO YOU TODAY, ZACCHEUS. IT IS TO HELP PEOPLE LIKE YOU THAT I HAVE COME TO THE WORLD.

ROM JERICHO THE CROWDS CONTINUE THEIR WAY TO JERUSALEM FOR THE GREAT PASSOVER FEAST. THE FESTIVAL IS STILL SIX DAYS AWAY, SO JESUS STOPS IN BETHANY TO VISIT HIS FRIENDS -- MARY, MARTHA, AND LAZARUS. AT A SUPPER IN THE HOME OF SIMON THE LEPER, MARY KNEELS BESIDE JESUS AND ANOINTS HIS FEET WITH COSTLY OIL -- THEN WIPES THEM WITH HER HAIR.

JUDAS ISCARIOT, TREASURER OF THE DISCIPLES, IS ANGERED BY WHAT HE THINKS IS A WASTE OF MONEY.

WHY WASN'T THE OIL SOLD AND THE MONEY GIVEN TO THE POOR?

I WANTED TO HONOR JESUS--

LET HER ALONE, SHE IS SHOWING HER LOVE FOR ME.

JUDAS IS ANGERED BY THIS REPRIMAND-- AND AN UGLY THOUGHT COMES TO HIS MIND.

WHEN THE TIME IS RIGHT I'LL GO TO THE PRIESTS AND PHARISEES-- **THEY'LL** BE GLAD TO LISTEN TO ME.

THE NEXT DAY JESUS AND HIS DISCIPLES JOIN THE CROWDS GOING UP TO JERUSALEM TO PREPARE FOR THE PASSOVER FEAST. ON THE WAY...

GO OVER INTO THAT VILLAGE AND AS YOU ENTER YOU WILL FIND A COLT. BRING IT TO ME. AND IF ANYONE QUESTIONS YOU, TELL HIM I NEED THE ANIMAL-- AND WILL RETURN IT.

PUZZLED, THE TWO DISCIPLES GO TO THE VILLAGE WHERE THEY FIND THE COLT. WHEN THEY START TO UNTIE THE ROPE...

WHAT DO YOU MEAN, TAKING MY ANIMAL?

JESUS SAID TO TELL YOU THAT HE NEEDED IT.

AT THE MENTION OF JESUS' NAME, THE MAN GLADLY GIVES HIS CONSENT

I WONDER WHY JESUS WANTS MY COLT. IT HAS NEVER BEEN RIDDEN-- BESIDES, IT'S NOT A VERY NOBLE BEAST FOR ANYONE AS IMPORTANT AS JESUS TO RIDE.

Triumphal Entry

FROM LUKE 19:36–38;
MATTHEW 21:10–17; 22:15–17

IT IS THE FIRST DAY OF THE WEEK. THE ROAD TO JERUSALEM IS FILLED WITH PEOPLE ON THE WAY TO CELEBRATE THE PASSOVER FEAST OF THE JEWS. AT JESUS' REQUEST HIS DISCIPLES BRING HIM A LOWLY BEAST OF BURDEN-- HE MOUNTS IT AND JOINS THE MULTITUDE OF PILGRIMS. EAGERLY THEY MAKE WAY FOR HIM--WAVING PALM BRANCHES AND CARPETING HIS PATH WITH THEIR GARMENTS. AND, WHILE THEY ESCORT HIM--TRIUMPHANTLY--UP THE ROAD AND INTO THE CITY, THE SOUND OF THEIR PRAISES FILLS THE AIR: "HOSANNA! BLESSED IS THE KING THAT COMETH IN THE NAME OF THE LORD!"

DURING ITS LONG HISTORY JERUSALEM HAS SEEN MANY PROCESSIONS ENTER ITS GATES-- KINGS ON HORSEBACK AND CONQUERORS WITH ARMED LEGIONS-- BUT NEVER ONE LIKE THIS.

WHO IS THIS MAN?

JESUS, THE PROPHET OF NAZARETH!

BUT THE NEWS THAT JESUS IS COMING HAS ALREADY SPREAD THROUGH THE CITY. WHEN HE REACHES THE TEMPLE, HE FINDS THE BLIND, LAME, AND SICK THERE WAITING.

RISE UP, MY CHILD, AND WALK.

HOSANNA TO THE SON OF DAVID!

LOOK! WE ARE IN CHARGE OF THE TEMPLE, BUT JESUS IS TAKING OVER. I SAY IF WE DON'T GET RID OF HIM NOW IT WILL BE TOO LATE.

NO--NO--THERE ARE TOO MANY PEOPLE IN THE CITY WHO BELIEVE IN HIM. WE MUST WAIT FOR THE RIGHT MOMENT.

WHEN JESUS BEGINS TO PREACH, PEOPLE CROWD INTO THE TEMPLE COURTS TO HEAR HIM. BUT BEHIND CLOSED DOORS THE PRIESTS AND PHARISEES PLOT THEIR STRATEGY. BY TUESDAY THEY ARE READY...

MASTER, WE KNOW YOU TEACH THE TRUTH. TELL US, IS IT RIGHT TO PAY TAXES TO CAESAR, OR NOT?

IF HE SAYS "YES," THE PEOPLE WILL TURN AGAINST HIM BECAUSE THEY HATE TO PAY TAXES TO ROME; IF HE SAYS "NO," ROME WILL ARREST HIM FOR TREASON.

HE'S TRAPPED THIS TIME FOR SURE!

The Great Commandment

FROM LUKE 20:23–26; MARK 12:28–34, 38–44; 13; MATTHEW 26:14–16

JESUS IS PREACHING IN A COURT OF THE TEMPLE, AND IN AN ATTEMPT TO GET HIM INTO TROUBLE, THE PHARISEES ASK: "IS IT RIGHT TO PAY TAXES TO CAESAR?" JESUS KNOWS THAT THIS IS A TRICK QUESTION. IF HE ANSWERS "YES," THE PEOPLE WILL TURN AGAINST HIM. IF HE SAYS "NO," THE ROMANS WILL ARREST HIM FOR TREASON. HE ASKS TO SEE A ROMAN COIN.

WHOSE IMAGE IS THIS?

CAESAR'S.

637

THEN JESUS WARNS THE PEOPLE AGAINST THOSE WHO DO GOOD DEEDS JUST TO BE SEEN BY OTHERS. WHEN HE HAS FINISHED SPEAKING HE LOOKS UP TO SEE A PROUD MAN PLACE A LARGE SUM OF MONEY IN THE TEMPLE TREASURY.

THE MAN IS FOLLOWED BY A POOR WIDOW WHO HUMBLY DROPS IN TWO SMALL COINS.

THE WIDOW HAS GIVEN MORE THAN ANYONE ELSE -- FOR SHE HAS GIVEN ALL SHE HAS TO GOD.

WITH THESE WORDS JESUS LEAVES THE TEMPLE -- FOR THE LAST TIME. OUTSIDE JERUSALEM, ON THE QUIET SLOPES OF THE MOUNT OF OLIVES, SOME OF HIS DISCIPLES ASK ABOUT THE FUTURE. JESUS EXPLAINS THAT HIS GOSPEL WILL BE PREACHED THROUGHOUT THE WORLD -- AND THEN HE WILL COME AGAIN TO JUDGE THE WORLD.

JESUS AND HIS DISCIPLES RETURN TO BETHANY. LATER THAT NIGHT JUDAS HURRIES TO JERUSALEM TO CARRY OUT AN IDEA THAT CAME TO HIM WHEN MARY ANOINTED JESUS WITH COSTLY OIL.

I WANT TO SEE THE CHIEF PRIEST.

A MAN NAMED JUDAS ISCARIOT WANTS TO SEE YOU. HE SAYS IT'S URGENT.

JUDAS ISCARIOT? WHY, HE'S ONE OF JESUS' DISCIPLES. SHOW HIM IN.

I KNOW HOW MUCH YOU WANT TO GET RID OF JESUS. WHAT WILL YOU GIVE TO HAVE HIM DELIVERED TO YOU -- AWAY FROM THE CROWDS THAT BELIEVE IN HIM?

THIRTY PIECES OF SILVER.

Secretly—In an Upper Room

FROM LUKE 22:7–13; JOHN 13:1–20, 27–30;
MATTHEW 26:21–25

IT IS LATE TUESDAY NIGHT WHEN JUDAS BARGAINS WITH THE CHIEF PRIESTS TO BETRAY JESUS. AFTER THE AGREEMENT IS MADE HE RETURNS TO BETHANY AND SPENDS WEDNESDAY WITH JESUS AND THE DISCIPLES-- NEVER SUSPECTING THAT JESUS KNOWS WHAT HE HAS DONE. THURSDAY, JESUS CALLS PETER AND JOHN ASIDE.

GO INTO JERUSALEM AND MAKE THINGS READY FOR THE PASSOVER FEAST.

WHERE CAN WE GO SO THAT YOUR ENEMIES WILL NOT SEE US?

WHEN YOU ENTER THE CITY YOU WILL SEE A MAN CARRYING A PITCHER. FOLLOW HIM AND ASK HIS MASTER TO SHOW YOU THE ROOM THAT WE MAY USE.

PETER AND JOHN GO AT ONCE TO JERUSALEM. THEY FIND THE SERVANT CARRYING A PITCHER AND FOLLOW HIM HOME.

WHERE IS THE ROOM IN WHICH JESUS AND HIS DISCIPLES CAN EAT THE PASSOVER?

COME WITH ME.

642

The Lord's Supper

FROM LUKE 22:17–20; JOHN 13:33–38; 14;
MATTHEW 26:30, 36–56

AFTER JUDAS, THE TRAITOR, LEAVES,
JESUS PICKS UP A PIECE OF BREAD,
THANKS GOD FOR IT, BREAKS IT,
AND GIVES IT TO HIS DISCIPLES,
SAYING, "THIS IS MY BODY."
WHEN THEY HAVE EATEN THE
BREAD, HE OFFERS THEM
A CUP.

DRINK OF IT, EACH ONE
OF YOU, FOR IT IS MY
BLOOD, WHICH WILL BE
SHED TO PAY THE PRICE OF
YOUR SINS. AFTER I'M
GONE, DO THIS IN
REMEMBRANCE OF ME.

SO JESUS MAKES A NEW
COVENANT BETWEEN GOD AND
CHRISTIANS. AS WE TAKE THE
BREAD AND CUP IN THE NAME
OF JESUS WE ARE REMINDED
THAT GOD, THROUGH HIS SON,
HAS DELIVERED US FROM THE
SLAVERY OF SIN.

645

QUIETLY, THEY LEAVE THE UPPER ROOM. THEY WALK THROUGH THE MOONLIT STREETS OF THE CITY, OUT AN EAST GATE, AND ACROSS A VALLEY TO THE GARDEN OF GETHSEMANE ON THE MOUNT OF OLIVES.

AT THE ENTRANCE JESUS ASKS EIGHT OF THE DISCIPLES TO WAIT WHILE HE TAKES HIS CLOSEST DISCIPLES, PETER, JAMES, AND JOHN FARTHER INTO THE GARDEN.

THIS IS A SAD NIGHT FOR ME -- STAY HERE AND WATCH WHILE I GO ALONE TO PRAY.

O MY FATHER, IF THOU BE WILLING, REMOVE THIS AGONY FROM ME; NEVERTHELESS, NOT MY WILL, BUT THINE BE DONE.

WHEN JESUS RETURNS TO HIS DISCIPLES, HE FINDS THEM SLEEPING. TWO MORE TIMES HE GOES ASIDE TO PRAY, AND EACH TIME HE FINDS HIS FRIENDS ASLEEP. AFTER WAKING THEM THE THIRD TIME...

ARISE -- THE ONE WHO IS TO BETRAY ME IS NEAR.

AS JESUS SPEAKS, JUDAS LEADS A BAND OF MEN INTO THE GARDEN. ACCORDING TO HIS AGREEMENT, HE IDENTIFIES JESUS WITH A KISS.

GREETINGS, MASTER!

AS THE SOLDIERS TAKE HOLD OF JESUS, PETER DRAWS HIS SWORD. SLASHING WILDLY, HE CUTS OFF THE EAR OF A SERVANT.

PETER, PUT UP YOUR SWORD. DO YOU THINK THAT I CANNOT CALL ON GOD TO SEND LEGIONS OF ANGELS TO PROTECT ME?

QUIETLY JESUS HEALS THE MAN'S EAR. WHEN THE DISCIPLES SEE THAT JESUS IS MAKING NO ATTEMPT TO SAVE HIMSELF, THEY RUN FOR THEIR LIVES. AT AN OFFICER'S COMMAND, THE SOLDIERS BIND JESUS AND TAKE HIM BACK TO JERUSALEM—THE CITY INTO WHICH HE HAD RIDDEN SO TRIUMPHANTLY ONLY A FEW DAYS BEFORE.

647

Tried and Denied!

FROM MATTHEW 26:57–75; JOHN 18:28–38;
LUKE 23:6–12

FOLLOWING HIS ARREST, JESUS IS BROUGHT TO THE PALACE OF THE HIGH PRIEST. FALSE WITNESSES BOLDLY ACCUSE HIM OF MANY THINGS --BUT THEY CAN PROVE NOTHING. FINALLY THE HIGH PRIEST QUESTIONS THE PRISONER.

ARE YOU THE CHRIST, THE SON OF GOD?

I AM.

THERE! YOU HEARD HIM. ANYONE WHO SPEAKS BLASPHEMY BY CLAIMING TO BE GOD'S SON DESERVES TO DIE.

INSTANTLY THE GUARDS TURN ON JESUS -- SPITTING ON HIM, COVERING HIS FACE AND DEMANDING THAT HE PROVE HIS POWER BY IDENTIFYING THOSE WHO STRIKE HIM.

FOR THE THIRD TIME PETER DENIES KNOWING JESUS-- AND THEN THE COCK CROWS! STARTLED, PETER RAISES HIS HEAD--TO LOOK STRAIGHT INTO THE EYES OF JESUS, WHO IS BEING LED OUT OF THE COURT.

SICK WITH SHAME, PETER RUSHES OUTSIDE, WEEPING BITTERLY.

THREE TIMES I DENIED MY LORD--JUST AS HE SAID I WOULD! O GOD, FORGIVE ME, FORGIVE ME!

IN THE EARLY HOURS OF FRIDAY MORNING THE MEMBERS OF THE JEWISH HIGH COURT, WHICH CANNOT SENTENCE A MAN TO DEATH, TAKE JESUS TO THE ROMAN GOVERNOR, PILATE. CLEVERLY, THEY CHARGE HIM-- NOT WITH BREAKING JEWISH LAWS--BUT WITH TREASON AGAINST ROME. PILATE QUESTIONS JESUS PRIVATELY AND THEN RETURNS HIM TO THE PRIESTS AND CROWDS THAT HAVE GATHERED OUTSIDE.

I DO NOT FIND THIS MAN GUILTY OF ANY CRIME.

NOT GUILTY? WHY, HE TRIED TO START REVOLTS ALL OVER JUDEA AND GALILEE!

AT THE MENTION OF GALILEE, PILATE SENDS JESUS TO HEROD, THE RULER OF GALILEE, WHO IS IN JERUSALEM FOR THE PASSOVER. HEROD IS CURIOUS AND ASKS JESUS TO PERFORM SOME MIRACLE. WHEN JESUS WILL NOT, HEROD AND HIS SOLDIERS MAKE FUN OF HIM -- AND THEN RETURN HIM TO PILATE.

PILATE HESITATES TO DECLARE JESUS GUILTY OF TREASON. HE DOES NOT BELIEVE JESUS IS GUILTY. "BUT, IF I LET HIM GO," HE ARGUES TO HIMSELF, "AND THE LOCAL LEADERS MAKE TROUBLE, THE EMPEROR IN ROME WILL HOLD ME RESPONSIBLE." FINALLY HE THINKS OF A WAY TO EASE HIS CONSCIENCE AND PROTECT HIMSELF....

THE PEOPLE! I'LL LET THEM DECIDE!

Condemned to Die

FROM JOHN 18:39—19:16;
MATTHEW 27:3–10

THE RELIGIOUS LEADERS HAVE CHARGED JESUS WITH TREASON AGAINST ROME. PILATE, THE ROMAN GOVERNOR, DOES NOT BELIEVE HE IS GUILTY--BUT HE IS AFRAID TO ANGER HIS OPPONENTS FOR FEAR THEY WILL STIR UP SO MUCH TROUBLE THAT THE REPORTS OF IT WILL REACH THE EMPEROR IN ROME. LOOKING AT THE CROWDS IN JERUSALEM FOR THE PASSOVER, HE SUDDENLY SEES A WAY OUT: LET THE PEOPLE DECIDE WHETHER OR NOT JESUS SHOULD DIE. BUT HE DOES NOT KNOW THAT THE PRIESTS ARE STIRRING UP THE CROWDS

IT IS THE CUSTOM TO RELEASE A PRISONER TO YOU DURING THE PASSOVER. WHICH SHALL I GIVE YOU-- JESUS, WHO IS CALLED THE CHRIST-- OR BARABBAS, THE MURDERER?

BARABBAS! GIVE US BARABBAS!

PILATE IS STUNNED. HE MAKES ANOTHER ATTEMPT TO SAVE JESUS.

SCOURGE HIM.

MAYBE THE PEOPLE WILL BE SATISFIED IF THE PRISONER IS PUNISHED.

SO JESUS IS WHIPPED WITH LEATHER THONGS. THEN, IN SPORT, THE SOLDIERS MAKE A CROWN OF THORNS AND PLACE IT ON HIS HEAD.

HAIL, THE KING OF THE JEWS!

HOPING THE SIGHT OF JESUS, BRUTALLY BEATEN, WILL AROUSE THE CROWD'S SYMPATHY, PILATE PRESENTS HIM TO THE MULTITUDE.

BEHOLD THE MAN!

CRUCIFY HIM!

CRUCIFY HIM!

654

I HAVE SINNED-- I HAVE BETRAYED AN INNOCENT MAN.

WHAT IS THAT TO US?

HERE-- TAKE IT. I WANT NO PART OF YOUR DIRTY MONEY.

DRIVEN BY GUILT TOO GREAT TO BEAR, JUDAS GOES OUT AND HANGS HIMSELF.

BUT RETURNING THE MONEY DOES NOT SAVE THE MAN HE HAS BETRAYED. JESUS IS NOW IN THE HANDS OF THE ROMAN SOLDIERS-- WHO PLACE A HEAVY CROSS ON HIS BACK AND FORCE HIM OUT INTO THE STREET THAT LEADS TO A HILL CALLED CALVARY...

A King Is Crucified

FROM LUKE 23:26–46; JOHN 19:25–27

HAPPY, EXCITED PILGRIMS FROM ALL OVER PALESTINE HAVE BEEN CROWDING INTO JERUSALEM FOR DAYS TO CELEBRATE THE PASSOVER FEAST. BUT ON FRIDAY MORNING STARTLING NEWS SWEEPS ACROSS THE CITY LIKE A CHILLING WIND: JESUS OF NAZARETH IS GOING TO BE CRUCIFIED -- FOR TREASON!

THE STREET THAT LEADS TO THE HILL OF EXECUTION IS SOON FILLED WITH A STRANGE MIXTURE OF PEOPLE-- PRIESTS AND PHARISEES WHO DEMAND JESUS' DEATH; WOMEN WEEPING FOR THE MAN WHO FORGAVE SINS AND HEALED THE SICK; AND THE CURIOUS WHO WANT ONLY TO SEE A CONDEMNED MAN CARRY HIS CROSS...

IT IS NOW NOON. SLOWLY, A STRANGE SHADOW COVERS THE LAND. FOR THREE HOURS THERE IS DARKNESS, THEN JESUS CRIES OUT TO GOD...

The Sealed Tomb

FROM MARK 15:38–39; LUKE 23:48–49;
JOHN 19:38–42; MATTHEW 27:62–66

AT ABOUT NINE O'CLOC
FRIDAY MORNING JE
OF NAZARETH IS
CRUCIFIED OUTSIDE
WALLS OF JERUSAL
FROM NOON UNTIL THRI
O'CLOCK DARKNESS COV
THE LAND. THEN -- SUDDE
AN EARTHQUAKE ROCK
THE GROUND. AND IN
JERUSALEM...

THE VEIL BEFORE
THE HOLIEST PLACE
IN THE TEMPLE HAS
BEEN RIPPED! WH
CAN IT MEAN?

THIS IS THE ANSWER: ON A HILL CALLED CALVARY THE SON OF GO
HAS GIVEN HIS LIFE FOR THE SINS OF THE WORLD. THE VEIL IN THE
TEMPLE NO LONGER SEPARATES US FROM THE PRESENCE OF GOD,
FOR JESUS, THE SON, HAS OPENED THE WAY TO GOD, THE FATHER.

OUTSIDE THE CITY, EVEN THE ROMAN OFFICER WHO DIRECTED THE CRUCIFIXION IS AWED BY WHAT HAS HAPPENED. REVERENTLY, HE LOOKS UP AT THE MAN WHO FORGAVE HIS ENEMIES.

TRULY THIS MAN WAS GOD'S SON!

THE PEOPLE, TOO, ARE SHAKEN BY THE EXECUTION. AS THEY TURN BACK TO THE CITY...

I HAD HOPED THAT HE WAS THE ONE WHO WOULD DELIVER US FROM THE ROMANS.

IN JERUSALEM JOSEPH OF ARIMATHEA, A MEMBER OF THE JEWISH HIGH COURT AND SECRETLY A FOLLOWER OF JESUS, GOES BOLDLY TO PILATE.

MAY I HAVE THE BODY OF JESUS SO THAT WE MAY BURY IT BEFORE THE SABBATH?

YES... I'LL GIVE ORDERS TO MY OFFICER IN CHARGE.

REVERENTLY, JOSEPH TAKES THE BODY OF JESUS FROM THE CROSS. THEN HE AND HIS FRIEND, NICODEMUS, WRAP IT IN LINEN CLOTH, AND PLACE IT IN JOSEPH'S GARDEN TOMB.

EARLY THE NEXT DAY THE PRIESTS AND PHARISEES ALSO GO TO PILATE...

WE REMEMBER JESUS SAID THAT AFTER THREE DAYS HE WOULD RISE FROM THE DEAD. ORDER YOUR SOLDIERS TO SEAL AND GUARD THE TOMB SO THAT HIS DISCIPLES CAN'T STEAL THE BODY AND CLAIM THAT JESUS MADE GOOD ON HIS BOAST.

TAKE THE SOLDIERS YOU NEED AND SET UP A GUARD UNTIL AFTER THE THIRD DAY.

SO THE TOMB IS SEALED, AND ROMAN SOLDIERS ARE PLACED ON GUARD.

THERE-- THAT'S THE LAST WE'LL HEAR OF THIS MAN WHO CALLED HIMSELF THE SON OF GOD!

Arresting a King

When Jesus is arrested, His friends think their hope is gone. In a short time, Jesus is arrested, tried, and crucified. Little do they realize, that He will rise a victorious King soon. Here are some of the things that happen:

▶ Jesus is about 33 years old when He dies.

▶ When soldiers arrest Jesus, Peter cuts off an ear of the guard. Jesus heals the ear immediately (p. 647).

▶ All of Jesus' friends desert Him when He is arrested (p. 647).

▶ When Jesus dies, an earthquake occurs and the heavy veil in the temple splits in half from top to bottom. This veil is 60 feet long and 30 feet high (p. 660).

▶ Judas betrays Jesus for 30 pieces of silver, the price paid for a slave (p. 640).

▶ Soldiers mock Jesus by giving Him a robe, a crown of thorns, and a reed for a scepter (p. 653).

Be sure to turn to the other side of this page to see where Jesus went during this time.

663

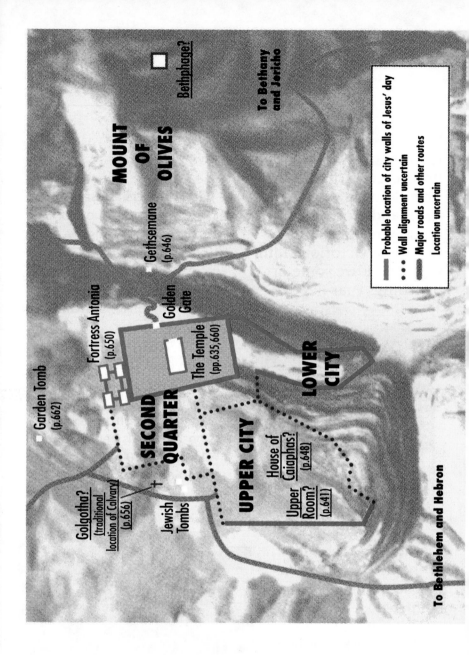

Bethphage?

To Bethany and Jericho

MOUNT OF OLIVES

Gethsemane (p.646)

Fortress Antonia (p.650)

Golden Gate

The Temple (pp.635,660)

Garden Tomb (p.662)

SECOND QUARTER

LOWER CITY

Golgotha? (traditional location of Calvary) (p.656)

Jewish Tombs

UPPER CITY

House of Caiaphas? (p.648)

Upper Room? (p.641)

To Bethlehem and Hebron

Probable location of city walls of Jesus' day
Wall alignment uncertain
Major roads and other routes
Location uncertain

Jerusalem
in the
First Century A.D.

The Lord Is Risen

FROM MARK 16:1–7; JOHN 20:2–18;
MATTHEW 28:11–15; LUKE 24:13–32

FRIDAY -- JUST OUTSIDE JERUSALEM -- JESUS OF NAZARETH IS CRUCIFIED AND BURIED. AT THE REQUEST OF THE PRIESTS AND PHARISEES, THE TOMB IS SEALED AND ROMAN SOLDIERS SET TO GUARD IT.

BUT ON THE MORNING OF THE THIRD DAY THE EARTH TREMBLES. AN ANGEL OF THE LORD DESCENDS -- AND ROLLS THE HEAVY STONE ASIDE. TERRIFIED, THE SOLDIERS FALL TO THE GROUND. WHEN THEY CAN GET TO THEIR FEET THEY RUSH BACK TO THE CITY.

THAT SAME MORNING MARY MAGDALENE AND OTHER FRIENDS OF JESUS HURRY TO THE TOMB WITH SPICES TO ANOINT HIS BODY. ON THE WAY, THEY WORRY ABOUT HOW THEY WILL GET THE STONE ROLLED AWAY. BUT WHEN THEY REACH THE GARDEN...

THE TOMB! IT IS OPEN!

BELIEVING THAT SOMEONE HAS STOLEN JESUS' BODY, MARY RUNS BACK TO JERUSALEM TO TELL PETER AND JOHN. BUT THE OTHERS ENTER THE TOMB-- TO FIND AN ANGEL SEATED THERE.

DON'T BE FRIGHTENED. JESUS IS RISEN. GO, TELL HIS DISCIPLES.

IN THE CITY PETER AND JOHN ARE SO STARTLED BY MARY'S NEWS THAT THEY RACE BACK AHEAD OF HER. WHEN THEY REACH THE TOMB--

ONLY HIS BURIAL CLOTHES. WHAT DO YOU MAKE OF IT?

THAT HE ROSE FROM THE DEAD-- AS HE SAID HE WOULD. OH, WHY DIDN'T WE BELIEVE HIM!

BY THE TIME MARY REACHES THE GARDEN THE OTHERS HAVE GONE. IN HER GRIEF SHE DOES NOT RECOGNIZE THE VOICE OF ONE WHO QUESTIONS HER.

WHY DO YOU WEEP?

IF YOU HAVE TAKEN JESUS' BODY, TELL ME WHERE YOU HAVE LAID IT.

FTLY JESUS SPEAKS HER NAME-- ARY!" SHE TURNS -- AND SEES HER EN LORD.

MASTER!

BUT JESUS' FRIENDS ARE NOT THE ONLY ONES WHO ARE EXCITED ABOUT WHAT HAPPENED IN THE GARDEN. IN JERUSALEM THE ROMAN SOLDIERS REPORT TO THE PRIESTS AND PHARISEES. AFRAID OF WHAT MAY HAPPEN IF THE TRUTH IS KNOWN, THEY ACT QUICKLY.

HERE, TAKE THIS MONEY. TELL PEOPLE THAT JESUS' DISCIPLES STOLE HIS BODY.

WHILE THE SOLDIERS SPREAD HEIR LIE, JESUS JOINS TWO OF IS DISCIPLES ON THE WAY TO MMAUS. THEY TALK WITH HIM, BUT THEY DO NOT KNOW WHO HE IS.

THAT EVENING AS THEY DINE IN EMMAUS, JESUS BLESSES THE BREAD -- AND WHEN HE HANDS IT TO THEM THEY SUDDENLY RECOGNIZE HIM.

JESUS!

AND JUST AS SUDDENLY HE VANISHES FROM THEIR SIGHT!

Behind Locked Doors

FROM LUKE 24:33–43; JOHN 20:19—21:6

IT IS LATE SUNDAY NIGHT-- THROUGHOUT JERUSALEM PEOPLE ARE STILL TALKING ABOUT THE STRANGE REPORT OF THE ROMAN SOLDIERS.

THEY SAY JESUS' DISCIPLES STOLE HIS BODY TO MAKE US BELIEVE HE ROSE FROM THE DEAD.

I WONDER WHAT THOSE BRAVE ROMAN GUARDS WERE DOING WHILE THE TOMB WAS ROBBED. AND WHAT DO THE DISCIPLES SAY?

BUT JESUS' FRIENDS HAVE ALSO HEARD THE SOLDIERS' REPORT. THEY ARE AFRAID THEY MAY BE ARRESTED, SO THEY LOCK THE DOORS IN THE UPPER ROOM WHERE ALL--BUT THOMAS-- HAVE GATHERED. TWO FRIENDS FIND THEM THERE.

JESUS IS ALIVE! WE WERE ON OUR WAY TO EMMAUS WHEN A STRANGER JOINED US. WE ASKED HIM TO HAVE SUPPER WITH US. AND WHEN HE BLESSED THE BREAD AND GAVE IT TO US, WE KNEW--ALL AT ONCE--THAT THE STRANGER WAS JESUS. THEN HE DISAPPEARED.

669

A WEEK LATER THOMAS IS WITH THE DISCIPLES WHEN THEY MEET AGAIN BEHIND LOCKED DOORS. ONCE MORE JESUS APPEARS TO THEM.

THOMAS, TOUCH MY HANDS AND MY SIDE.

MY LORD AND MY GOD!

BECAUSE YOU HAVE SEEN, THOMAS, YOU BELIEVE. BLESSED ARE THOSE WHO HAVE NOT SEEN AND YET HAVE BELIEVED.

AGAIN JESUS DISAPPEARS FROM THEIR SIGHT.

OBEYING A COMMAND THAT JESUS HAD GIVEN THEM, THE DISCIPLES GO NORTH TO GALILEE. ONE EVENING THEY GO FISHING. THEY FISH ALL NIGHT BUT CATCH NOTHING. AT DAYBREAK THEY SEE THE FIGURE OF A MAN STANDING ON THE SHORE.

CAST YOUR NET ON THE RIGHT SIDE OF THE BOAT.

THEY OBEY—AND SUDDENLY THE NET IS SO FULL OF FISH THEY CANNOT PULL IT IN.

he Last Command

ROM JOHN 21:7–18; MATTHEW 28:16–20;
UKE 24:44–51

LL NIGHT THE DISCIPLES OF JESUS FISH IN
HE SEA OF GALILEE--AND CATCH NOTHING. AT
AYBREAK THEY SEE A MAN ON SHORE WHO TELLS
HEM TO CAST THEIR NET ON THE RIGHT SIDE
F THE BOAT. THEY OBEY--AND SUDDENLY
HE NET IS SO FULL THAT THE RUGGED
ISHERMEN CANNOT DRAW IT UP. JOHN
OOKS AGAIN AT THE FIGURE
N THE SHORE...

LOOK, PETER, IT IS THE LORD!

PETER IS SO EAGER TO REACH JESUS
THAT HE JUMPS INTO THE WATER AND
SWIMS TO LAND. THE OTHERS BRING THE
BOAT IN AND ANCHOR IT OFFSHORE.
AFTER THE NET IS PULLED IN, JESUS
CALLS TO HIS HUNGRY DISCIPLES.

COME AND EAT.

WHEN THEY FINISH EATING, JESUS TURNS TO PETER.

PETER, DO YOU LOVE ME?

YES, LORD, YOU KNOW I DO.

TWICE MORE JESUS ASKS PETER THE SAME QUESTION, AND EACH TIME PETER DECLARES HIS LOYALTY. THEN JESUS GIVES HIM A GREAT ASSIGNMENT.

TAKE CARE OF MY FOLLOWERS, PETER.

A FEW DAYS LATER JESUS APPEARS TO FIVE HUNDRED OF HIS FOLLOWERS, GATHERED AT HIS COMMAND, ON A MOUNTAIN NEAR THE SEA OF GALILEE. HE GIVES THEM A GREAT COMMISSION:

GO YE THEREFORE, AND TEACH ALL NATIONS, BAPTIZING THEM IN THE NAME OF THE FATHER, AND OF THE SON, AND OF THE HOLY SPIRIT, TEACHING THEM TO OBSERVE ALL THINGS WHATSOEVER I HAVE COMMANDED YOU: AND, LO, I AM WITH YOU ALWAYS, EVEN UNTO THE END OF THE WORLD.

DURING THE TIME BETWEEN JESUS'
RESURRECTION AND ASCENSION,
JESUS MEETS WITH HIS FOLLOWERS
AND EXPLAINS HOW--BY HIS DEATH
AND RESURRECTION--HE HAS FULFILLED
GOD'S MISSION FOR HIM TO BE THE
SAVIOR OF THE WORLD. HE CHARGES
THEM TO CARRY ON THE WORK.
"BUT WAIT IN JERUSALEM," HE
ADDS, "UNTIL THE POWER OF
GOD'S HOLY SPIRIT COMES
UPON YOU."

ON THE FORTIETH DAY
AFTER HIS RESURRECTION,
JESUS TAKES HIS DISCIPLES
TO THE MOUNT OF OLIVES
NEAR BETHANY. AND WHILE
HE IS BLESSING THEM, HE
ASCENDS INTO HEAVEN.

The Acts of the Apostles,

THE FIFTH BOOK OF THE NEW TESTAMENT, TELLS HOW JESUS'
DISCIPLES OBEYED HIS COMMAND TO GO INTO ALL THE WORLD
AND PREACH THE GOSPEL.

Waiting for a Promise FROM ACTS 1:1–26

FORTY DAYS AFTER HIS RESURRECTION JESUS
TAKES HIS ELEVEN DISCIPLES TO THE MOUNT OF
OLIVES, NEAR BETHANY. WHILE HE IS GIVING
THEM HIS FINAL BLESSING, HE IS LIFTED UP OUT
OF THEIR SIGHT. IN AWE AND WONDER
THEY STAND LOOKING UP INTO HEAVEN
AS IF TO CATCH ONE MORE GLIMPSE
OF THE MASTER THEY LOVE. SUDDENLY
TWO ANGELS APPEAR.

YOU MEN OF GALILEE,
WHY DO YOU STAND HERE
LOOKING UP INTO HEAVEN?
JESUS WILL COME AGAIN-- IN
THE VERY WAY YOU HAVE
SEEN HIM GO.

THE DISCIPLES ASK GOD'S GUIDANCE IN THE CHOICE THEY MAKE-- AND MATTHIAS IS NAMED.

THE LORD HAS BLESSED YOU, MATTHIAS.

FOR THE NEXT TEN DAYS THE DISCIPLES MEET TOGETHER IN PRAYER--WAITING FOR THE COMING OF THE HOLY SPIRIT. AT THE SAME TIME FAITHFUL JEWS FROM ALL OVER PALESTINE, AND EVEN DISTANT COUNTRIES, CROWD INTO JERUSALEM TO CELEBRATE THE FEAST OF THANKSGIVING CALLED PENTECOST.

MANY OF THE PILGRIMS PASS BY THE PLACE CALLED CALVARY, AND ARE REMINDED OF JESUS' CRUCIFIXION.

ROMAN SOLDIERS SAY JESUS' DISCIPLES STOLE HIS BODY FROM THE TOMB AND CLAIM HE ROSE FROM THE DEAD AS HE PROPHESIED HE WOULD.

BUT I'VE ALSO HEARD THAT A LOT OF PEOPLE SAW JESUS --ALIVE. I HOPE I CAN FIND SOMEONE IN JERUSALEM WHO DID.

I'M SEEKING THE TRUTH--BUT IT WILL TAKE A SIGN FROM GOD TO MAKE ME BELIEVE THAT JESUS' DISCIPLES SPEAK IT.

Like Tongues of Fire! FROM ACTS 2:1–38

AS JESUS RAISED FROM THE DEAD? OR DID HIS DISCIPLES STEAL HIS BODY FROM THE TOMB AND CLAIM THAT HE WAS?

THESE QUESTIONS ARE STILL BEING ASKED AS JEWS COME TO JERUSALEM TO CELEBRATE THE HARVEST FEAST CALLED PENTECOST. JESUS' DISCIPLES KNOW THE TRUTH; BUT THEY ARE WAITING FOR POWER FROM GOD TO HELP THEM PREACH IT TO THE WORLD.

EARLY ON THE DAY OF PENTECOST, 120 FOLLOWERS OF JESUS ARE GATHERED IN A SECRET ROOM, PRAYING. SUDDENLY THERE IS A SOUND LIKE A RUSHING, MIGHTY WIND, AND GOD'S PRESENCE FILLS THE ROOM. THEN, LIKE TONGUES OF FIRE, HIS SPIRIT RESTS ON EACH ONE.

IN THAT SACRED MOMENT JESUS' FOLLOWERS ARE FILLED WITH STRENGTH AND COURAGE THEY HAVE NEVER KNOWN. RUSHING OUT OF THE UPPER ROOM AND INTO THE STREET BELOW, THEY BEGIN TO PREACH -- EACH IN A DIFFERENT LANGUAGE AS THE SPIRIT OF GOD DIRECTS.

THE CROWDS LISTEN WITH AMAZEMENT. AS THE STORY OF THIS STRANGE EVENT SPREADS, IT REACHES TWO MEN WHO HAVE COME TO JERUSALEM SEEKING THE TRUTH ABOUT JESUS.

LET'S FIND THE DISCIPLES AND SEE FOR OURSELVES IF WHAT THE PEOPLE ARE SAYING IS TRUE.

THEY FIND THE DISCIPLES, AND AS THEY LISTEN...

IT **IS** TRUE! EVERYONE IN JERUSALEM -- EVEN THOSE MEN FROM ARABIA, EGYPT, ROME, CRETE -- CAN UNDERSTAND WHAT THE DISCIPLES SAY. HOW DO YOU EXPLAIN IT?

THEY'VE BEEN DRINKING TOO MUCH NEW WINE.

DRUNKEN MEN DO NOT SUDDENLY SPEAK IN FOREIGN LANGUAGES -- AND WITH SUCH WISDOM.

678

IN ANSWER TO THIS INSULT, PETER SPEAKS OUT FOR ALL THE DISCIPLES.

WE ARE NOT DRUNK! WE ARE FILLED WITH THE HOLY SPIRIT AS THE PROPHET JOEL PROPHESIED. YOU MEN OF JERUSALEM, YOU CRUCIFIED JESUS, THE CHOSEN ONE OF GOD. BUT GOD RAISED HIM FROM THE DEAD, AND WE ARE WITNESSES TO THAT RESURRECTION!

THIS BOLD CHARGE CUTS DEEP INTO THE HEARTS OF THE PEOPLE, FOR THEY REMEMBER HOW THEY CALLED FOR JESUS' CRUCIFIXION.

REPENT OF YOUR SINS, AND BE BAPTIZED IN THE NAME OF JESUS CHRIST. THEN YOU SHALL RECEIVE THE GIFT OF THE HOLY SPIRIT AS WE HAVE!

YOU SAID IT WOULD TAKE A SIGN FROM GOD TO CONVINCE YOU THAT JESUS' DISCIPLES SPEAK THE TRUTH. WHAT DO YOU SAY NOW?

Three Thousand in a Day

FROM ACTS 2:38—3:7

WHEN PETER BOLDLY TELLS THE PEOPLE IN JERUSALEM THAT THEY CONDEMNED GOD'S CHOSEN ONE TO DIE, THEY ASK, "WHAT CAN WE DO?" "REPENT AND BE BAPTIZED IN THE NAME OF THE ONE YOU CRUCIFIED," PETER REPLIES. ONE BY ONE THE PEOPLE CRY OUT...

O GOD, FORGIVE MY SINS, IN THE NAME OF YOUR SON, JESUS CHRIST, WHO CAME TO SAVE ME!

YOU SAID ONLY A SIGN FROM GOD COULD MAKE YOU BELIEVE JESUS' DISCIPLES SPOKE THE TRUTH--

YES, AND I HAVE SEEN THAT SIGN. I BELIEVE JESUS LIVES. I BELIEVE HE IS THE SON OF GOD AND THAT THROUGH HIM MY SINS CAN BE FORGIVEN. HOW GOOD GOD IS TO GIVE ME A CHANCE TO BEGIN A NEW LIFE -- WITH JESUS!

BEFORE THE DAY OF PENTECOST IS OVER, THREE THOUSAND PEOPLE ARE BAPTIZED. AND AS THE DAYS PASS MORE AND MORE JOIN THE GROUP OF JESUS' FOLLOWERS. THE UPPER ROOM IS NOT LARGE ENOUGH TO HOLD THE CROWDS, SO PEOPLE MEET IN HOMES.

I'VE BROUGHT SOME FRIENDS WHO WANT TO LEARN ABOUT JESUS.

COME IN-- YOU ARE WELCOME.

HAVE YOU HEARD-- THE POOR WIDOW WE TALKED WITH NEEDS FOOD FOR HER CHILDREN.

I'LL GIVE THE APOSTLES SOME MONEY TO HELP HER.

THE FOLLOWERS OF JESUS ARE SO HAPPY WORSHIPING TOGETHER AND TAKING CARE OF ONE ANOTHER'S NEEDS THAT SOON ALL JERUSALEM IS TALKING ABOUT THEM.

WHAT DO YOU MAKE OF THESE FRIENDS OF JESUS?

I DON'T UNDERSTAND THEM--BUT I WISH I COULD BE AS HAPPY AS THEY ARE.

ONE AFTERNOON WHEN PETER AND JOHN GO TO THE TEMPLE FOR PRAYER THEY FIND A LAME MAN BEGGING AT THE BEAUTIFUL GATE.

HAVE MERCY-- A COIN FOR THE POOR.

LOOK AT US!

MAYBE **BOTH** OF THEM WILL GIVE ME SOMETHING...

I HAVE NO MONEY, BUT I'LL GIVE YOU WHAT I HAVE. IN THE NAME OF JESUS CHRIST, RISE UP AND WALK!

WALK? THE MAN WHO HAS NEVER TAKEN A STEP IN HIS LIFE CANNOT BELIEVE WHAT HE HAS HEARD. BUT AS PETER REACHES OUT HIS HAND TO HIM, THE MAN STRETCHES FORTH HIS OWN...

Miracle at the Gate

FROM ACTS 3:7—4:17

TO THE LAME BEGGAR AT THE TEMPLE GATE, PETER HOLDS OUT HIS HAND AND SAYS, "IN THE NAME OF JESUS CHRIST, RISE UP AND WALK!" AT ONCE THE MAN FEELS STRENGTH COME TO HIS LEGS AND ANKLES. HE LEAPS TO HIS FEET!

I CAN WALK! PRAISE GOD, I CAN WALK!

IN HIS EXCITEMENT THE MAN RUSHES INTO THE TEMPLE, LEAPING AND SHOUTING FOR JOY.

LOOK! ISN'T THAT THE LAME MAN WHO WAS AT THE GATE?

YES, BUT--

GRATEFULLY, THE MAN TURNS TO PETER AND JOHN. THE CROWDS GATHER AROUND-- EAGER TO KNOW WHAT HAS HAPPENED.

WHY DO YOU LOOK AT US AS THOUGH **WE** MADE THIS MAN WALK? THE HEALING POWER CAME FROM GOD, WHO HAS DONE THIS TO HONOR JESUS WHOM **YOU** CRUCIFIED, BUT GOD RAISED FROM THE DEAD.

SEEING THAT HE HAS THE ATTENTION OF THE CROWD, PETER CONTINUES...

REPENT, AND TURN TO GOD SO THAT YOUR SINS MAY BE WIPED OUT. PREPARE YOURSELVES, FOR CHRIST WILL COME AGAIN...

AT THE BACK OF THE CROWD THE PRIESTS LISTEN. THEY ARE ANGRY—AND THEIR ANGER INCREASES AS THEY WATCH THE GROWING INTEREST OF THE PEOPLE.

HE MUST BE STOPPED AT ONCE--OR HE'LL HAVE ALL OF JERUSALEM BELIEVING THAT JESUS ROSE FROM THE DEAD.

WITH THE HELP OF THE CAPTAIN OF THE TEMPLE GUARDS, THE PRIESTS PUSH THEIR WAY THROUGH THE CROWDS.

YOU ARE UNDER ARREST!

WITHOUT ANOTHER WORD, PETER AND JOHN ARE MARCHED AWAY TO PRISON-- BUT ALREADY FIVE THOUSAND MEN HAVE DECLARED THEIR BELIEF IN JESUS.

THE NEXT MORNING THEY ARE BROUGHT BEFORE THE SANHEDRIN, THE SAME JEWISH COURT THAT CON-DEMNED JESUS TO DEATH. BESIDE THEM-- PERFECTLY WELL-- STANDS THE MAN WHO HAD BEEN LAME FROM BIRTH.

BY WHAT POWER AND IN WHOSE NAME HAVE YOU HEALED THIS MAN?

685

FILLED WITH THE HOLY SPIRIT, PETER SPEAKS OUT COURAGEOUSLY.

LET IT BE KNOWN TO YOU, AND ALL THE PEOPLE OF ISRAEL -- THIS MAN WAS HEALED BY THE NAME OF JESUS CHRIST OF NAZARETH, WHOM **YOU** CRUCIFIED!

THE COURT, IS STUNNED. PETER AND JOHN ARE UNEDUCATED FISHERMEN, YET THEY SPEAK AND ACT WITH AUTHORITY AND POWER.

TAKE THEM AWAY --UNTIL WE CALL FOR THEM AGAIN.

THE MINUTE THE PRISONERS ARE OUT OF SIGHT, THE COURT HOLDS A MEETING.

EVERYONE KNOWS A MIRACLE HAS TAKEN PLACE. WE CANNOT DENY IT, BUT WE MUST KEEP THE NEWS FROM SPREADING. WHAT CAN WE DO?

TELL THESE "PREACHERS" THAT IF THEY SPEAK AGAIN IN THE NAME OF JESUS THEY WILL BE PUT TO DEATH AS HE WAS!

686

The Pretenders

FROM ACTS 4:18—5:18

PETER TELLS THE PEOPLE THAT HE HEALED THE LAME MAN IN THE NAME OF JESUS, WHOM THEY AND THEIR LEADERS CRUCIFIED AND WHOM GOD RAISED FROM THE DEAD. THIS ANGERS THE PRIESTS; THEY HAVE PETER AND JOHN ARRESTED AND BROUGHT BEFORE THE COURT. THE PRIESTS WANT TO PUNISH THE DISCIPLES BUT ARE AFRAID THIS WILL STIR THE CROWDS TO RIOT.

WE WILL RELEASE YOU THIS TIME, BUT DON'T EVER PREACH ABOUT JESUS AGAIN.

688

THE PRAISE THAT IS SHOWERED ON BARNABAS FOR HIS GENEROUS GIFT PROMPTS A MAN NAMED ANANIAS AND HIS WIFE, SAPPHIRA, TO SEEK SUCH HONOR FOR THEMSELVES.

WE, TOO, HAVE SOLD OUR LAND AND WE WANT TO GIVE THE MONEY TO HELP THE CHURCH.

ANANIAS, THE MONEY WAS YOURS TO DO WITH AS YOU PLEASED. BUT WHY DO YOU PRETEND TO GIVE ALL, WHEN YOU KNOW THAT IS NOT TRUE? DON'T YOU SEE -- YOU ARE LYING TO GOD?

WHEN ANANIAS HEARS THESE WORDS, HE FALLS DOWN DEAD. SOME YOUNG MEN TAKE HIS BODY AWAY, AND AS THEY ARE RETURNING SAPPHIRA COMES IN. LIKE HER HUSBAND, SHE LIES ABOUT THE MONEY.

SAPPHIRA, YOUR HUSBAND IS DEAD BECAUSE HE LIED TO GOD. AND YOU WILL PAY THE SAME PENALTY.

INSTANTLY SAPPHIRA FALLS TO THE FLOOR -- AND DIES. THE FOLLOWERS OF JESUS LOOK ON THIS SEVERE PUNISHMENT AS A WARNING TO ANYONE WHO THINKS HE CAN PRETEND LOYALTY TO GOD.

IN SPITE OF THREATS, THE DISCIPLES KEEP ON HEALING IN THE NAME OF JESUS. THE PRIESTS WATCH--ANGRY BUT HELPLESS--AS FAMILIES BRING THEIR SICK ONES OUT INTO THE STREETS, WAITING FOR THE DISCIPLES TO PASS BY AND HEAL THEM.

HE IS LAME— PLEASE MAKE HIM STRONG SO THAT HE CAN RUN AND PLAY LIKE OTHER CHILDREN.

I CANNOT HEAL HIM, BUT JESUS, THE SON OF GOD, CAN. IN HIS NAME, I SAY TO YOU, YOUR SON IS HEALED.

THE FAME OF THE DISCIPLES SPREADS-- AND SOON PEOPLE FROM THE TOWNS ROU ABOUT CROWD INTO JERUSALEM, BEGGIN TO BE HEALED. AT LAST THE PRIESTS CA STAND IT NO LONGER. IN A FIT OF RAGE THEY HAVE THE DISCIPLES ARRESTED AN THROWN INTO JAIL.

THIS TIME THERE WILL BE NO RELEASE!

Missing Prisoners

FROM ACTS 5:19—6:10

AFRAID THAT THE CROWDS MIGHT TURN AGAINST THEM, THE PRIESTS ARE FORCED TO STAND BY WHILE JESUS' DISCIPLES CONTINUE TO TEACH AND HEAL THE SICK. BUT WHEN PEOPLE FROM OTHER CITIES BEGIN TO POUR INTO JERUSALEM ASKING FOR THE DISCIPLES, THE PRIESTS CAN CONTROL THEIR JEALOUSY NO LONGER. THEY HAVE THE DISCIPLES ARRESTED AND THROWN INTO PRISON. DURING THE NIGHT AN ANGEL FROM GOD RELEASES THEM.

GO-- STAND IN THE TEMPLE AND TELL PEOPLE ABOUT THE NEW LIFE GOD HAS PROMISED THOSE WHO BELIEVE IN HIS SON, JESUS CHRIST.

692

WE MUST OBEY GOD RATHER THAN MEN!

AT THIS REPLY THE COURT IS SO ANGRY THAT IT WANTS THE DISCIPLES KILLED AT ONCE. BUT GAMALIEL, A FAMOUS TEACHER, QUICKLY ORDERS THE DISCIPLES TAKEN OUTSIDE. THEN HE TURNS TO THE COURT.

BE CAREFUL OF THE ACTION YOU TAKE AGAINST THESE MEN. IF THIS TEACHING IS THEIR OWN IDEA, IT WILL FAIL. BUT IF IT IS FROM GOD YOU CANNOT DEFEAT THEM-- AND YOU WILL FIND YOURSELVES IN THE AWFUL POSITION OF FIGHTING GOD.

THE COURT IS FORCED TO ADMIT THE WISDOM OF THIS ADVICE. ANGRILY IT ORDERS THE DISCIPLES BEATEN, THEN RELEASES THEM WITH A THREAT OF MORE PUNISHMENT IF THEY CONTINUE PREACHING ABOUT JESUS.

THE DISCIPLES LEAVE...

I'M PROUD TO BE ABLE TO SUFFER FOR JESUS. WE'LL KEEP RIGHT ON WORKING FOR HIM.

ONE OF THEM -- STEPHEN -- IS SOON RECOGNIZED AS A FINE PREACHER.

IN SPITE OF THREATS THE DISCIPLES GO ON PREACHING AND HEALING. THE NUMBER OF FOLLOWERS INCREASES SO MUCH THAT THE TWELVE DISCIPLES DECIDE OTHERS MUST BE CHOSEN TO HELP WITH THE WORK. SEVEN DEACONS ARE SELECTED.

HIS FORMER FRIENDS IN THE SYNAGOGUE CHALLENGE HIM TO A DEBATE ABOUT JESUS. TO THEIR EMBARRASSMENT THEY FIND THEY ARE NO MATCH FOR STEPHEN'S WISDOM AND ABILITY TO DEFEND HIS FAITH. SECRETLY THEY PLOT THEIR REVENGE.

WE MUST BE CAREFUL NOT TO TURN THE PEOPLE AGAINST US.

RIGHT -- BUT IF WE HANDLE IT PROPERLY WE CAN USE THE PEOPLE THEMSELVES TO HELP US DESTROY STEPHEN.

Martyr for Christ

FROM ACTS 6:11—8:4

STEPHEN PREACHES SUCH POWERFUL SERMONS THAT MANY PEOPLE IN JERUSALEM BECOME FOLLOWERS OF JESUS. THE LOCAL TEACHERS CHALLENGE HIM TO DEBATES, BUT THEY ARE NO MATCH FOR HIM. THIS MAKES THEM ANGRY, AND THEY PLOT TO GET RID OF HIM.

SPREAD THE WORD AROUND JERUSALEM THAT STEPHEN IS PREACHING AGAINST THE LAW GOD GAVE TO MOSES.

THAT WILL TURN EVERY GOOD CITIZEN IN JERUSALEM AGAINST STEPHEN.

THE PLOT WORKS -- STEPHEN IS ARRESTED AND BROUGHT BEFORE THE SANHEDRIN, THE SAME COURT THAT CONDEMNED JESUS TO DEATH.

BOLDLY STEPHEN ANSWERS HIS ENEMIES...

YOUR FATHERS PERSECUTED THE PROPHETS WHO TOLD ABOUT THE COMING OF GOD'S CHOSEN ONE-- AND NOW **YOU** HAVE MURDERED **HIM**. **YOU** ARE THE ONES WHO RECEIVED GOD'S LAW, AND **YOU** ARE THE ONES WHO HAVE DISOBEYED IT**!**

REMEMBERING THE APOSTLES' STRANGE ESCAPE FROM PRISON, THE PERSECUTORS SEEM AFRAID TO ARREST THEM. BUT RAIDS AGAINST THE OTHER DISCIPLES CONTINUE, AND THEY ARE FORCED TO FLEE FOR THEIR LIVES.

WE MUST ESCAPE AT ONCE. I'M NOT A COWARD, BUT MY FAMILY--

JESUS SAID THAT IF WE WERE PERSECUTED IN ONE CITY WE SHOULD FLEE TO ANOTHER.

TWO BIG CARAVANS ARE LEAVING BY THE NORTH GATE TOMORROW MORNING. IF WE'RE CAREFUL WE CAN JOIN THEM AND NOT BE SEEN.

EARLY THE NEXT MORNING TRADERS LEAD THEIR CAMEL TRAINS OUT OF THE CITY, AND IN THEIR MIDST...

WHEREVER WE GO WE'LL TAKE OUR FAITH IN JESUS WITH US.

AND AS WE TEACH OTHERS WE'LL BE HELPING TO SPREAD THE GOSPEL AS JESUS ASKED US TO DO.

AND SO, BY DRIVING JESUS' FRIENDS OUT OF JERUSALEM, LOCAL LEADERS, UNKNOWINGLY, CAUSE HIS TEACHINGS TO BE SPREAD THROUGHOUT ALL PALESTINE--EVEN AMONG THEIR ENEMIES, THE SAMARITANS!

Simon, the Magician

FROM ACTS 8:5–26

TO ESCAPE PERSECUTION AT THE HANDS OF THE RELIGIOUS LEADERS, THOUSANDS OF JESUS' FOLLOWERS FLEE FROM JERUSALEM. PHILIP, ONE OF THE DEACONS OF THE JERUSALEM CHURCH, GOES NORTH TO SAMARIA.

SAMARITANS HATE JEWS. BUT THEY, TOO, ARE LOOKING FOR A SAVIOR, SO I MUST TELL THEM THAT HE HAS COME.

TO PHILIP'S SURPRISE THE SAMARITANS LISTEN EAGERLY AS HE TELLS THEM ABOUT JESUS, AND THEY WATCH WITH WONDER AS HE LOVINGLY HEALS THEIR SICK.

IN THE NAME OF JESUS CHRIST, STAND UP AND WALK!

WHEN REPORTS OF PHILIP'S WORK REACH THE DISCIPLES IN JERUSALEM, PETER AND JOHN GO TO VISIT SAMARIA. AND AS THEY LAY THEIR HANDS ON THESE NEW FRIENDS OF JESUS, THE HOLY SPIRIT COMES UPON THEM.

THIS IS THE MOST WONDERFUL THING I HAVE EVER SEEN.

SELL ME THIS POWER THAT YOU HAVE.

SIMON! MONEY WILL NOT BUY THIS HOLY GIFT. YOU HAVE NO PLACE IN GOD'S WORK, FOR I CAN SEE THAT YOUR HEART IS FILLED WITH WICKEDNESS. REPENT, AND PRAY THAT GOD WILL FORGIVE YOU.

THE BIBLE DOES NOT SAY WHETHER SIMON TRULY REPENTS. HIS NAME IS NEVER MENTIONED AGAIN.

SOON AFTER THIS PETER AND JOHN RETURN TO JERUSALEM. BUT PHILIP REMAINS, AND ONE NIGHT GOD SENDS HIM NEW INSTRUCTIONS.

PHILIP! ARISE AND GO DOWN THE ROAD THAT RUNS FROM JERUSALEM TO GAZA.

WITHOUT KNOWING THE REASON FOR HIS JOURNEY, OR WHERE IT MAY TAKE HIM, PHILIP OBEYS...

On the Gaza Road

FROM ACTS 8:26–40; 9:32–35

"GO DOWN TO THE ROAD THAT LEADS TO GAZA," AN ANGEL OF GOD TELLS PHILIP. PHILIP OBEYS, AND AS HE WALKS ALONG THE HOT DESERT HIGHWAY A CHARIOT COMES UP BEHIND HIM. HE LOOKS BACK, AND AT THAT MOMENT THE HOLY SPIRIT SPEAKS UP TO HIM: "GO UP TO THE CHARIOT--AND KEEP CLOSE TO IT."

WHO COULD BE IN THAT CHARIOT THAT GOD HAS SENT ME ALL THIS WAY TO MEET?

AGAIN PHILIP OBEYS. NEARING THE CHARIOT, HE HEARS A MAN READING FROM THE SCRIPTURES.

"HE WAS LED AS A SHEEP TO THE SLAUGHTER."

DO YOU UNDERSTAND WHAT THE PROPHET ISAIAH IS SAYING?

HOW CAN I UNLESS SOMEONE HELPS ME? WILL YOU?

EAGERLY PHILIP GETS INTO THE CHARIOT. THE MAN INTRODUCES HIMSELF AS TREASURER FOR CANDACE, QUEEN OF ETHIOPIA. THEN HE TURNS BACK TO THE SCROLL.

IS THE PROPHET TALKING ABOUT HIMSELF-- OR SOMEONE ELSE?

ABOUT JESUS CHRIST, THE SON OF GOD. HIS ENEMIES CRUCIFIED HIM, BUT GOD RAISED HIM FROM THE DEAD.

AS THEY RIDE ALONG PHILIP EXPLAINS THAT GOD LOVED THE WORLD SO MUCH THAT HE SENT HIS SON JESUS TO DIE FOR OUR SINS, AND WHOEVER TRUSTS IN HIM WILL LIVE FOREVER WITH GOD.

I BELIEVE IN JESUS, AND I'M SORRY FOR EVERYTHING WRONG I HAVE DONE. IS THERE ANY REASON WHY I CANNOT BE BAPTIZED AND BECOME ONE OF HIS FOLLOWERS?

I'M SURE THAT'S WHAT GOD SENT ME HERE TO DO.

SO THE MAN FROM ETHIOPIA IS BAPTIZED... AND THEN HE CONTINUES HIS JOURNEY, EAGER TO TELL THE GOOD NEWS ABOUT JESUS TO HIS OWN PEOPLE.

PHILIP GOES NORTH, PREACHING IN THE TOWNS ALONG THE RIM OF THE MEDITERRANEAN SEA. IN CAESAREA, THE ROMAN CAPITAL IN PALESTINE, HE MAKES HIS HOME.

ABOUT THIS TIME A MIRACULOUS THING HAPPENS--PAUL, WHO HAS BEEN PERSECUTING JESUS' FRIENDS, HAS A WONDERFUL EXPERIENCE. ON THE WAY TO DAMASCUS, JESUS APPEARS TO HIM. PAUL KNOWS THAT JESUS IS THE SAVIOR WHOM GOD RAISED FROM THE DEAD. SO, INSTEAD OF PERSECUTING JESUS' FOLLOWERS, PAUL BECOMES A FOLLOWER, TOO.

WHEN THE DISCIPLES HEAR THIS THEY REJOICE, FOR NOW THEY CAN TRAVEL ALL OVER PALESTINE TEACHING AND HEALING IN THE NAME OF JESUS WITH-OUT FEAR OF PAUL ARRESTING THEM.

Sea of Galilee

CAESAREA

JOPPA

LYDDA

JERUSALEM

GAZA

MEDITERRANEAN SEA

Dead Sea

704

Mission to Joppa

FROM ACTS 9:36—10:2

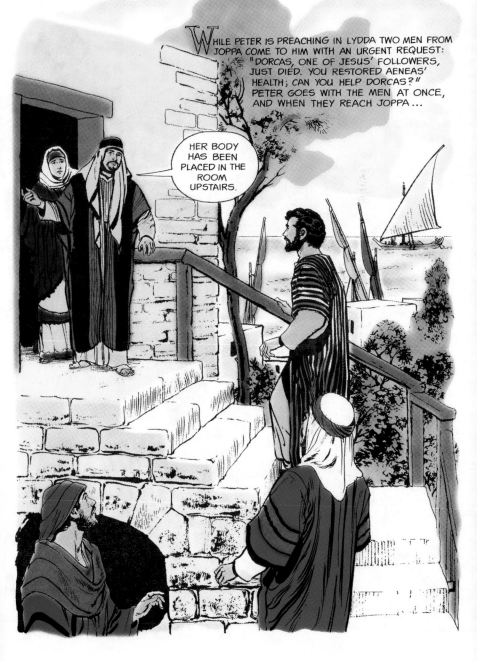

WHILE PETER IS PREACHING IN LYDDA TWO MEN FROM JOPPA COME TO HIM WITH AN URGENT REQUEST: "DORCAS, ONE OF JESUS' FOLLOWERS, JUST DIED. YOU RESTORED AENEAS' HEALTH; CAN YOU HELP DORCAS?" PETER GOES WITH THE MEN AT ONCE, AND WHEN THEY REACH JOPPA...

HER BODY HAS BEEN PLACED IN THE ROOM UPSTAIRS.

AT THE SIGHT OF DORCAS SOME OF THE WOMEN FALL ON THEIR KNEES, WEEPING FOR JOY. OTHERS RUSH OUT INTO THE STREETS TO TELL THE EXCITING NEWS.

DORCAS IS ALIVE!

SHH-- PEOPLE WILL THINK YOU'RE LOSING YOUR MIND. DORCAS IS DEAD-- AND EVERYONE KNOWS IT.

NO! NO! PETER, THE DISCIPLE OF JESUS, BROUGHT HER BACK TO LIFE. COME, SEE FOR YOURSELF!

NOT BELIEVING, BUT CURIOUS, THE WOMAN HURRIES TO DORCAS' HOME.

IT'S TRUE! IT'S TRUE! OH, GOD BE PRAISED!

ONE DAY A STRANGE THING HAPPENS IN THE HOME OF CORNELIUS, A ROMAN CENTURION LIVING IN THE SEACOAST CITY OF CAESAREA, SOME THIRTY MILES NORTH. IT IS THREE O'CLOCK IN THE AFTERNOON. CORNELIUS, WHO IN HIS YEARS OF SERVICE IN PALESTINE HAS LEARNED TO WORSHIP GOD, KNEELS TO PRAY.

THE NEWS SPREADS QUICKLY THROUGHOUT JOPPA, AND SOON GREAT CROWDS COME TO PETER, BEGGING TO BE TAUGHT ABOUT JESUS. PETER CONTINUES TO PREACH IN JOPPA UNTIL...

707

God, a Roman, and a Jew

FROM ACTS 10:2—1[

ONE AFTERNOON AS CORNELIUS, AN OFFICER OF THE ROMAN ARMY, KNEELS TO PRAY, HE HAS A VISION--AN ANGEL OF GOD APPEARS AND CALLS HIM BY NAME.

WHAT IS IT?

YOUR PRAYERS AND GOOD WORKS ARE PLEASING TO GOD. SEND MEN TO JOPPA FOR A MAN NAMED PETER. HE IS STAYING WITH SIMON, THE TANNER, WHOSE HOUSE IS BY THE SEA.

WHEN THE ANGEL DISAPPEARS, CORNELIUS SENDS THREE OF HIS MOST TRUSTED MEN AT ONCE TO JOPPA. AS THEY APPROACH THE CITY, THE MAN FOR WHOM THEY ARE SEARCHING GOES TO THE ROOFTOP TO PRAY...

HE, TOO, HAS A VISION. AND A VOICE COMMANDS HIM: "GET UP, PETER; KILL AND EAT."

NEVER, LORD. IN ALL MY LIFE I HAVE NEVER EATEN ANYTHING THAT THE JEWISH LAW CALLS UNCLEAN.

THE VOICE REPLIES: "YOU MUST NOT CALL WHAT GOD HAS CLEANSED UNCLEAN." ALL THIS IS REPEATED THREE TIMES; THEN THE VISION DISAPPEARS. WHILE PETER IS WONDERING WHAT IT MEANS THE HOLY SPIRIT SPEAKS TO HIM: "THREE MEN ARE HERE LOOKING FOR YOU. GO WITH THEM AND HAVE NO DOUBTS, FOR I HAVE SENT THEM TO YOU."

PETER HURRIES DOWNSTAIRS-- AND FINDS THREE MEN AT THE GATE INQUIRING FOR HIM.

I AM THE MAN YOU ARE LOOKING FOR. WHAT DO YOU WANT?

CORNELIUS, A ROMAN CENTURION WHO WORSHIPS GOD, WAS COMMANDED BY AN ANGEL TO SEND FOR YOU.

THE NEXT DAY PETER AND SIX OF HIS FRIENDS SET OUT WITH THE THREE MEN FOR CAESAREA. AS THEY ENTER THE HOME OF CORNELIUS, THE ROMAN CENTURION FALLS ON HIS KNEES TO WORSHIP PETER.

NO--NO-- I AM A MAN LIKE YOURSELF.

Angel—Open Gate

FROM ACTS 11:1—12:14

THE NEWS THAT PETER HAS BEEN ASSOCIATING WITH GENTILES REACHES JERUSALEM BEFORE HE DOES--AND SEVERAL OF THE CHURCH MEMBERS ARE WAITING TO QUESTION HIM.

IS IT TRUE THAT YOU ARE BREAKING OUR JEWISH LAWS AND BEING FRIENDLY TOWARD GENTILES--EVEN EATING WITH THEM AND VISITING IN THEIR HOMES?

GOD DIRECTED A ROMAN CENTURION TO SEND FOR ME, AND GOD TOLD ME TO GO TO HIM. I OBEYED, AND WHILE I WAS TELLING THE GENTILES ABOUT JESUS, THE HOLY SPIRIT CAME TO THEM -- THE SAME AS TO US ON THE DAY OF PENTECOST. IF GOD GAVE THEM THE SAME GIFT THAT HE GAVE TO US, WHO WAS I TO STAND IN THE WAY?

THE MEMBERS AGREE WITH PETER -- AND PRAISE GOD FOR GIVING ETERNAL LIFE TO THE GENTILES. THE CHURCH CONTINUES TO GROW...

AND AS IT DOES, THE ANGER OF THE LOCAL LEADERS GROWS. TO WIN THEIR FAVOR, KING HEROD AGRIPPA BEGINS TO PERSECUTE JESUS' FOLLOWERS.

ARREST THE DISCIPLE CALLED JAMES. CHARGE HIM WITH STIRRING UP TROUBLE AND PUT HIM TO DEATH-- AT ONCE!

SO JAMES, ONE OF THE FOUR FISHERMEN WHO LEFT THEIR NETS TO FOLLOW JESUS, IS SLAIN TO SATISFY A WICKED KING'S STRUGGLE FOR POWER.

THIS PLEASES THE RELIGIOUS LEADERS WHO CONDEMNED JESUS TO DEATH. EAGER TO GAIN MORE OF THEIR FAVOR, HEROD ORDERS PETER ARRESTED AND PUT IN PRISON--TO BE EXECUTED AFTER THE FEAST OF THE PASSOVER.

CHAIN EACH HAND TO A GUARD. KEEP FOUR SOLDIERS ON WATCH AT ALL TIMES. THIS PRISONER **MUST NOT** ESCAPE!

BUT ON THE NIGHT BEFORE HEROD PLANS TO SENTENCE PETER, AN ANGEL OF GOD ENTERS THE PRISON CELL...

GET UP! PUT ON YOUR SANDALS, WRAP YOUR CLOAK AROUND YOU, AND FOLLOW ME.

AS PETER OBEYS THE CHAINS FALL FROM HIS WRISTS -- AND THE ANGEL LEADS HIM OUT OF THE PRISON CELL.

WHEN THEY APPROACH THE GREAT IRON GATE IN THE PRISON WALL, IT OPENS! THEY GO OUT INTO THE CITY STREETS, AND -- SUDDENLY -- THE ANGEL VANISHES!

SCARCELY BELIEVING WHAT HAS HAPPENED, PETER HURRIES TO THE HOME OF MARY, THE MOTHER OF HIS YOUNG FRIEND, MARK. THERE HE POUNDS ON THE DOOR OF THE GATE UNTIL RHODA, A SERVANT GIRL, ANSWERS.

IT'S PETER!

BUT INSTEAD OF LETTING HIM IN, RHODA TURNS AND RUNS BACK INTO THE HOUSE...

Fall of a Tyrant

FROM ACTS 12:14–24

IT IS NIGHT IN JERUSALEM. PETER HAS JUST BEEN RESCUED FROM PRISON BY AN ANGEL AND IS SEEKING ADMITTANCE AT THE HOME OF A FRIEND. WHEN THE SERVANT GIRL RECOGNIZES HIS VOICE, SHE RUSHES BACK INTO THE HOUSE.

IT'S PETER!

PETER? O RHODA, YOU'RE SO UPSET THAT YOU'RE IMAGINING THINGS.

THE GIRL INSISTS. FINALLY SOME OF THE GROUP, WHO HAVE GATHERED TO PRAY FOR PETER, ACCOMPANY HER TO THE GATE.

IF YOU KNEW IT WAS PETER, WHY DIDN'T YOU LET HIM IN?

I WAS SO EXCITED--I HAD TO TELL YOU.

CAUTIOUSLY THEY OPEN THE DOOR...

PETER! IT *IS* YOU! COME IN--QUICKLY!

DID HEROD RELEASE YOU?

NO-- BUT GOD DID. AN ANGEL AWAKENED ME AND TOLD ME TO FOLLOW. I DID-- AND THE PRISON GATES OPENED BEFORE US. IN THE STREET, THE ANGEL DISAPPEARED. TELL THE OTHERS THAT I AM FREE. AND NOW I MUST GET OUT OF JERUSALEM BEFORE HEROD LEARNS WHAT HAS HAPPENED.

THE FRIENDS OF PETER REJOICE AND THANK GOD FOR HIS ESCAPE, BUT THE NEXT MORNING WHEN HEROD DISCOVERS THAT HIS PRISONER IS GONE--

YOU SAY HE WAS CHAINED TO TWO GUARDS, AND OTHERS WERE GUARDING THE DOOR, YET YOU EXPECT ME TO BELIEVE THAT HE JUST DISAPPEARED? WHAT WERE THE GUARDS DOING? SEARCH THE CITY. FIND PETER OR THOSE TRAITORS WILL PAY FOR THIS WITH THEIR LIVES!

BUT THE SEARCH FAILS.

A FEW DAYS LATER HEROD APPEARS AT A PUBLIC CELEBRATION IN CAESAREA. THERE, DRESSED IN A DAZZLING ROBE OF SILVER, HE GOES OUT AND SPEAKS TO THE PEOPLE. TO FLATTER HIM, THEY SHOUT:

IT IS THE VOICE OF A GOD--NOT A MAN!

HEROD ACCEPTS THE PRAISE WHICH SHOULD HAVE BEEN GIVEN ONLY TO GOD. SUDDENLY GOD STRIKES HIM DOWN, AND A FEW DAYS LATER HE DIES.

WITH THE DEATH OF HEROD, THE PERSECUTION OF THE CHURCH STOPS FOR A TIME. THE GOOD NEWS OF JESUS CHRIST CONTINUES TO SPREAD THROUGHOUT THE LAND OF THE JEWS...

The Story of Paul

FROM ACTS 7:58—8:4; 9:1–3A; 22:3

Adventurer for Christ

BOLDLY HE FACES ANGRY MOBS... CROSSES MOUNTAINS... AND SAILS THE STORMY SEAS TO PREACH THE GOOD NEWS THAT JESUS IS THE SON OF GOD AND SAVIOR OF THE WORLD.

THE EXCITING STORY OF THIS GREAT MISSIONARY BEGINS LONG AGO...

A FEW YEARS AFTER THE BIRTH OF JESUS PAUL* IS BORN IN TARSUS. THE SON OF GOOD JEWISH PARENTS, HE IS BROUGHT UP TO WORSHIP AND OBEY GOD.

WHAT WILL YOU DO WHEN YOU GROW UP, PAUL?

I DON'T KNOW YET. BUT WHATEVER I DO, IT WILL BE FOR GOD, AND IT WILL BE EXCITING.

*HIS JEWISH NAME IS SAUL.

HE TAKES THE FIRST STEP TOWARD MAKING HIS DREAM COME TRUE WHEN HE GOES TO JERUSALEM TO STUDY. THERE HE MEETS SOME OF THE SAME TEACHERS THAT JESUS TALKED WITH ONLY A FEW YEARS BEFORE.

IN TIME PAUL BECOMES THE MOST BRILLIANT PUPIL OF THE FAMOUS TEACHER, GAMALIEL. TOGETHER THEY DISCUSS THE SCRIPTURES-- ESPECIALLY THE PARTS THAT TELL ABOUT THE COMING OF THE SAVIOR.

LIKE KING DAVID, HE WILL MAKE OUR COUNTRY STRONG AND POWERFUL. IF ONLY HE WOULD COME NOW -- I'D SPEND MY LIFE SERVING HIM.

718

BUT LIKE MOST JEWISH LEADERS, PAUL REFUSES TO ACCEPT JESUS AS THE SAVIOR FOR WHOM THE JEWS ARE WAITING. WHEN THEY STONE STEPHEN, ONE OF JESUS' FOLLOWERS, PAUL STANDS BY -- WATCHING.

ANY MAN WHO FOLLOWS JESUS DESERVES TO DIE!

PAUL SOON BEGINS HIS OWN ATTACK ON JESUS' FOLLOWERS. HE RAIDS THEIR HOMES AND DRAGS THEM OFF TO BE QUESTIONED, PUNISHED, EVEN PUT TO DEATH.

NO! NO! MY CHILDREN!

THE FOLLOWERS OF JESUS FLEE FOR THEIR LIVES. WHEN PAUL LEARNS THAT THEY ARE SPREADING THEIR TEACHING WHEREVER THEY GO, HE IS EVEN MORE FURIOUS.

THEY MUST BE STOPPED BEFORE THEY STIR UP PEOPLE EVERYWHERE. ALREADY THEY ARE AS FAR NORTH AS DAMASCUS.

WHAT CAN WE DO?

WITH SOME STRONG-ARMED MEN, PAUL SETS OUT ON A 190-MILE JOURNEY TO DAMASCUS. HIS EXCITEMENT MOUNTS WITH EVERY MILE, FOR HE BELIEVES WITH ALL HIS HEART THAT IN DESTROYING JESUS' FOLLOWERS HE IS SERVING GOD...

A Light and a Voice

FROM ACTS 9:3–22

PAUL RIDES TOWARD DAMASCUS WITH THE EAGERNESS OF A HUNTER ON THE TRACK OF HIS PREY. AT THE SIGHT OF THE CITY IN THE DISTANCE, HE URGES HIS HORSE ON -- AS IF EVERY MINUTE COUNTED IN HIS SEARCH TO DESTROY JESUS' FOLLOWERS.

SUDDENLY HE IS SURROUNDED BY A LIGHT BRIGHTER THAN THE NOONDAY SUN. HE FALLS TO THE GROUND -- AND

A VOICE CALLS HIM BY HIS JEWISH NAME: "SAUL! SAUL, WHY ARE YOU PERSECUTING ME?"

WHO ARE YOU?

I AM JESUS OF NAZARETH, WHOM YOU ARE PERSECUTING.

WHAT DO YOU WANT ME TO DO?

"GO INTO THE CITY," JESUS ANSWERS, "AND YOU WILL BE TOLD WHAT TO DO."

THE MEN WITH PAUL ARE TERRIFIED BY WHAT HAS HAPPENED.

PAUL, WHAT'S THE MATTER?

MY EYES—I CAN'T SEE! HELP ME INTO THE CITY.

SO, BLIND, AND AWED BY HIS EXPERIENCE, TH ONCE-PROUD PAUL IS LED INTO DAMASCUS DOWN A STREET CALLED STRAIGHT.

WHERE ARE YOU TAKING ME?

TO THE HOME OF JUDAS, A FRIEND OF MINE.

IN DARKNESS PAUL PRAYS AND WAITS. ON THE THIRD DAY HE CALLS TO HIS HOST.

HAS A MAN NAMED ANANIAS ASKED TO SEE ME?

NO. WHAT MAKES YOU EXPECT HIM?

I HAVE BEEN PRAYING, AND IN A VISION I HAVE SEEN A MAN BY THAT NAME COMING TO RESTORE MY SIGHT.

IF HE COMES I'LL BRING HIM TO YOU AT ONCE.

Man with a Mission

FROM ACTS 9:27–30; 11:22–25

PAUL RETURNS TO JERUSALEM ONLY TO FIND THAT JESUS' FRIENDS BELIEVE HE IS STILL THEIR ENEMY. AT THE SIGHT OF HIM THEY HIDE. BUT BARNABAS, THE MAN WHO SOLD HIS FARM AND GAVE THE MONEY FOR THE POOR, IS NOT AFRAID. HE LISTENS TO PAUL—AND TAKES HIM TO PETER.

PAUL SAYS HE IS NOW A FOLLOWER OF JESUS--AND I BELIEVE HIM.

BRING HIM IN.

FOR DAYS AND NIGHTS PAUL, THE BRILLIANT STUDENT OF JEWISH LAW, AND PETER, THE RUGGED FISHERMAN FROM GALILEE, TALK ABOUT THEIR LORD AND SAVIOR.

JESUS' LAST COMMAND DIRECTED US TO GO INTO ALL THE WORLD AND PREACH THE GOSPEL.

I'M GLAD HE TRUSTS ME TO HELP CARRY OUT THAT COMMAND.

BUT JESUS' FOLLOWERS AGAIN LEARN OF THE PLOT AGAINST PAUL'S LIFE, AND WARN HIM.

YOUR ENEMIES ARE POWERFUL MEN, PAUL, AND THEY WILL NOT STOP UNTIL THEY HAVE PUT AN END TO YOUR WORK IN JERUSALEM. LET US HELP YOU ESCAPE.

YOU ARE RIGHT! I CAN SERVE MY LORD ELSEWHERE.

WITH THE HELP OF FRIENDS, PAUL ESCAPES TO THE SEACOAST. THEN HE SAILS NORTH TO HIS BOYHOOD HOME OF TARSUS. THERE HE EARNS HIS LIVING BY MAKING TENTS -- AND DEVOTES THE REST OF HIS TIME TO TELLING PEOPLE THAT JESUS IS THE PROMISED SAVIOR.

ONE DAY A SHIP DOCKS AT TARSUS... A PASSENGER HURRIES DOWN THE PLANK.

NOW TO FIND PAUL!

Foreign Assignment

FROM ACTS 11:25–30; 12:25—13:7

AFTER ESCAPING FROM HIS ENEMIES IN JERUSALEM, PAUL RETURNS TO HIS BOYHOOD HOME OF TARSUS. FOR SEVERAL YEARS HE WORKS AND PREACHES THE GOSPEL. ONE DAY AN OLD FRIEND COMES TO SEE HIM...

BARNABAS! WHAT BRINGS YOU TO TARSUS?

YOU, PAUL! I HAVE BEEN PREACHING IN ANTIOCH, AND THE CHURCH HAS GROWN SO MUCH THAT I NEED HELP. WILL YOU COME?

EAGERLY PAUL ACCEPTS THE INVITATION.

THE CHURCH WAS STARTED BY PEOPLE WHO FLED FROM YOUR PERSECUTION IN JERUSALEM.

THANK GOD YOU ARE GIVING ME THE CHANCE TO ASK THEIR FORGIVENESS AND WORK WITH THEM IN SPREADING THE GOSPEL.

IN ANTIOCH, THE THIRD LARGEST CITY OF THE ROMAN EMPIRE, PAUL AND BARNABAS WIN BOTH JEWS AND GENTILES TO FAITH IN CHRIST. HERE THE FOLLOWERS OF JESUS ARE GIVEN THE NAME OF CHRISTIANS!

AFTER A TIME TEACHERS FROM JERUSALEM COME TO VISIT THE GROWING CHURCH ONE OF THEM, AGABUS, MAKES A TRAGIC PROPHECY.

I HAVE RECEIVED A WARNING FROM GOD THAT A GREAT FAMINE IS COMING. MANY OF OUR PEOPLE IN JERUSALEM ARE POOR. THEY WILL STARVE UNLESS--

PAUL INTERRUPTS EXCITEDLY.

LET US ALL GIVE WHAT MONEY WE CAN. I'LL HELP DELIVER IT!

BUT YOU HAVE ENEMIES IN JERUSALEM!

AND OUR LORD HAS FOLLOWERS THERE! WE MUST HELP THEM IN SPITE OF THE DANGER.

The Enemy Strikes

FROM ACTS 13:7-50

AFTER A TOUR ACROSS THE ISLAND OF CYPRUS, PAUL, BARNABAS, AND YOUNG MARK REACH THE CAPITAL. TO THEIR SURPRISE, THE ROMAN GOVERNOR CALLS THEM BEFORE HIM AND ASKS TO HEAR ABOUT JESUS. EAGERLY PAUL TELLS ABOUT JESUS AND HOW GOD RAISED HIM FROM THE DEAD. AT THIS THE COURT MAGICIAN RISES UP IN ANGER...

Paul, A Champion Who Switches Sides!

Did You Know?

Paul is a great man of God who first kills Christians because he honestly believes they are going against God. Then when Jesus speaks to him directly on the road to Damascus, Paul realizes he has been on the wrong side. He becomes a great champion for the Gospel.

Here are some other interesting facts about him:

▶ He has two names—Paul (Roman) and Saul (Hebrew).

▶ Paul is a Jew and a Roman citizen (Acts 22:27).

▶ As a boy, he learns to make tents (Acts 18:3).

▶ At his conversion, he is blind for three days (p. 722).

▶ He writes 13 letters called the Pauline Epistles, which become part of the Bible.

▶ Paul and Barnabas are the first Christian missionaries (p. 730).

▶ When Paul and Silas are thrown in jail for disturbing the peace, they sing praises to God and God sends an earthquake (page 752).

▶ He faces danger and hardship as a missionary . . .
5 times whipped
3 times beaten with rods
1 time stoned with rocks
3 times shipwrecked
plus bandits, hunger, thirst, cold.
From 2 Corinthians 11:23-27

But he later said . . .
I have kept the faith . . . a crown of righteousness awaits me.
From 2 Timothy 4:7-8

Spreading the Good News . . .

Many people throughout history have chosen to follow Jesus' command to take the Gospel to all nations (see p. 672). Here are just a few:

▶ **William Carey** (1761-1834) went to India from England. Besides preaching the Gospel, Carey set up mission stations, schools, translated the Bible into several languages, and brought agricultural improvements to the Indian people.

▶ **Adoniram Judson** (1788-1850) was an American who went to Burma After years of struggle and imprisonment, he translated the entire Bible into Burmese.

▶ **James Hudson Taylor** (1832-1905) was an English medical missionary to China. Unlike other missionaries, he ate and dressed like the Chinese people he served. Under his leadership, 800 missionaries served the China Inland Mission from several church denominations.

▶ **Mary Slessor** (1848-1915) left Scotland to help the people of Nigeria, Africa. She taught the people to read the Bible and became a peacemaker among tribal chiefs. She wanted to reach tribes that had never heard of Jesus.

▶ **Amy Carmichael** (1867-1951) grew up teaching Sunday classes to mill workers in Northern Ireland. In 1895, she went to India. As well as preaching the Gospel, she rescued many children from evil temple practices.

Miracle in Lystra
FROM ACTS 13:51—14:19

TO ESCAPE PERSECUTION, PAUL AND BARNABAS ARE FORCED TO LEAVE ANTIOCH. THEY GO SOUTHEAST ABOUT 80 MILES TO ICONIUM, ANOTHER CITY IN THE PROVINCE OF GALATIA. HERE JEWS AND GENTILES ALIKE ACCEPT THE GOOD NEWS OF JESUS. THIS UPSETS PAUL'S ENEMIES.

PAUL! BARNABAS! YOU MUST LEAVE AT ONCE! THERE'S A PLOT UNDER WAY TO STONE YOU!

DON'T WORRY -- YOU HAVE FRIENDS HERE WHO WILL FIGHT TO PROTECT YOU.

WE CANNOT LET YOU RISK YOUR LIVES FOR US. WE MUST LEAVE -- BUT KEEP STRONG IN YOUR FAITH, AND HELP THE OTHERS.

BUT YOU ARE LIKE THE GODS JUPITER AND MERCURY.

JUPITER AND MERCURY ARE FALSE GODS. WORSHIP THE TRUE GOD WHO HAS SENT YOU RAIN FROM HEAVEN AND FRUIT IN ITS SEASON.

THE PEOPLE LISTEN EAGERLY. BUT, UNKNOWN TO PAUL AND BARNABAS, THEIR ENEMIES FROM ANTIOCH AND ICONIUM FOLLOW THEM TO LYSTRA. THEY SPREAD THEIR LIES AMONG THE SIMPLE PEOPLE.

PAUL AND BARNABAS CAUSE TROUBLE WHEREVER THEY GO. GET RID OF THEM AS WE DID!

THERE'LL BE NO TROUBLE IN LYSTRA. I'LL SEE TO THAT!

SO A MOB IS WHIPPED INTO ACTION!

THERE'S PAUL! STONE HIM!

Storm Warning

FROM ACTS 14:19—15:1

Whipped into a rage by men from Antioch and Iconium, the people of Lystra turn against Paul and stone him.

THIS WILL BE A LESSON TO ANYONE WHO TRIES TO MAKE TROUBLE IN **OUR** CITY!

THE NEXT MORNING PAUL AND BARNABAS SET OUT FOR DERBE WHERE THEY WIN MANY FOLLOWERS TO JESUS. ONE DAY PAUL STATES THAT IT IS TIME TO START THEIR HOMEWARD JOURNEY.

I AGREE. THE SHORTEST ROUTE IS THROUGH THE MOUNTAINS BY THE WAY OF YOUR BOYHOOD HOME OF TARSUS.

NO-- WE MUST GO BACK THE WAY WE CAME. OUR CHRISTIAN FRIENDS MAY NEED OUR HELP.

SO, IN SPITE OF THE DANGERS, PAUL AND BARNABAS RETRACE THEIR STEPS, VISITING THE CITIES OF GALATIA AND ORGANIZING THE CHURCHES THEY STARTED BEFORE. AT LAST THEY SAIL TOWARD THEIR HOME BASE-- ANTIOCH IN SYRIA.

ON THEIR FIRST MISSIONARY JOURNEY TO THE GENTILES, PAUL AND BARNABAS TRAVELED SOME 1400 MILES BY LAND AND SEA, AND WERE GONE FROM HOME ABOUT TWO YEARS.

ANTIOCH
ICONIUM
LYSTRA
DERBE
TARSUS
Galatia
ANTIOCH
PERGA
ATTALIA
Syria
Mediterranean Sea
Cyprus
SALAMIS
PAPHOS

IN ANTIOCH THEY RECEIVE A ROYAL WELCOME. THE CHURCH IS PROUD OF ITS MISSIONARIES AND THANKFUL TO HAVE A PART IN HELPING OTHERS KNOW JESUS.

I AM GLAD SO MANY GENTILES HERE IN ANTIOCH HAVE BECOME CHRISTIANS.

YES, AND THEY ARE LOYAL, TOO!

743

Council in Jerusalem

FROM ACTS 15:1–13; GALATIONS

LIKE A VIOLENT WIND, A DISAGREEMENT BETWEEN THE JEWISH AND GENTILE CHRISTIANS RIPS THROUGH THE ANTIOCH CHURCH, DIVIDING THE MEMBERS. UNKNOWN TO PAUL AND BARNABAS, WHO ARE STRUGGLING TO KEEP THE CHURCH UNITED, ANOTHER STORM IS BUILDING UP IN THE AREA OF THEIR FIRST MISSIONARY JOURNEY...

744

Second Journey

FROM ACTS 15:13—16:8

THE JERUSALEM COUNCIL FACES A PROBLEM THAT IS DIVIDING THE CHURCH: MUST GENTILES BECOME JEWS AND OBEY ALL THEIR RULES BEFORE THEY CAN BECOME CHRISTIANS? THE ARGUMENTS ARE PRESENTED. THE COUNCIL TURNS TO JAMES, BROTHER OF JESUS AND HEAD OF THE COUNCIL.

BROTHERS, LET US NOT MAKE IT HARD FOR GENTILES TO BECOME CHRISTIANS. WE SHOULD ASK ONLY THAT THEY OBEY A FEW NECESSARY RULES. THEY MUST AVOID EATING FOOD THAT HAS BEEN OFFERED TO IDOLS, AND THEY MUST LEAD PURE LIVES.

THE COUNCIL AGREES, AND TWO OF ITS MEMBERS, JUDAS BARSABAS AND SILAS, JOIN PAUL AND BARNABAS IN TAKING THE DECISION TO ANTIOCH.

THE NEWS IS RECEIVED WITH JOY IN ANTIOCH THAT JEWS AND GENTILES CAN GO ON WORKING TOGETHER FOR JESUS. WITH THIS SETTLED, PAUL IS FREE TO CONTINUE HIS MISSIONARY WORK IN GENTILE COUNTRIES.

BARNABAS, LET'S MAKE A TRIP TO VISIT THE CHURCHES WE STARTED.

GOOD IDEA-- I'D LIKE TO ASK MARK TO GO WITH US AGAIN.

NO -- MARK LEFT US BEFORE.

I KNOW, BUT WE SHOULD GIVE HIM ANOTHER CHANCE.

PAUL DISAGREES, SO BARNABAS TAKES MARK AND SAILS TO THE ISLAND OF CYPRUS. PAUL TAKES SILAS WITH HIM BY LAND TO VISIT THE CHURCHES HE STARTED.

IN LYSTRA, THE CITY IN WHICH HE HAD BEEN STONED, PAUL FINDS A GROWING CHURCH.

PAUL, I WANT YOU TO MEET TIMOTHY. HE'S BECOME ONE OF OUR BEST YOUNG LEADERS.

I'VE HEARD MANY FINE REPORTS OF YOU, TIMOTHY. WOULD YOU LIKE TO GO WITH SILAS AND ME?

Call from across the Sea

From Acts 16:9–19

749

SOON ALL OF THE MEMBERS OF LYDIA'S HOUSE-HOLD ACCEPT JESUS AS THEIR SAVIOR. LYDIA INVITES THE MISSIONARIES TO MAKE HER HOME THEIR HEADQUARTERS WHILE IN PHILIPPI.

THE ROMANS LOVE PURPLE-- I SELL MOST OF MY CLOTH TO THEM.

AS YOU SELL TO THEM, TELL THEM ABOUT JESUS.

ONE DAY AS PAUL AND SILAS WALK THROUGH THE STREETS OF PHILIPPI...

THE POOR GIRL IS UNDER THE INFLUENCE OF AN EVIL SPIRIT. HER MASTERS ARE USING HER AS A FORTUNETELLER.

IN CHRIST'S NAME, COME OUT!

YOU ARE A MAN OF GOD!

LOOK! SHE CAN'T TELL FORTUNES ANY MORE. OUR BUSINESS IS RUINED. WHAT'LL WE DO?

WHOEVER THAT MAN IS, HE'LL PAY FOR MEDDLING IN OUR AFFAIRS. COME ON!

Earthquake

FROM ACTS 16:20–37

PAUL REMOVES AN EVIL SPIRIT FROM A GIRL WHO WAS A FORTUNETELLER FOR SOME GREEDY MEN. ANGRY BECAUSE THEIR BUSINESS HAS BEEN RUINED, THE MEN DRAG PAUL AND SILAS BEFORE THE JUDGES IN THE PUBLIC SQUARE. A CROWD GATHERS.

THESE MEN ARE JEWS. THEY ARE TRYING TO MAKE TROUBLE BY TEACHING THINGS AGAINST ROMAN LAW.

YES! WE ALL HEARD HIM!

BUT I--

SILENCE! THERE'LL BE NO TROUBLE IN THIS CITY. GIVE THESE MEN A BEATING AND THROW THEM IN JAIL. AND SEE THAT THEY DON'T ESCAPE.

753

Out of Trouble . . . Into Trouble

FROM ACTS 16:38—17:13

THE ROMAN JUDGES, WHO ORDERED PAUL AND SILAS RELEASED FROM PRISON, ARE SURPRISED WHEN THE OFFICER RETURNS WITH A MESSAGE FROM THE PRISONERS.

THOSE MEN ARE ROMAN CITIZENS. THEY DEMAND THAT YOU COME TO THE PRISON AND RELEASE THEM AS PUBLICLY AS YOU PUNISHED THEM.

ROMAN CITIZENS? AND WE SENTENCED THEM WITHOUT A TRIAL! THIS COULD MEAN TROUBLE FOR US.

FORGETTING THEIR DIGNITY THE JUDGES GO IMMEDIATELY TO THE PRISON.

WE ARE TRULY SORRY FOR THE WAY WE TREATED YOU. NOW PLEASE LEAVE THE CITY TO AVOID FURTHER TROUBLE.

WE FORGIVE YOU-- AND WE WILL LEAVE TODAY.

AT THE HOUSE OF LYDIA, PAUL, SILAS, AND TIMOTHY BID THEIR FRIENDS GOOD-BYE.

THANK YOU FOR LEAVING DR. LUKE HERE TO LEAD OUR CHURCH.

WE WILL RETURN SOMEDAY. HOLD FAST TO YOUR FAITH IN JESUS AND HELP OTHERS TO KNOW HIM.

TRAVELING ON SOME 90 MILES, THE MISSIONARIES REACH THESSALONICA ON THE AEGEAN SEA. PAUL GOES AT ONCE TO THE SYNAGOGUE TO PREACH.

THE SCRIPTURES PROMISED THAT A SAVIOR WOULD COME. JESUS, WHO DIED ON THE CROSS AND ROSE FROM THE DEAD, IS THAT SAVIOR.

MANY PEOPLE LISTEN AND BELIEVE -- BUT SOME OF THE JEWISH LEADERS DO NOT.

WE'VE GOT TO GET RID OF HIM BEFORE HE HAS THE WHOLE CITY BELIEVING WHAT HE SAYS.

HE'S STAYING AT JASON'S HOUSE. LET'S GET HIM THERE.

GATHERING A STRONG-ARMED MOB, THE RELIGIOUS LEADERS CALL ON JASON.

IF YOU'RE LOOKING FOR PAUL, HE'S NOT HERE.

YOU'RE HIDING HIM. IF YOU WON'T LET US HAVE HIM, WE'LL TAKE YOU.

Paul Explains the "Unknown God"

FROM ACTS 17:13—18:12; 1 AND 2 THESSALONIANS

ON THE SABBATH PAUL PREACHES TO THE JEWS, BUT DURING THE WEEK HE CARRIES HIS MESSAGE OF JESUS TO THE GREEKS IN THE MARKET PLACE.

HE SAYS THERE IS ONLY ONE GOD, AND THAT HE SENT HIS ONLY SON, JESUS, TO SAVE US.

I'D LIKE TO HEAR MORE ABOUT A GOD WHO CARES FOR PEOPLE. LET'S ASK THIS MAN TO SPEAK BEFORE THE COURT OF MARS' HILL.

PAUL ACCEPTS THE INVITATION EAGERLY.

GENTLEMEN OF ATHENS, SINCE YOU WORSHIP A GOD YOU DO NOT KNOW, I'LL TELL YOU WHO HE IS -- THE TRUE GOD, WHO MADE ALL THINGS. HE DOES NOT LIVE IN TEMPLES MADE BY HUMAN HANDS. HE IS NOT FAR FROM EACH ONE OF US, FOR IN HIM WE LIVE, AND MOVE, AND HAVE OUR BEING.

THE MEN OF ATHENS LISTEN EAGERLY -- UNTIL PAUL SAYS THAT JESUS ROSE FROM THE DEAD.

NOBODY CAN BE RAISED FROM THE DEAD. WHAT A SILLY IDEA!

I'M NOT SO SURE...

IT IS DOING WELL, BUT THE PEOPLE ARE HAVING A HARD TIME.

I'LL WRITE TO THEM AT ONCE.

PAUL'S First Letter to the Thessalonians, WHICH IS A BOOK OF THE NEW TESTAMENT.

To the church of the Thessalonians-- from Paul, Silas, and Timothy

We remember how joyfully you turned from idols to serve the true God. Though we had to leave, it was good to receive news that you are standing true to your faith, even though people have been making it hard for you.

As we urged you when we were with you, live in the way that will please God, who invited you to have a place in His Kingdom. Keep on praying, and love one another more and more. I know you have worried about Christians who have died, but you need not. For Jesus promised that when He comes back from Heaven these will meet Him.

Be sure this letter is read to all the members of the church.

PAUL GETS FURTHER WORD FROM HIS FRIENDS IN THESSALONICA. HE WRITES A Second Letter to the Thessalonians. THIS ALSO IS A BOOK OF THE NEW TESTAMENT.

To the church of the Thessalonians-- from Paul, Silas, and Timothy

Don't get a mistaken idea of what I told you. No one should quit working because he thinks Jesus will return right away. If anyone will not work, he should not be fed. Before Jesus comes, there will be a time when an evil man tries to rule the world, taking the place of God. But God will keep you from evil. Don't get discouraged in doing what is right.

In any letter that I send to you, I write a few words at the close in my own handwriting-- like this-- so that you will be sure the letter is from me. May Christ's love be with you all.

FOR A YEAR AND A HALF PAUL PREACHES IN CORINTH. A STRONG CHRISTIAN CHURCH IS STARTED. BUT THE JEWISH LEADERS ARE ANGRY AT PAUL AND LOOK UPON HIM AS A TRAITOR TO HIS RELIGION.

GALLIO IS A NEW GOVERNOR. HE WON'T RISK HAVING TROUBLE BREAK OUT RIGHT AWAY. I THINK WE CAN WORK THINGS SO THAT HE WILL GET RID OF PAUL FOR US!

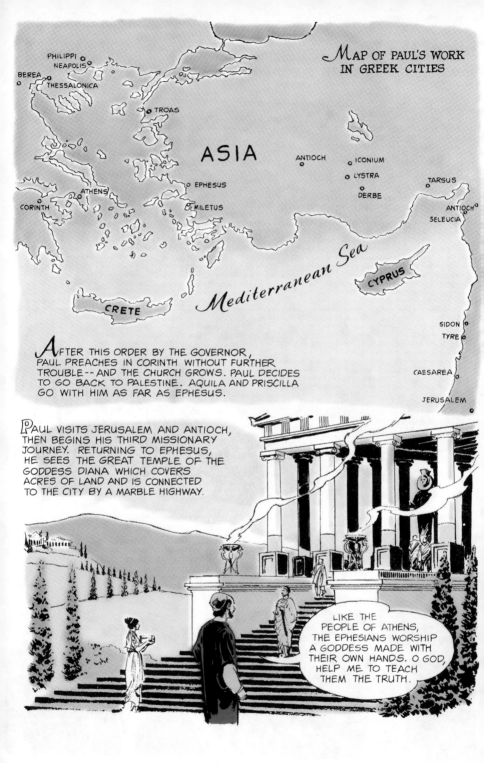

MAP OF PAUL'S WORK IN GREEK CITIES

PHILIPPI
NEAPOLIS
BEREA
THESSALONICA

TROAS

ASIA

ANTIOCH
ICONIUM
LYSTRA
DERBE

TARSUS

ATHENS
CORINTH
EPHESUS
MILETUS

ANTIOCH
SELEUCIA

CYPRUS

CRETE
Mediterranean Sea

SIDON
TYRE

CAESAREA

JERUSALEM

AFTER THIS ORDER BY THE GOVERNOR, PAUL PREACHES IN CORINTH WITHOUT FURTHER TROUBLE-- AND THE CHURCH GROWS. PAUL DECIDES TO GO BACK TO PALESTINE. AQUILA AND PRISCILLA GO WITH HIM AS FAR AS EPHESUS.

PAUL VISITS JERUSALEM AND ANTIOCH, THEN BEGINS HIS THIRD MISSIONARY JOURNEY. RETURNING TO EPHESUS, HE SEES THE GREAT TEMPLE OF THE GODDESS DIANA WHICH COVERS ACRES OF LAND AND IS CONNECTED TO THE CITY BY A MARBLE HIGHWAY.

LIKE THE PEOPLE OF ATHENS, THE EPHESIANS WORSHIP A GODDESS MADE WITH THEIR OWN HANDS. O GOD, HELP ME TO TEACH THEM THE TRUTH.

The Angry Mob

FROM ACTS 19:17—20; 1 CORINTHIANS

THE PEOPLE OF EPHESUS SEE THAT WHAT PAUL SAYS IS TRUE AND THAT THE MAGICIANS ARE FAKES. MANY PERSONS BELIEVE IN CHRIST AND BURN THEIR BOOKS OF MAGIC.

THOSE MEN ARE BURNING A FORTUNE.

YES, BUT NOW THEY WILL HAVE A NEW LIFE!

PAUL IS STILL REJOICING WITH THE GROWTH OF THE CHURCH IN EPHESUS WHEN NEWS COMES FROM CORINTH...

THE CHURCH IN CORINTH IS HAVING ALL SORTS OF TROUBLES. THE MEMBERS ARE TAKING SIDES AGAINST ONE ANOTHER. SOME OF THEM SAY YOU ARE THE HEAD OF OUR CHURCH. OTHERS SAY APOLLOS IS THE BEST PREACHER -- AND STILL OTHERS SAY PETER IS THE REAL LEADER CHOSEN BY JESUS.

PAUL DICTATES A LETTER TO THE CHURCH OF CORINTH. KNOWN AS 1 Corinthians, IT IS A BOOK OF THE NEW TESTAMENT.

Paul, to the church at Corinth...

I beg of you, my brothers, do not quarrel and divide the church. There is only one head of the Christian Church -- Christ! It was Christ -- not Paul or Apollos or Peter -- who died for you on the cross.

Keep yourselves pure. Don't you see that you yourselves are the temple of God -- and that God's Spirit lives in you? God will destroy anyone who defiles his temple, for his temple is holy -- and that is what you are!

If I knew everything and could speak like an angel but did not have Christian love, I would amount to nothing. Be kind and love one another in the church. I send my love to all of you.

THE CHURCH IN EPHESUS GROWS — ALMOST AS RAPIDLY AS THE BLAZE WHICH DESTROYED THE BOOKS OF MAGIC. IT HAS ITS EFFECT ON THE IDOL MERCHANTS OF THE CITY...

BUSINESS IS NO GOOD. PEOPLE AREN'T BUYING SILVER TEMPLES OF DIANA.

IT'S BECAUSE OF THAT CHRISTIAN PREACHER, PAUL. HE IS LEADING THE PEOPLE TO BELIEVE IN JESUS.

765

THE CROWD GROWS AS IT PUSHES THROUGH THE STREETS -- SOON THE WHOLE CITY IS IN AN UPROAR...

GREAT IS DIANA OF THE EPHESIANS!

AND THE MOB TAKES PAUL'S FRIENDS TO THE GREAT OUTDOOR THEATER.

A FEW MINUTES LATER IN ANOTHER PART OF THE CITY...

PAUL! THE SILVERSMITHS ARE AFTER YOU FOR DESTROYING THEIR BUSINESS. THEY HAVE SEIZED GAIUS AND ARISTARCHUS AND...

WHERE ARE THEY?

NO! PAUL! THAT MOB WILL KILL YOU!

Riot in Ephesus

FROM ACTS 19:31—20:3; 2 CORINTHIANS; ROMANS

CITY OFFICIALS BEG PAUL TO STAY AWAY FROM THE MOB. FOR TWO HOURS THE RIOTERS SHOUT, "GREAT IS DIANA OF THE EPHESIANS." FINALLY THE TOWN CLERK MAKES HIMSELF HEARD...

GENTLEMEN OF EPHESUS -- IF THE SILVERSMITHS HAVE A COMPLAINT, LET THEM BRING IT BEFORE THE COURTS. I WARN YOU -- IF THE ROMAN GOVERNMENT ASKS THE REASON FOR THIS RIOTING, THERE IS NO EXCUSE WE CAN GIVE FOR IT.

IN FACE OF THIS THREAT, THE RIOT BREAKS UP. PAUL SENDS FOR HIS FRIENDS.

THE MOB WAS REALLY AFTER ME -- SO TO PREVENT TROUBLE FOR ALL OF YOU, I WILL GO TO PHILIPPI.

OUR PRAYERS WILL GO WITH YOU.

SOON AFTER PAUL REACHES PHILIPPI, TITUS JOINS HIM WITH NEWS FROM CORINTH.

PAUL, YOUR LETTER TO THE CHRISTIANS AT CORINTH MADE THEM CORRECT THEIR WRONG-DOING. BUT NOW SOME PEOPLE HAVE COME TO CORINTH WHO CLAIM YOU ARE NOT A TRUE APOSTLE OF JESUS.

ONCE AGAIN PAUL WRITES TO THE CHURCH IN CORINTH. THE LETTER--KNOWN AS II *Corinthians* --IS A BOOK OF THE NEW TESTAMENT.

I can see that my letter upset you, but I am glad I sent it. Not because I want to hurt you, but to make you sorry as God would have you sorry for the things that were wrong.

We are taking a collection for poor Christians in Jerusalem. Other churches have given large sums. I trust you will be able to do the same. Let everyone give what he has decided in his own heart to give, for God loves a cheerful giver.

And now, for those who question whether or not I am a true minister of Christ. I have been imprisoned, I have been beaten many times, I have often faced death. I have been stoned, I have been shipwrecked three times--all to carry out the work of Christ. When I visit you again, I hope it will be a happy meeting. Good-bye till then.

WHILE TITUS TAKES THE LETTER TO CORINTH, PAUL CONTINUES VISITING CHURCHES IN MACEDONIA, COLLECTING MONEY FOR THE POOR IN JERUSALEM. MONTHS LATER HE REACHES CORINTH WHERE HE IS GREETED BY FRIENDS WHO HAVE GIVEN EAGERLY TO HIS COLLECTION.

THIS MONEY WILL SHOW THE CHRISTIANS IN JERUSALEM THAT YOU'RE CONCERNED FOR THEM.

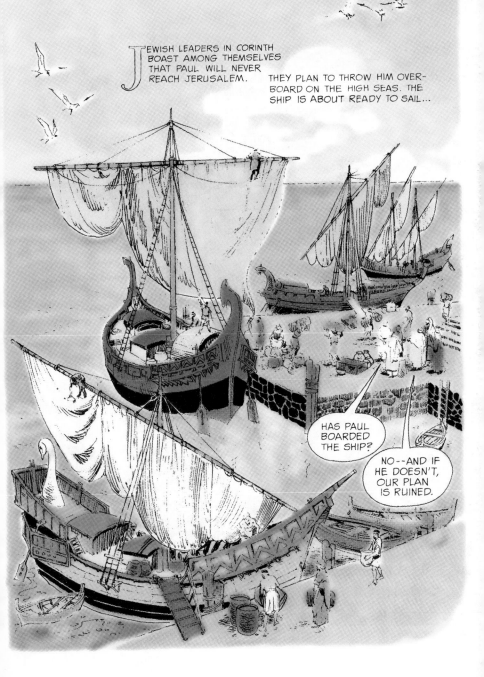

JEWISH LEADERS IN CORINTH BOAST AMONG THEMSELVES THAT PAUL WILL NEVER REACH JERUSALEM. THEY PLAN TO THROW HIM OVERBOARD ON THE HIGH SEAS. THE SHIP IS ABOUT READY TO SAIL...

HAS PAUL BOARDED THE SHIP?

NO--AND IF HE DOESN'T, OUR PLAN IS RUINED.

769

THANK GOD!

HE WAS DEAD -- I'M SURE HE WAS. WHAT POWER GOD HAS GIVEN PAUL!

AFTER PREACHING UNTIL DAYBREAK, PAUL SAYS GOOD-BY TO HIS FRIENDS.

MUST YOU GO, PAUL?

YES, I HAD PLANNED TO BE IN JERUSALEM FOR THE FEAST OF THE PASS-OVER, BUT I COULD NOT. NOW I WANT TO REACH THERE FOR THE FEAST OF PENTECOST.

AT MILETUS, PAUL SENDS WORD FOR THE ELDERS OF EPHESUS TO MEET HIM. EAGERLY THEY TRAVEL THE 35 MILES TO SEE HIM.

I MUST GO TO JERUSALEM -- EVEN IF MY LIFE IS IN DANGER. I DO NOT CONSIDER MY LIFE IMPORTANT SO LONG AS I COMPLETE THE MINISTRY WHICH THE LORD GAVE ME. YOU ARE NOW SHEPHERDS OF THE CHURCH OF CHRIST -- WHICH HE BOUGHT WITH HIS OWN LIFE. HELP THE WEAK -- AND REMEMBER THE WORDS OF JESUS: TO GIVE IS BETTER THAN TO RECEIVE.

PAUL GOES ON TO TYRE, WHERE HE PREACHES FOR A WEEK. WHEN HE LEAVES, THE CHRISTIANS FOLLOW HIM TO THE BEACH FOR A PRAYERFUL GOOD-BY

DON'T GO TO JERUSALEM. SOME THERE ARE WAITING TO KILL YOU BECAUSE YOU SAY JESUS IS THE SON OF GOD.

I MUST GO. I HAVE MONEY WHICH GENTILE CHRISTIANS HAVE GIVEN ME FOR THE POOR IN JERUSALEM. I AM NOT AFRAID...

FARTHER DOWN THE COAST AT CAESAREA, PAUL VISITS WITH PHILIP THE EVANGELIST. THE PROPHET AGABUS JOINS THEM, AND--SUDDENLY-- WHILE THEY ARE TALKING HE TAKES PAUL'S BELT AND BEGINS TO BIND HIS OWN HANDS AND FEET.

WHAT DOES THIS MEAN?

THE HOLY SPIRIT TELLS ME THAT THE MAN TO WHOM THE BELT BELONGS WILL BE BOUND--LIKE THIS--BY SOME JEWS IN JERUSALEM AND HANDED OVER TO THE GENTILES.

PAUL-- GIVE UP YOUR PLANS TO GO TO JERUSALEM. FOR OUR SAKE--

WHY DO YOU TRY TO WEAKEN ME WITH YOUR TEARS? I AM PREPARED NOT ONLY TO BE BOUND, BUT TO DIE FOR THE SAKE OF THE LORD JESUS.

772

A Boy and a Secret

FROM ACTS 21:15—23:24

THE DAY AFTER PAUL REACHES JERUSALEM, HE MEETS WITH JAMES AND OTHER LEADERS OF THE JERUSALEM CHURCH. HE DELIVERS THE MONEY FOR THE POOR AND TELLS WHAT GOD HAS DONE IN OTHER LANDS.

I MUST WARN YOU, PAUL, YOU HAVE ENEMIES HERE WHO THINK YOU ARE A TRAITOR. EVEN THE CHRISTIAN JEWS HAVE QUESTIONS BECAUSE OF YOUR WORK AMONG THE GENTILES.

I'LL WORSHIP WITH THEM IN THE TEMPLE TO SHOW THAT I AM TRUE TO THE FAITH OF OUR FATHERS.

JAMES' WARNING COMES TRUE WITHIN THE WEEK. WHILE PAUL IS WORSHIPING IN THE TEMPLE HIS ENEMIES ACCUSE HIM, FALSELY, OF BRINGING GENTILES INTO GOD'S HOUSE WHERE ONLY JEWS ARE ALLOWED.

THERE HE IS -- THE TRAITOR!

HE HAS DEFILED THIS HOLY PLACE OF GOD!

IN ANGER THE PEOPLE TURN AGAINST PAUL. A MOB DRAGS HIM FROM THE TEMPLE AND STARTS TO BEAT HIM.

LOOK OUT-- ROMAN SOLDIERS ARE COMING!

THE SOLDIERS CARRY PAUL TO THE PRISON. ON ITS STEPS PAUL STOPS AND TELLS THE PEOPLE HOW HE BECAME A CHRISTIAN, BUT WHEN HE MENTIONS PREACHING TO THE GENTILES, THE MOB GOES WILD.

NOW, TELL US WHAT THIS MAN HAS DONE.

TAKE HIM AWAY-- KILL HIM!

HE IS NOT FIT TO LIVE!

KILL HIM!

KILL HIM!

774

Paul Pleads His Case

FROM ACTS 23:25—28:4

TO PROTECT PAUL'S LIFE, THE ROMAN COMMANDER AT JERUSALEM SENDS HIM TO CAESAREA, WHERE PAUL IS KEPT IN PRISON. AFTER TWO YEARS PAUL APPEARS BEFORE FESTUS, THE ROMAN GOVERNOR, AND DEMANDS HIS RIGHT TO BE TRIED BY THE EMPEROR NERO AT ROME. BUT FIRST FESTUS BRINGS PAUL BEFORE A NEIGHBORING RULER, KING AGRIPPA, WHO IS VISITING THE CITY.

I ONCE THOUGHT IT MY DUTY TO OPPOSE JESUS. I HAD MANY OF HIS FOLLOWERS IMPRISONED. BUT ON MY WAY TO DAMASCUS I SAW A LIGHT FROM HEAVEN... AND JESUS SAID TO ME, "I SEND YOU TO TURN PEOPLE OF ALL NATIONS FROM THE POWER OF SATAN TO GOD... O KING AGRIPPA, I COULD NOT DISOBEY THE HEAVENLY VISION.

YOU'RE TRYING TO PERSUADE ME TO BE A CHRISTIAN.

FESTUS AND AGRIPPA WOULD HAVE SET PAUL FREE IF HE HAD NOT DEMANDED A TRIAL IN ROME. SO -- UNDER ROMAN GUARD AND ACCOMPANIED BY LUKE -- PAUL IS TAKEN ABOARD A SHIP BOUND FOR ROME. AT THE ISLAND OF CRETE...

THE WINTER STORMS WILL SOON BE HERE. IT WILL BE DANGEROUS TO GO ON UNTIL SPRING.

THE HARBOR AT PHOENIX IS NOT FAR AWAY -- WE'LL SPEND THE WINTER THERE.

THE SHIP SETS SAIL -- ONLY TO BE STRUCK BY A RAGING "NORTHEASTER."

TAKE DOWN THE MAINSAIL!

ON THE 14TH NIGHT OF THE STORM THE SAILORS TRY TO DESERT THE SHIP.

UNLESS THOSE MEN STAY WITH THE SHIP, YOU CANNOT BE SAVED!

IN ANSWER TO PAUL'S PRAYERS, ALL 276 MEN ON BOARD REACH LAND SAFELY. PEOPLE ON THE ISLAND OF MALTA RUSH DOWN TO THE SHORE TO HELP THE VICTIMS OF THE WRECK.

I'LL GET SOME MORE WOOD.

WE'LL HAVE A FIRE GOING SOON.

AS PAUL LAYS SOME STICKS ON THE FIRE A SNAKE CRAWLS OUT OF THE BUNDLE-- AND STRIKES!

A VIPER!

THE MAN ACTS AS IF HE DOESN'T KNOW THAT A VIPER'S BITE MEANS AGONY AND DEATH!

HE MUST BE A MURDERER! HE ESCAPED THE SEA --BUT JUSTICE WILL NOT LET HIM LIVE.

PAUL SHAKES OFF THE SNAKE INTO THE FIRE AND IS UNHARMED. THE PEOPLE WAIT FOR HIM TO BEGIN SWELLING OR SUDDENLY FALL DEAD, BUT AFTER THEY HAD WAITED A LONG TIME, THEY CHANGE THEIR MINDS AND BRING SICK PEOPLE TO HIM TO BE HEALED. THREE MONTHS LATER PAUL SAILS FOR ROME AND A LONG STAY IN PRISON.

Apostle on the March

FROM PHILIPPIANS; 1 TIMOTHY; TITUS

AS SOON AS HE IS WELL, EPAPHRODITUS GOES TO SEE PAUL.

THE CHURCH IN ROME IS GROWING RAPIDLY. UNLESS YOU NEED ME HERE, I WOULD LIKE TO GO BACK HOME.

YES, THAT'S WHAT YOU SHOULD DO. I HAVE WRITTEN A LETTER TO MY FRIENDS IN PHILIPPI. YOU CAN TAKE IT BACK WITH YOU.

PAUL'S LETTER TO THE *Philippians* IS A BOOK OF THE NEW TESTAMENT.

To the church at Philippi,
I don't know yet how my trial will come out, but I believe God will let me visit you again. Make me happy by living in harmony among yourselves. Think as Christ did. Though divine, He was willing to humble Himself and become a Man-- willing even to die on the cross.

Thank you for your gift which Epaphroditus brought. You have been generous. God will also supply all that you need. Always be glad, since you are Christians, and think about the things that are good. The Christians here send greetings, especially the ones who are working in Caesar's palace.

TWO YEARS--AND FINALLY PAUL'S CASE IS BROUGHT TO COURT.* BEFORE NERO, THE MOST POWERFUL RULER IN THE WORLD, PAUL MAKES HIS DEFENSE, AND IN A FEW DAYS...

THANK GOD! NOW I CAN CARRY OUT MY DREAM TO TAKE THE GOSPEL OF CHRIST TO THE FARTHEST CORNERS OF THE EMPIRE!

PAUL! PAUL! THE COURT HAS SET YOU FREE!

*ALTHOUGH THE BIBLE DOES NOT TELL ABOUT PAUL'S RELEASE, THE LETTERS HE WROTE AFTER- WARD SHOW THAT IT MUST HAVE TAKEN PLACE.

he Burning of Rome

ₒOM 2 TIMOTHY; HEBREWS 13:23

TORICAL BACKGROUND . . .

T IS THE YEAR 64. NERO, THE CRUEL
EMPEROR OF ROME, HAS MANY ENEMIES
AMONG HIS OWN PEOPLE. THERE ARE
₁ORS OF PLOTS AGAINST HIS LIFE.
N, STRANGELY, A FIRE SWEEPS
₂OSS THE CITY. FOR NINE DAYS
₂AGES--BURNING GREAT SECTIONS
THE CITY AND DRIVING THOUSANDS
ₒM THEIR HOMES. FROM
PALACE, NERO WATCHES . . .

WHEN LUKE RETURNS, PAUL TELLS HIM WHAT TO WRITE. THE LETTER, **II Timothy**, IS A BOOK OF THE NEW TESTAMENT.

Dear Timothy,

Be strong, like a good soldier for Christ. Remember the truth as you learned from me and from the Holy Scriptures. Keep preaching it, even though the time will come when people don't want to hear the truth.

I want to see you very much. Do your best to come before winter. Bring the coat I left at Troas, and the books. I have almost reached the end of my life. Soon I will be with the Lord and He will give me a place in His heavenly Kingdom. Try to come soon.

Paul

WHEN TIMOTHY RECEIVES THE LETTER, HE SAILS AT ONCE TO ROME. THERE HE FINDS LUKE, WHO TAKES HIM TO THE PRISON. BUT AS TIMOTHY GREETS PAUL...

I HAVE JUST RECEIVED ORDERS -- YOU ARE UNDER ARREST!

So TIMOTHY, TOO, IS ARRESTED FOR TEACHING ABOUT JESUS. IN THEIR PRISON CELLS THE TWO MISSIONARIES WAIT FOR ROMAN LAW TO BRING THEM TO TRIAL IN TIME PAUL'S CASE IS CALLED. ALONE, HE IS MARCHED TO THE COURT OF NERO

Soldier Victorious

FROM 2 TIMOTHY 4:6–8

IN ROME, PAUL IS ON TRIAL FOR HIS LIFE BEFORE THE CRUEL EMPEROR, NERO.

I FIND YOU GUILTY OF STIRRING UP TROUBLE IN THE EMPIRE. THE SENTENCE IS DEATH-- BY THE SWORD.

QUICKLY SOLDIERS TAKE PAUL OUTSIDE THE CITY--TO BEHEAD HIM.

I HAVE FOUGHT THE GOOD FIGHT. I HAVE FINISHED MY COURSE. I HAVE KEPT THE FAITH.

SO DEATH COMES TO PAUL, WHO FOUNDED CHRISTIAN CHURCHES ON TWO CONTINENTS AND WHO WAS LED BY GOD TO WRITE NEARLY HALF OF THE BOOKS OF THE NEW TESTAMENT.

BUT PAUL'S DEATH DOES NOT BRING A HALT TO THE GOSPEL. CHRIST'S CHURCH MARCHES ON--THROUGHOUT THE ROMAN EMPIRE, AND THEN ACROSS THE WORLD.

The End of an Era

HEBREWS THROUGH REVELATION

JESUS' DISCIPLES WHO WERE STILL ALIVE WERE GROWING OLD IN THE LATTER HALF OF THE FIRST CENTURY AFTER HIS BIRTH. THEY COULD NOT TRAVEL TO ALL THE CHURCHES, SO THEY TURNED TO WRITING LETTERS TO JESUS' FOLLOWERS.

THE LAST NINE BOOKS OF THE NEW TESTAMENT, HEBREWS THROUGH REVELATION, ARE MESSAGES THESE MEN WROTE TO GIVE ADVICE, COURAGE, AND COMFORT TO THE EARLY CHRISTIANS.

The Book of Hebrews

THE LETTER TO THE HEBREWS WAS WRITTEN AT A TIME WHEN JEWISH CHRISTIANS WERE BEING PRESSURED BY THE ROMANS AND JEWS TO GIVE UP THEIR FAITH IN JESUS.

THEY ASKED THEMSELVES: WHICH IS RIGHT, FAITH IN JESUS OR FAITH IN THE RELIGION OF OUR FOREFATHERS ABRAHAM, MOSES, AND DAVID?

"GOD HAS SPOKEN TO US THROUGH HIS SON, JESUS," THE LETTER SAID. "ABRAHAM, MOSES, AND DAVID WERE GREAT MEN WHO LIVED BY FAITH. THEY DIED; BUT JESUS CHRIST WILL LIVE FOREVER. HOLD FAST TO YOUR FAITH IN HIM."

THE LETTER ALSO BROUGHT THE GOOD NEWS THAT TIMOTHY HAD BEEN RELEASED FROM PRISON.

The Book of James

AS LEADER OF THE CHURCH IN JERUSALEM, JAMES, THE BROTHER OF JESUS, WROTE A LETTER OF ADVICE TO CHRISTIANS LIVING IN OTHER COUNTRIES.

"True religion is shown by what you do. Help those who need help. Be fair to all people. Ask God for wisdom, and keep your lives pure."

THUS THE BROTHER OF JESUS, WHO WAS KNOWN AS JAMES THE JUST, CONTINUED TO SPREAD THE GOSPEL.

The Book of I Peter

PETER WAS NOW AN OLD MAN. HE COULD SEE THAT THE ROMANS WERE TURNING AGAINST THE CHRISTIANS AND THAT JESUS' FOLLOWERS WOULD BE IN GREAT DANGER. HE HAD SILAS WRITE A LETTER FOR HIM.

"Face your hardships bravely," Peter told the people. "There is one thing no one can take from you -- the hope of living in Heaven with Christ. Trust in Him; He will reward those who follow Him faithfully."

The Book of II Peter

PETER KNEW THAT HE DID NOT HAVE MANY YEARS TO LIVE. HE WANTED TO HELP THE FOLLOWERS OF JESUS TO BE TRUE TO HIM, SO HE SENT THEM THIS LETTER.

"You believe in Jesus," he wrote. "Then act the way His followers should." Then he warned the Christians not to be upset by people who laughed at them because they believed that Jesus would return.

"When the time is right," Peter wrote, "Christ will return.

"God is giving people a chance to repent. He has promised a new world for those who love and obey Him.

"See how important it is for you to live for God!"

THESE ARE THE LAST WORDS WE HEAR FROM THE FISHERMAN WHO GAVE UP HIS NETS TO FOLLOW JESUS.

The Book of I John

JOHN, WHO HAD BEEN SO CLOSE TO JESUS IN EARLIER YEARS, WAS NOW THE LEADER OF THE CHRISTIANS AROUND EPHESUS.

"I have been with Jesus," John wrote to his people, "and I want you to have the same joy in knowing Him that I have. Don't believe anyone who says that God's Son did not come to the world as a real Person. God loved us and sent His Son to be our Savior. As He loved us, we should love one another."

The Book of II John

"I was very glad," John wrote, "to find some of your children living by the truth and obeying God's command to love one another. If any enemies of the truth come to you teaching that Christ was not a real man, do not receive them into your house. If you do, you will be helping in this evil work."

The Book of III John

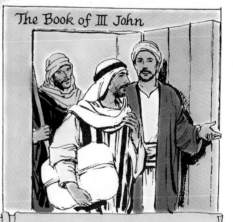

"Dear Gaius," John wrote to his Christian friend, "I have heard good things about you. You are doing right in receiving Christians into your home, especially traveling preachers. Your kindness helps in their work. Don't pay attention to anyone who tries to stop you from doing this."

The Book of Jude

JUDE, ANOTHER BROTHER OF JESUS, DID NOT BELIEVE THAT JESUS WAS THE SON OF GOD--UNTIL HE ROSE FROM THE DEAD. THEN JUDE BECAME A CHRISTIAN AND AFTER THAT HE WAS A STRONG WORKER FOR CHRIST.

ONE DAY HE RECEIVED BAD NEWS--THAT PEOPLE IN SOME OF THE CHURCHES WERE TEACHING THINGS THAT WERE NOT TRUE.

JUDE WROTE THE CHURCHES A LETTER:

"*You must defend our Christian faith. You have been warned that people would try to turn you away from Christ. I understand some of these false teachers are with you now. Pray that God will keep you strong, and that He will help you strengthen others.*"

The Book of Revelation

JOHN, WHO WROTE THE BEST-LOVED GOSPEL AND THREE LETTERS TO THE FOLLOWERS OF JESUS, ALSO WROTE THE BOOK OF REVELATION--TO HELP CHRISTIANS FACE THE ANGRY POWER OF ROME.

THE ROMANS HAD ARRESTED JOHN AND SENT HIM AS A PRISONER TO THE ISLAND OF PATMOS. THERE HE SAW A VISION OF HEAVEN, AND HE HEARD JESUS SAY:

"BEHOLD, I STAND AT THE DOOR, AND KNOCK: IF ANYONE HEARS MY VOICE, AND OPENS THE DOOR, I WILL COME INSIDE."

IN HEAVEN, JOHN SAW THE BOOK OF LIFE--IN WHICH WERE WRITTEN THE NAMES OF THOSE WHO LOVE CHRIST. AND FINALLY, THE OLD DISCIPLE SAW THE HOLY CITY, WHERE THERE IS NO SICKNESS, NO SORROW, NO DEATH. THOSE WHOSE NAMES ARE IN THE BOOK OF LIFE WILL ENTER THE GLORIOUS CITY AND LIVE FOREVER WITH CHRIST!

AND WITH JOHN'S VISION ENDS THE GREATEST STORY EVER TOLD, THE STORY OF THE BIBLE.

Life in Bible Times

It's easy to take some of our modern-day conveniences for granted, isn't it? Have you ever wondered what it would have been like to live when Jesus did? If you wanted a drink, a trip to the local well was in order.

In this section, you'll see what life was like two thousand years ago in Palestine.

When it's time for bed and the fire has died down to a few glowing coals, a board will be laid over it and then a carpet. This keeps the room warm for hours. The family sleeps on mattresses spread on the floor.

AT HOME IN PALESTINE

The lower floor of the average house was used as a stable for animals when they couldn't be left outdoors. At other times it served as a workshop or a playroom.

ST HOMES IN PALESTINE
WO FLOORS. THE PEOPLE
THEIR FLAT ROOFS
MANY ACTIVITIES, BUT
SECOND FLOOR WAS
MAIN LIVING QUARTERS.
RE THEY SLEPT AT
T, DID THEIR COOKING
ORED THEIR BELONGINGS.
PICTURE WE SEE A TYPICAL
ILY IN THE SECOND
OR OF THEIR HOME.

ER IS BRINGING HOME
CK OF WHEAT. THE GIRL
Y ARE GRINDING FLOUR.
R IS TAKING SOMETHING
UT OF ONE OF THE
TS" (THEIR CLOSETS WERE
PIGEON HOLES" IN THE
WALLS). THE FIRE IS
RGE HOLE IN THE FLOOR,
LED WITH BURNING
CHARCOAL.

ONE THING TO BE SAID IN FAVOR OF THE
CLOTHING STYLES IN JESUS' TIME IS THAT
THEY DIDN'T CHANGE FROM YEAR TO YEAR
AS OURS DO TODAY. SOME PEOPLE LIVING
IN THAT PART OF THE WORLD TODAY
DRESS ALMOST THE SAME AS THEY
DID IN BIBLE TIMES.

LABORERS USUALLY
WORE ONLY THE
UNDERGARMENT—
WITH OR WITHOUT
SLEEVES—OR
MERELY A WAIST-
LOTH WHICH REACHED
TO THEIR KNEES.

A WIDE GIRDLE
AROUND THEIR
WAIST SERVED AS
"POCKETS" IN WHICH
THEY CARRIED MONEY,
FOOD, A SWORD OR
DAGGER, ETC.

"FAMILY FASHIONS in the FIRST CENTURY"

SOME WORE A PLAIN
SHEET WOUND AROUND
THE BODY WITH ONE
END FLUNG OVER
THE SHOULDER. JESUS
IS USUALLY
PICTURED DRESSED
THAT WAY.

GIRLS WORE THE SAME
KIND OF CLOTHING AS
THEIR MOTHERS WORE...
WHICH, BY THE WAY, WAS
PRACTICALLY THE SAME AS
THE MEN WORE. IN FACT,
SOME OF THE GARMENTS
WERE SO MUCH ALIKE
THAT THEY COULD BE WORN BY
EITHER MEN OR WOMEN,
AND NO ONE WOULD KNOW
THE DIFFERENCE, EXCEPT
FOR THE HEADDRESS. WOMEN
AND GIRLS WORE LONG
HEAD SCARFS.

THE CITY OF GATES

At LEAST TWENTY GATES LEADING INTO JERUSALEM ARE RECORDED IN HISTORY. BECAUSE OF THE TRAFFIC PASSING THROUGH THEM, SOME OF THE GATES HAD COLORFUL NAMES SUCH AS FISH GATE, HORSE GATE, FOUNTAIN GATE, CORNER GATE, WATER GATE, SHEEP GATE AND SO ON. THE BUSY CARAVAN ROAD TO DAMASCUS ENTERED JERUSALEM THROUGH THE DAMASCUS GATE, PICTURED HERE.

Sometimes FOREIGN TRADERS WOULD HAVE A SPECIAL QUARTER OF THE CITY SET APART FOR THEM. USUALLY, HOWEVER, TRAVELING TRADESMEN DISPLAYED THEIR WARES BOTH IN AND OUTSIDE OF THE CITY'S GATES.

When you go to a supermarket today, you go to the right section and choose the food you want. But in Bible days all the shops that sold bread would be on "Baker's Street," ... all the meat shops on "Butcher's Row," ... candy shops on "The Street of Sweets."

So shopping in those days meant a lot of walking from street to street.

Streets of Bible-time towns were usually narrow, crowded and noisy. They wound their way through the city, twisting and turning uphill and down. Through these streets went merchants with their heavily loaded camels, horses and donkeys...porters carrying heavy bundles on their backs ...women balancing water jars on their heads...beggars...peddlers— all pushing, bumping and jostling.

There were no price tags. What you paid was determined by how good you were at bargaining and how anxious the merchant was to make a sale.

A SHEKEL COINED ABOUT 140 B.C.

The shekel was the most common coin used in Palestine in Bible days. A gold shekel was worth about fifteen silver shekels. A silver shekel was equal to a day's worker's pay for four days. One half and one quarter silver shekels were also used.

OCCUPATIONS IN BIBLE TIMES

FARMERS IN JESUS' TIME DIDN'T LIVE ON THEIR FARMS. THEY LIVED IN THE VILLAGES FOR MUTUAL PROTECTION FROM WILD ANIMALS AND BANDITS. EACH MORNING THE FARMERS WOULD DRIVE THEIR ANIMALS TO THEIR FIELDS FOR THE DAY'S WORK, WHICH BEGAN AT SUNRISE AND ENDED AT SUNSET.

MOST OF THE SMALL FARMS IN PALESTINE WERE WORKED BY THE FARMER'S FAMILY. BUT MANY MEN WHO DID NOT OWN FARMS WOULD HIRE THEMSELVES OUT AS FARM WORKERS.

A SHEPHERD'S LIFE IN BIBLE TIMES WAS FILLED WITH DANGER AND HARDSHIP. HE WAS ON GUARD DAY AND NIGHT PROTECTING HIS SHEEP FROM RUSTLERS AND WILD ANIMALS. HIS DEFENSES AGAINST THESE LURKING DANGERS WERE HIS STAFF, HIS SLING AND HIS COURAGE.

SHEPHERDS USED A SLING WITH AMAZING ACCURACY. THE SMALL STONES THEY HURLED STRUCK WITH TERRIFIC FORCE. DAVID SLEW THE GIANT GOLIATH WITH A SHEPHERD'S SLING. (1 SAMUEL 17:32-51)

THE SLING WAS A SHORT STRIP OF LEATHER. A WIDE PIECE IN THE CENTER HELD THE SMALL STONE. AFTER WHIRLING THE SLING AROUND HIS HEAD A FEW TIMES, THE SHEPHERD LET GO OF ONE END, SENDING THE STONE SPEEDING LIKE A BULLET TOWARD THE TARGET.

AT NIGHT FLOCKS WERE BROUGHT INTO A SHEEPFOLD FOR PROTECTION. AS EACH SHEEP ENTERED, IT WAS COUNTED—EVEN CALLED BY NAME. THROUGHOUT THE NIGHT THE SHEPHERD SLEPT AT THE OPENING OF THE FOLD, ACTING AS THE VERY GATE ITSELF.

LIFE IN BIBLE TIMES WAS QUITE DIFFERENT FROM TODAY. BUT THE WORDS JESUS PREACHED IN THE NEW TESTAMENT APPLY TO US AS MUCH AS THEY DID TO THESE PEOPLE WHO LIVED 2,000 YEARS AGO.

Scripture Index

~A~

Acts 1:1-26 674
Acts 2:1-38 677
Acts 2:38–3:7 680
Acts 3:7–4:17 683
Acts 4:18–5:18 687
Acts 5:19–6:10 691
Acts 6:11–8:4 695
Acts 7:58–8:4 717
Acts 8:5-26 698
Acts 8:26-40 701
Acts 9:1-3a 717
Acts 9:3-22 721
Acts 9:27-30 724
Acts 9:32-35 701
Acts 9:36–10:2 705
Acts 10:2–11:1 708
Acts 11:1–12:14 711
Acts 11:22-25 724
Acts 11:25-30 727
Acts 12:14-24 714
Acts 12:25–13:7 727
Acts 13:7-50 731
Acts 13:51–14:19 737
Acts 14:19–15:1 740
Acts 15:1-13 744
Acts 15:13–16:8 746
Acts 16:9-19 749
Acts 16:20-37 752
Acts 16:38–17:13 755
Acts 17:13–18:12 757
Acts 18:13–19:16 761
Acts 19:17-20 763
Acts 19:31–20:3 767
Acts 20:3–21:14 769
Acts 21:15–23:24 773
Acts 22:3 717
Acts 23:25–28:4 775
Amos 534

~C~

1 Chronicles 11:6 324
1 Chronicles 13 327
1 Chronicles 15–16 327
2 Chronicles 2:16 366
2 Chronicles 24:1-23 445
2 Chronicles 24:20-27 448
2 Chronicles 32:1-20 451
2 Chronicles 32:21–33:12 . . .454

2 Chronicles 33:13–34:18 . . .457
2 Chronicles 34:19–36:16 . . .460
2 Chronicles 36:17-20 463
1 Corinthians 763
2 Corinthians 767

~D~

Daniel 1–2:13 515
Daniel 2:16-48 518
Daniel 3:1-25 521
Daniel 3:26–5:6 524
Daniel 5 466
Daniel 5:7–6:14 527
Daniel 6:16-28 531
Deuteronomy 34 189

~E~

Esther 1:1–2:11 475
Esther 2:11–3:6 476
Esther 3:8–4:16 479
Esther 5:1–6:10 482
Esther 6:11–10 485
Exodus 1:1–2:2 121
Exodus 2:3-11 125
Exodus 2:11–3:4 129
Exodus 3:4–5:21 133
Exodus 5:22–6:5 137
Exodus 11:6–14:12 142
Exodus 14:10–16:10 146
Exodus 16:11-17 150
Exodus 17:12–19:20 154
Exodus 20–32:19 157
Exodus 25–40:18-38 164
Exodus 32:20–40:17 161
Ezekiel 1 509
Ezekiel 1–48 512
Ezra 1–2 466
Ezra 3–10 469

~G~

Galatians 744
Genesis 1–2 13
Genesis 3 19
Genesis 4:1-8 22
Genesis 4:8-26 25
Genesis 5 25
Genesis 6:1-8 25
Genesis 6:7-22 28
Genesis 7:1-10 28

Genesis 7:16-24 31
Genesis 8 31
Genesis 9 31
Genesis 11 . . . . .31, 41, 43
Genesis 12:1-15 46
Genesis 12:16-20 48
Genesis 13 48
Genesis 14:1-13 48
Genesis 15 51
Genesis 16–19:1-10 51
Genesis 19:11-30 55
Genesis 21:1-16 55
Genesis 21:17-21 59
Genesis 22:1-10 59
Genesis 22:11-18 65
Genesis 23:1-2, 19-20 65
Genesis 24:1-10 65
Genesis 24:11-67 68
Genesis 25:7-8 68
Genesis 25:9-33 72
Genesis 25:32-34 75
Genesis 26 75
Genesis 27:1-41 75
Genesis 27:42-46 80
Genesis 28 80
Genesis 29:1-25 80
Genesis 29:26–32:6 85
Genesis 32:7-33 89
Genesis 35:1-20 89
Genesis 35:27-29 92
Genesis 37:1-26 92
Genesis 37:27-36 97
Genesis 39:1-20 97
Genesis 39:21-23 101
Genesis 40–42:6 101
Genesis 42:6-38 105
Genesis 43:1–44:12 109
Genesis 44:13–45:26 113
Genesis 45:27-28 117
Genesis 47–48 117
Genesis 50:1-15 117
Genesis 50:15-26 121

~H~

Habakkuk 536
Hebrews 786
Hebrews 13:23 781
Hosea 534

~I~

Isaiah 491
Isaiah 45:1, 2, 13 466

~J~

James 786
Jeremiah 1 493
Jeremiah 18–20:2 496
Jeremiah 20–36 497
Jeremiah 27 500
Jeremiah 28:1-12 500
Jeremiah 29:1-14 509
Jeremiah 37:1-10 500
Jeremiah 37–38:6 503
Jeremiah 38:7–43:7 506
John 1:35-46 570
John 1:47-51 573
John 2:1-11, 23-25 573
John 3:1-2 573
John 3:3–4:6 576
John 4:6-44 579
John 6:1-10 596
John 6:10-15 601
John 6:22-71 604
John 7:11-52 611
John 8:21-59 611
John 9:1–10:21 614
John 10:22-40 620
John 11:1-8 623
John 11:38-54 626
John 12:1-8 630
John 13:1-20 641
John 13:27-30 641
John 13:33-38 644
John 14 644
John 18:28-38 648
John 18:39–19:16 652
John 19:25-27 656
John 19:38-42 660
John 20:2-18 665
John 20:19–21:6 668
John 21:7-18 671
Joel 534
1 John 787
2 John 787
3 John 787
Jonah 535
Joshua 1 189
Joshua 2:1–4:10 193
Joshua 4:1–6:20 197
Joshua 6:20–7:4 201
Joshua 7:5–9:16 205
Joshua 9:17–11:7 209
Joshua 11:8–24:33 211
Judges 1:1–4:2 211
Judges 4–5 214
Judges 6–7 218

Judges 7:22-25 224
Judges 8:28 224
Judges 13:2–14:5 227
Judges 14:19–15:12 232
Judges 15:13–16:2 235
Judges 16:3-5 238
Judges 16:6-21 241
Judges 16:21-30 244
Jude 788

~K~

1 Kings 1:1-9 360
1 Kings 1:9-49 363
1 Kings 1:49–2:46 366
1 Kings 8:1–10:1 371
1 Kings 10:2–11:8 374
1 Kings 11:29–12:3 377
1 Kings 12:4-27 380
1 Kings 12:28–16:34 385
1 Kings 17:1-7 389
1 Kings 18:17-37 391
1 Kings 18:38–19:2 395
1 Kings 19:3-18 399
1 Kings 19:19-21 402
1 Kings 21:1-8 402
1 Kings 21:9–22:29 405
1 Kings 22:30–2 Kings 2:10 . .409
2 Kings 2:11-18 412
2 Kings 4:1 412
2 Kings 4:2-7 415
2 Kings 5:1-14a 418
2 Kings 5:14-16 421
2 Kings 6:8-16 421
2 Kings 6:17-24 424
2 Kings 6:25–7:5 427
2 Kings 7:8-16 430
2 Kings 7:5-7, 14–9:12 433
2 Kings 9:13-32 436
2 Kings 9:32–11:3 439
2 Kings 11:1-12 442
2 Kings 11:13-21 445
2 Kings 12–18:10 448
2 Kings 22:1-10 457
2 Kings 22:1–23:29 493
2 Kings 22:11–24:20 460
2 Kings 23:29-37 496
2 Kings 24–25:4 500
2 Kings 25:1-11 463

~L~

Leviticus 1–10:2 164
Luke 1:23-55 549
Luke 1:57-80 552

Luke 2:1-5 552
Luke 2:1-15 555
Luke 2:7, 16-20 558
Luke 2:40-52 564
Luke 3:1–4:4 567
Luke 4:16-28 579
Luke 6:12-16 589
Luke 9:37-45 608
Luke 10:25 614
Luke 10:25-40 617
Luke 10:40–11:2 620
Luke 15:1-19 620
Luke 15:20-32 623
Luke 18:15-23 626
Luke 19:1-3 626
Luke 19:4-10 630
Luke 19:29-35 630
Luke 19:36-38 633
Luke 20:23-26 636
Luke 22:7-13 641
Luke 22:17-20 644
Luke 23:6-12 648
Luke 23:26-46 656
Luke 23:48-49 660
Luke 24:13-32 665
Luke 24:33-43 668
Luke 24:44-51 671

~M~

Malachi 536, 537
Mark 1:16-20 579
Mark 2:1-14 583
Mark 3:26, 33 608
Mark 4:35-37 589
Mark 4:37-41 593
Mark 5:1-24, 35 593
Mark 5:38-43 596
Mark 6:14-17 576
Mark 7:1-23 604
Mark 9:26, 33 608
Mark 12:28-34, 38-44 637
Mark 13 637
Mark 15:38-39 660
Mark 16:1-7 665
Matthew 2:1-8 558
Matthew 2:9-14 561
Matthew 2:16-23 564
Matthew 4:5-11 570
Matthew 5–7 589
Matthew 6:9-13 620
Matthew 8:5-13 589
Matthew 9:9-13 586
Matthew 9:35–11:1 596

Matthew 12:9-14 586
Matthew 13:45-46 589
Matthew 14:1-12 596
Matthew 14:22-30 601
Matthew 14:30-36 604
Matthew 16:13-26 604
Matthew 17:1-2 604
Matthew 17:3-23 608
Matthew 18:1-14, 21-22 611
Matthew 21:10-17 633
Matthew 22:15-17 633
Matthew 26:14-16 637
Matthew 26:21-25 641
Matthew 26:30, 36-56 644
Matthew 26:57-75 648
Matthew 27:3-10 652
Matthew 27:62-66 660
Matthew 28:11-15 665
Matthew 28:16-20 671
Micah 535

~N~

Nahum 535
Nehemiah 472
Numbers 10–11:2 167
Numbers 11:2–12:10 169
Numbers 12:11–14:10 173
Numbers 14:10–16:5 177
Numbers 16:5–21:9 181
Numbers 21:21-35 181
Numbers 21:33–27:18 189

~O~

Obadiah 535

~P~

1 Peter 786
2 Peter 787
Philippians 779

~R~

Revelation 788
Romans 767
Ruth 2:6–3:18 247
Ruth 4 250

~S~

1 Samuel 1:1–3:17 253
1 Samuel 3:18–5:2 255
1 Samuel 5:3–7:10 258
1 Samuel 7:10–9:20 261
1 Samuel 9:20–11:7 264
1 Samuel 11–13:9 269

1 Samuel 13:10–15:14 272
1 Samuel 15:15–16:11 275
1 Samuel 16:12-19 278
1 Samuel 16:23–17:26 281
1 Samuel 17:28-48 284
1 Samuel 17:48–18:9 287
1 Samuel 19:22–20:33 290
1 Samuel 21:13–24:5 293
1 Samuel 24:5–25:13 295
1 Samuel 26:6–28:2 297
1 Samuel 28:5-11 300
1 Samuel 28:11-25 303
1 Samuel 29 300
1 Samuel 30:1-3 303
1 Samuel 30:1-11 306
1 Samuel 30 307
1 Samuel 31:1-6 303
2 Samuel 1:1-3 307
2 Samuel 1:2–2:9 310
2 Samuel 2:12–3:25 315
2 Samuel 3:26–4:5 318
2 Samuel 4:6–5:4 321
2 Samuel 5:5-9 324
2 Samuel 6–9:5 327
2 Samuel 9:6–11:14 330
2 Samuel 11:14-27 333
2 Samuel 12:1-14 336
2 Samuel 12:15–13:29 339
2 Samuel 13:30–14:30 342
2 Samuel 14:31–15:4 345
2 Samuel 15:7-13 348
2 Samuel 15:13–17:13 351
2 Samuel 17:14-23 354
2 Samuel 17:24–18:9 357
2 Samuel 18–24 360

~T~

1 Thessalonians 757
2 Thessalonians 757
1 Timothy 779
2 Timothy 781
2 Timothy 4:6-8 784
Titus 779

~Z~

Zechariah 536
Zephaniah 536

Look for each of these *Picture Bible* products from Chariot Victor ...

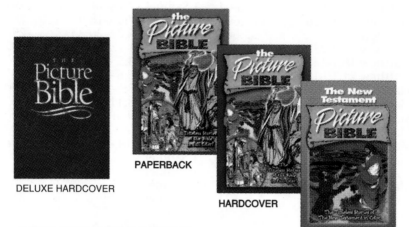

PAPERBACK

DELUXE HARDCOVER

HARDCOVER

THE PICTURE BIBLE

NEW TESTAMENT

The Picture Bible makes a good first Bible for young readers, though this classic best-seller is loved by people of all ages. The full-text version contains 233 Bible stories in full-color comic format that makes Bible stories exciting for kids. Newly revised, the new information pages, maps, and an improved index give this classic Bible storybook fresh significance for today!

DELUXE HARDCOVER
ISBN: 0-78143-057-7
PAPERBACK
ISBN: 0-78143-058-5
HARDCOVER
ISBN: 0-78143-055-0
THE NEW TESTAMENT
ISBN: 0-78143-056-9

PICTURE BIBLE DEVOTIONS

ISBN: 0-78143-067-4

Interactive activities and full-color pictures from *The Picture Bible* make this an innovative approach to devotions. Kids learn to apply Bible knowledge to their lives through 30 Old Testament and 30 New Testament stories.